Sense and Senses i

Edited by
Per Bäckström and Troels Degn Johansson

Sense and Senses
in Aesthetics

 **NSU Press**

NSU Press
Nordisk Sommeruniversitet
Box 12024
SE-402 41 Göteborg
Tlf. +46 31 69 56 39
Fax. +46 31 69 09 50
Email: sekretariatet@nsuweb.net

NSU Press publishes academic papers produced for Nordisk sommeruniversitet (NSU).
These publications are on sale in bookshops, or can be ordered directly from NSU.

Distrubutors: Söderströms, Georgsgatan 29 A, PB 870,
FIN-00101 Helsingfors/Helsinki, Finland.
mail to: www.soderstrom.fi

ISBN 91-88484-24-6
© 2003 Nordisk sommeruniversitet & the authors
Coverdesign: Helena Kajander
Printed by Nord Print Ab
Helsingfors/Helsinki, Finland 2003

Contents

Introduction

The Senses, Aesthetic Experience, and Art

OUR FIVE SENSES have traditionally been divided into two groups, those of distance (sight and hearing) and the senses of proximity: smell, touch and taste. In art, it has been maintained that the so-called "fine arts" were based on the distant senses (music, "art", i.e., painting, sculpture, etc.) while the "lower arts" such as perfumery and gastronomy were associated with the proximate senses. In a broader understanding, this division has undoubtedly been associated with a dualism between the ideals and eternal values of the fine arts and the more short-lived material joys brought on by the lower "vital arts". Our ability to grasp the ideal and the eternal had to take place with the help of reflexivity, contemplation and intuition, mental aspects which, in the concepts of philosophy and with the metaphors of generalized language, have revolved around "insight" or "listening to reason" when it concerns the "spoken word" (*logos*), i.e., linguistic transmission in itself. Here the senses live up to the deep kinship with the sense or meaning apparently indicated by the Latin "sens", which in both French and English signifies both meaning and sensing. Jean-Luc Nancy takes this duality as his point of departure in his *Le sense du monde*, linking it to the aesthetic and the sensing on the one hand, and to understanding and ontology on the other.

Traditionally more marginalized mental aspects, such as memory and amnesia, seem to have been associated with the proximate senses, in any case if we judge from the literature where these factors can be determined poetically, and from the brain research which is supposed to have demonstrated a special connection between the centers of smell and memory. That the emotions, in contrast, are intimately connected with the tactile senses, with touching, may be revealed from language, which seems not to know the difference; hence, we say "to feel" when we talk about touching and about emotions. The question, however, is whether this traditional division is still reasonable. There is no doubt that in modern times, the senses have become the object of renewed interest by aesthetic studies. Thus, today's conception of the aesthetic concerns not only our immediate experience of the world, but also the sensory modality by which we experience the world. It is no longer absurd to concern oneself with the aesthetics of the senses on the basis of the idea that the aesthetic experience of the world can be sensorially conditioned.

The senses and the aesthetic experience: mediation or immediacy?

As concerns sensory mediation or conditioning of the aesthetic environmental experience, it is possible to establish a relevant parallel to semiotics and its interest in the sign-related mediation of a meaning in the environment or in communications. In the phenomenological understanding of sign in Hegel and Husserl, when it concerns the great questions of the manifestation of the spirit in nature, we can demonstrate a gradually increasing interest in the sign aspect itself; an interest which culminates in Derrida's ideas of trace and difference. For Merleau-Ponty, the question of sign has given rise to a phenomenology of the body and, thus, an investigation of the way in which the senses mediate the world for the mental apparatus. A similar development seems to be occurring within media research, where studies of the computer media's interfaces reveal an increasingly closer technical linkage between media technology and the sensory apparatus. This social actuality of this topic appears with all desirable clarity in modern popular cultural forms of presentation such as those films and novels having a thematicization of the body's melting together with the machine. Further study could demonstrate a gradually increasing emphasis on precisely the perceptual relationship rather than the purely mechanical aspects (as could be presented by a Chaplin or a Tati, for example).

The perceptual relation is a popular topic in the cyberpunk literature, where the possible digital communication between the brain and the computer has led, in the works of William Gibson and other authors, to strong popular cultural fantasies. Media research's emerging interest in the senses as concerns the electrification of communication and the subsequent acceleration of information, is immediately led back to Marshall McLuhan, who described the conditions of the sensory apparatus in the media age of electricity. Electric, "hot" media contain an intensity, which must provoke a protective reaction among the masses, a response utilizing the "cooler" media, e.g., a corresponding reduction in the intensity of information. One finds again in McLuhan the Freudian concept of the protective shield (*Reizschutz*), which would protect the mental apparatus against the intensities of the environment and from the drives. This idea also inspired Walter Benjamin's critique of modernity, and was perhaps already existent prior to Freud (*Beyond the Pleasure Principle*) in the work of Georg Simmel, who indicated "blasé", detachment, the cool attitude *par excellence*, as the natural reaction to what McLuhan terms the hot media. Later on, the McLuhan-inspired Paul Virilio has compared the domains of war, communication, and the body with a point of departure in a general, intensifying acceleration of technologies related to the body's motoric and perceptual horizon. Here technologies can perhaps further be considered as a "level of mediation" which to an especially high degree problematises the senses, in that relations to the environment are variously disturbed by the technical acceleration.

The question, however, is whether these fundamentally modern traditions are still relevant, or whether, with a still wider pragmatic thinking, they can be rejected as "mentalistic" projects which really do not concern actual experience of the environment, but only its representations, say in literature and art. This pragmatism has – correctly – criticized the sign- and representation oriented "mediation thinking" as hermeneutic or speculative projects, instead proposing a more "immediate" approach to the sensory experience of the environment. This proposal leads to a positivistic demand for scientific objectivity and within the human sciences, having placed the psychology of perception in a privileged position. Notably brain research and the interdisciplinary studies of emotion and cognition have been pathbreaking in recent years as concerns the question of the functionality of the senses in relation to the experience of the environment and the mental apparatus.

Conversely, this functional orientation, which has also characterized much research in the human sciences today, can be criticized for not belonging to the study of aesthetics as such, inasmuch as the aesthetic is conceptualized as an artistic or in the special sense disinterested relation to the world, which is conceptually determined by the essential purposeless of art. A dialogue between the more aesthetically oriented "mediation thinking", which in a very general sense can be termed as being "semiotic" – insofar as semiotics must in principle seek a fundamental discreteness or mediation level ("the sign") – and a more "immediate", non-semiotic approach seems to be more pertinent as to more holistic approaches, such as James Gibson's perceptual ecology, Edmund Husserl's conception of the "life-world", Maurice Merleau-Ponty's late idea of a pre-phenomenological level ("flesh of the world"), or the psychoanalytic notion of a primordial imaginary (Jacques Lacan,

Melanie Klein, etc.). These ideas are all characterized by their focus on a direct, and immediate experience of the world, which allows itself to be conceived by a reflexive "looking back", i.e., by a semiotics, such that understanding, the immediate experience (*Erlebniss*) and the mediating experience (empiricism) in a more generalized sense can be considered as an integrated context. This condition takes semiotics as its point of departure. As an example, we may cite visual semiotics, and its dialogue between the phenomenology of art perspectives and linguistic semiotics (Roland Barthes, etc.), where the experience of meaning (*sens*) is explicated in the textual analytical construction of meaning (*signification*). Another example is recent system analysis (Göran Sonesson), where an immediately recognizable relationship to the environment finds its justification in logical relations of signs. There are indications that something similar operates for the senses and the aesthetic experience. The point of departure for such a study will be to allow the senses (or sensing) to assume "the sign's" eternally problematic place in semiotics; a mediating position which on the one hand makes the immediate in its totality inconceivable, but on the other hand inscribes the basis for the "mentalistic" – or better, reflexive – experience of the environment.

As concerns sensing, it will certainly be useful here to distinguish between "reflexive" and "non-reflexive" senses. Reflexive senses are in this case defined by being contained in a close, reflexive self-awareness. As such, as to the subject of vision, one may say that "(one sees oneself) see" (Merleau-Ponty). Something similar will not apply to non-reflexive senses, such as the sense of touch. Here the sensing subjectivity will only be able to convert its experience to the sentence: "I touch". It does not make sense to state: "I touch myself touch". This difference could indicate that the reflexive senses suspend the sensory mediation in an experience of proximity, which apparently, and not only in a metaphorical sense, transforms sight into the sense of intuition.

11

The senses and art: Conceptual art versus affective art

Within a modernity context in both art and popular culture, there seems to be a clear parallel with the aforementioned relation between "mediation thinking" and unmediated approaches to the question of aesthetic experience. We can perhaps find justification in the very popular, art-critical distinction between art, which functions as such by being immediately at "work" by creating affects in the spectator's mind, and conceptual art which operates by referring to a conceptual context, including even the institution of art itself. Affective art (*Wirkungskunst*) should thus constitute the form of art, which offers an immediate, sensory involvement and possibly further an empathy with a "level of content" (e.g., narrative art forms). Affective art must in this sense be related to popular cultural phenomena such as the early urbanity's panoramic forms and Hollywood films with the "invisible" montage. In art theory, conceptual art would be emancipated by the sensory acquisition unless this question is precisely thematicized conceptually.

However, questions begin to appear, if one attempts on this basis to approach modern art only as a project that problematises the naturalness of sensing and representation in the classical and renaissance traditions, which normally would been considered as affective art. For example, the meaning of the impressionistic pictorial art consists, naturally, not in its artists' environmental experiences having been at that time essentially different than ours today, but that it was in its time artistically interesting to thematicize the concept of visual perception, and subsequently also representation. Conversely, Andy Warhol's serial art, for which there has been a strong tendency to categorize as conceptual art, has in a current critique been connected to affective art, in that the seriality, instead of exclusively being a problematisation of the art work's uniqueness, should instead be viewed immediately, as an endless reaction and generalization of the trauma of modernity in art (cf. Hal Foster's notion of "traumatic realism"). In this context, the emphasis on complexity in these polar extremes can serve as an example of how the distinction between immediate and mediated thinking, insofar as it also applies to art, but that it is precisely a case of an integrated relationship. In a broader sense, the great challenge will be to identify the general condition for that integral relationship with special reference to the sensory aspect of art in the aesthetic experience.

The arts' sensory condition: plurality and synaesthesia

Art's relationship to humankind seems to exist through the senses. The fact that we have different types of art can be associated with the fact that we have different senses. The differentiation of the senses and the focus on the specificities of the senses leads to a focus on the different ways in which the aesthetic experience is transmitted. Through the different senses, the experience of the different types of art is transmitted. The arts can thus be necessarily understood in their plurality, i.e., as a fundamental plurality. There is no single way to experience art, but several ways due to the differences among the senses. Jean-Luc Nancy develops this point in his *Les Muses* (1994), posing the very basic question, "Why are there several arts and not just one?" Nancy's answer is advertised by his book's title. The muses simply exist in the plural; there exists a fundamental plurality in the arts. Nancy connects this plurality to the senses, and to the differentiation of the sensory apparatus, a notion already found in Classical Greek thought.

In this connection, an especially interesting form of aesthetic experience related to the senses is "synaesthesia". In this experience, a "recipient" appreciates a work of art using another sense (or at least with the help of concepts linked to another sense) than that with which the work would ordinarily be associated. In music, for example, composers such as Alexander Scriabin and Olivier Messiaen are known for linking their music to colors. This is not a case of the more metaphorical concept of *timbre (Klangfarbe)* (even though this can be said to be related to the problem), but of a concrete experience asserted by the composers. Messiaen makes use of several different scales and chords, which he immediately links to color experiences. In Scriabin's "Prometheus", from 1910, rhe inserts into the score a special "voice" for light (this work was first performed with light early in the 1990s, where it became possible to link its "light voice" to a keyboard with the help of MIDI technology). Theories of synaesthesia have also emerged in connection with different forms of perception research; a condition that can be explained by the challenges posed by such a theory to our understanding of perception and the sensory apparatus generally. Regarding synaesthesia, it is asserted that this experience should not be understood metaphorically, but literally as a concrete sensory experience. If it were "just" a matter of a metaphorical understanding, the theoretical problems would be of another character. The metaphorical application of the term "synesthesia" is also found in music in the concept of the timbre. This concept is quite current in music from the early part of the 20th century and perhaps especially with reference to a so-called "second Vienna School". The different instruments are here viewed as a coloring of the orchestral chords and the orchestration and arranging thereby understood analogously with the painter's palette. A number of different colors are chosen to form the orchestral chord, creating the orchestra's timbre.

When the different senses are placed in connection with something like an aesthetic experience and aesthetic theory, a problem emerges for aesthetics. To what degree can one subordinate these different sensory experiences into a single theory with a common conceptual apparatus? Is it at all possible with a single theoretical apparatus to treat essentially different forms of aesthetic experience? Inasmuch as aesthetics constitutes a meta-discipline, it already presumes this possibility, even though a theoretical basis is not always given for this. One way of defending the existence of such a foundation has been to defend the existence of a *sensus communis*, which should guarantee an internal consistency between the experiences linked to the individual senses. This communal sense must be understood as being independent of empirical sensing; it is not linked to the empirical data but is, rather, a theoretical construction, and possibly a kind of transcendental justification of aesthetics.

The concept of the *sensus communis* has an actuality beyond aesthetics as a meta-discipline. The community, which is assumed to have the concept must also be conceived as a community of actors; a society by which the meaning or the judgments are based on a communicative community. We find this variant of the concept in Kant as well as in Lyotard's readings of Kant. According to Lyotard, *sensus communis* contains a paradox. If *sensus* is conceptualized as a singularity, *communis* must consist of a form of generality. In Lyotard's reading, this generality is placed in connection with the judge-concept (in the Kantian sense), but the content may also be extended and more immediately linked to the question of aesthetic experience. The work of art is understood as a singularity, what Adorno, referring to Leibniz, calls a monad. In the interpretation, however, this singularity will be subordinated to the general (or at least a form of generality). The work is interpreted on the background of a language, a conceptual and theoretical apparatus which often has pretensions of generality. We can thereby assert that aesthetics contains an irresolvable paradox between the singular and the general, between the work of art and its interpretation or theory. We rediscover this problem in every concrete interpretation of works of art. To what degree is it possible within the interpretation to allow the work of art's uniqueness to become prominent, i.e., to bring forth its unique qualities so that they can be discussed? In aesthetic theory and in the work of interpretation, are we required to ignore some of the work's unique qualities in favor of a more general consideration, in which the general, i.e., that which is possible for aesthetic theory, can become the central aspect? In this sense, these questions must stand at the very core of an investigation of the sensory-related essential conditions for art.

Sense and senses in art

The intention of this anthology, therefore, is to address and – hopefully – answer some of the questions that our discussion above raises, by presenting a wide range of articles on different aesthetic fields. The anthology has its roots in the seminars of the *AISTHESIS: Aesthetics of the Senses* circle (1999–2001), at the Nordic Summer University, which has held regular meetings for three years. The themes of the seminars have varied, ranging from the problem of "synaesthesia" to the role of the "disgusting" in the arts, touching upon a variety of subjects, some of which are presented in this collection. The articles in the book are presented in a way that makes it possible to drift from a broad, philosophical analysis on the subject, through discussions of fine arts, literature, and cinema, as well as more simple "joys of life", such as dirty language, or cooking, in a discussion of the different senses and their presupposed hierarchy.

*

In the first article "Being Touched by Art: Art and Sense in Jean-Luc Nancy", Erik Steinskog gives a discussion of what can be said to be the main theme of this anthology, a problem based on the question that Jean-Luc Nancy puts forward in his book *The Muses*: "Why are there several arts and not just one?" Steinskog's study therefore can be read as a direct continuation of this introduction, and he takes the question further in a deeper analysis, as well as a broad presentation of Jean-Luc Nancy's thinking on the subject. Steinskog's main concern is to analyse the relation between aesthetics, art and sensation, and to leave behind the fact that the old division between body and mind still is present in aesthetics. Through a historical exposée of the problem, an investigation of the *Gesamtkunstwerk*, in which the senses work together, and a deeper analysis of the sense of touch and the exposure to which it leads, he finally arrives at a conclusion in which he formulates a more consistent view on the issue.

A recent theory of another philosopher is presented in Michael Penzold's article "Challenging Modernism in Sloterdijk's Spheres", which deals with the German thinker Peter Sloterdijk's ideas about spheres as – among other things – the spaces which science is unable to describe and the spaces which people share and have in common. Thus far, Sloterdijk has released the two first (mammoth) parts of a thrilogy, which is to explore the importance of spheres in human thinking, from the micro- to the macrosphere, and in relation to the history of philosophy and ideas. Sloterdijk is a little known philosopher in Scandinavia, which makes Penzold's article both an analysis and an introduction in our cultural sphere.

In her article "Orpheus as Socrates Practicing Music: On the Synaesthetic Origin of Literary Philosophy", Mischa Sloth Carlsen proposes the thesis that: "sense does not exist in advance. Rather, sense is suggested by the senses in the event of the work of art". She thereafter studies the synaesthetic origin of the Orphean myth through an historical exposée of the myth whose origin is lost. This leads to a discussion in which she involves the theoreticians Maurice Blanchot and Friedrich Nietzsche. The myth has both metapoetical and Socratic qualities, which makes it an ideal starting point for an analysis of the origin of literary philosophy, where the themes of creation and the *disjecta membra poetae* in the myth parallels early German romanticist ideas on wit (*Witz*) and irony. The death of Orpheus thus makes way for the birth of the possibilities of philosophical aesthetics.

In his article "Suspicion in the Ear: The Phonemic Reading of Garrett Stewart in a Scandinavian Context", Per Bäckström presents Stewart's theory about two different layers in written language, as proposed in

Stewart's book *Reading Voices: Literature and the Phonotext*. These are strata which speak to two separate senses at the same time, namely seeing and hearing. These two layers can cooperate in bringing meaning to a text, but they can also produce separate interpretations of the same passage. Bäckström discusses this phenomenon in relation to the English language, according to Garrett Stewart's investigations, and then furthermore transfers it to the context of Scandinavian language and literature.

Karen Hvidtfeldt Madsen discusses the synaesthetic value of colours for the interpretation of literature and music in her article "In Rot getaucht: Elias Canettis *Die gerettete Zunge* and the colour 'red' in modern art". Madsen takes as her point of departure the first volume of Elias Canetti's autobiographical trilogy, *Die gerettete Zunge*, and his characteristic use of the red colour. She presents an historical and contextual exposée with the help of the theories of Newton, Goethe and Jung, and also makes a comparison with the poetry of Sylvia Plath and the film *Rouge* by the Polish director Krzysztof Kieslowski. Madsen thus makes it clear that Canetti, by using the colour red in a characteristic mix of autobiography and fiction, at the same time gives expression to both his own identity and the modernity of his time.

The dialogue between art and philosophy in the beginning of the book is taken up again in Troels Degn Johansson's contribution, "The Tactile Image: A Veronican Approach to Pictorality in Michel Serres's Aesthetics of the Senses". Here, Johansson demonstrates that cinema, which for obvious reasons has been theorized mainly as a visual – and only recently as an audiovisual – medium, might paradoxically also help us to understand better French philosopher Michel Serres' peculiar concept of a general tactility, a concept which is pivotal for the perception of his aesthetics of the senses. In his main philosophical treaty on aesthetics, *Les Cinq Sens*, Serres places the five senses in a general philosophical system by identifying tactility as the most fundamental sense for the human soul and its experience of itself and its environment.

In the second article on cinema "Prosthesis Unbound", Esben Krohn discusses further the question of the relation of the different senses to the arts of photography and film, by rethinking the function of the double scene in early Danish silent film. In a comparison with the ideas of Edgar Allan Poe, the inventor of the detective story, he dwells on the characteristic play-within-the the-play of the early films, where scenes are staged with an intriguing complexity, containing up to three different layers of fictive scenes in one. Krohn explains this with reference to the fact that the silent film was an expression of modernity. Today this is easy to overlook, since silent cinema might appear as an antiquated aesthetic expression, while it was actually among the foremost of the arts in revealing modernity.

In the third article on film, "Holy Shit!: Quentin Tarantino's Excremental Aesthetics", Claus Krogholm Sand takes a firm grip on postmodernity and the postmodern film, as manifested by the films of the American director Quentin Tarantino. Sand makes a point out of the fact that the word "shit" is used with an unusual frequency throughout the film, and, based on the theories of Georges Bataille and Mircea Eliade, among others, concludes that this excessive use of the word is a means of describing an alternative way to attain the sacred. Throughout the film the existential ground of one of the main characters shifts from the profane to the sacred, which is prefigured and described by means of the excremental vocabulary of the film.

Finally, Helle Brønnum Carlsen, in her article "Taste as a matter of pedagogical concern", transgresses the subject of the preceding article, and widens the subject of this anthology, by discussing taste as both a matter of pedagogical concern and as a subject for aesthetics. Her primary point of departure is Caroline Korsmayer's book *Making Sense of Taste*, where Korsmayer discusses the supposed hierarchy of the senses, and its implications for a discussion of the "lower" senses, such as

19

touch, taste, and smell, in relation to the "higher" senses of hearing and seeing. The latter are understood as none-bodily, while the former are thought of as bodily, and therefore of lesser cognitive significance. Carlsen shows – with Korsmayer – that this is not the case, and that "the lower senses" can be as cognitive and aesthetic as "the higher senses".

Finally, we editors wish to thank the Nordic Summer University, the *AISTHESIS: Aesthetics of the Senses* circle, and the contributors who have made this publication possible.

Per Bäckström and Troels Degn Johansson

Being Touched by Art

Art and Sense in Jean-Luc Nancy

Erik Steinskog

IN HIS INFLUENTIAL book *The Ideology of the Aesthetic*, Terry Eagleton opens with the claim that "aesthetics is born as a discourse of the body" (Eagleton 1992: 13). While this claim seems valid enough, I would like to approach the question of aesthetics from a somewhat different, albeit related, angle, discussing the relation between aesthetics, art and sensation. The question is about the relation between aesthetics and the discourse of sensation and of sense. The double reference to the term "sense", referring both to sensation and to meaning, is of utmost importance to this approach. Such a double reference also implies that the discourse is related both to the body, as a sensing body, but also to what is often seen as its opposite or complement, the soul, here understood as the mind's establishing of meaning. In this sense, I do not wish to unnecessarily reintroduce a dichotomy, but it seems clear that the dichotomy of body and mind is still operative within the aesthetic discourse. However, by focusing on sense and its double reference, I believe that the two dimensions can be seen as interrelated at least in the aesthetic discourse.

One of the contemporary philosophers or aestheticians who has discussed this theme most thoroughly is Jean-Luc Nancy, not least in his two books *The Muses* and *The Sense of the World*. The discussion in the present article will focus on some of the themes in these books. However, to discuss the notion of sensation related to aesthetics, it is also important to discuss sensation in a rather general way. One dimension that inevitably appears is the relation between the different senses, a relation often found to be a hierarchy. An interesting aspect of aesthetic discourse in the last decades of the twentieth century, and the so-called "visual turn", was the emphasis on the importance of the sense of vision, and the domination this sense has had both on aesthetic discourse and the vocabulary used to think and express aesthetic judgements. As a side effect, there also arose the question of an adequate vocabulary to discuss art works not primarily related to the eyes and to vision.

There is more to art than meets the eye. This statement is obvious when we recall that art is a discourse for the senses. Thus, any art that "speaks" to senses other than vision obviously does so through the other senses. The statement then becomes an actualisation of the other art forms, the art forms related to senses other than vision. Differentiations of the senses seem to follow some common threads. Firstly, the senses are most often divided into five. However, they are then sub-divided into the higher and lower senses – an incipient hierarchy is already present – where vision and hearing are the higher senses, and the other three are lower. A consequence of this division is that hearing becomes "the second sense". It is not as elevated as vision, and not as low as the other senses, which are more closely related to the body and demand proximity between the sensing body and what is sensed. This latter consequence is also one of the key features of this division: the higher senses can sense at a distance, whereas the lower senses require that what is sensed is "close-up". In this division, we find a replica of the split between mind/soul and body.

Art and the arts

The question of the language we use in discussing the terms related to sensation is especially actualised when the various art forms are related to the different senses. This is one of the themes in Nancy's essay "Why Are There Several Arts and Not Just One?" from The Muses. When the art forms are related to the different senses, and when a strong relation is established between the art forms and the senses, such that each sense has its own art form, there arises a problem for aesthetic theory, not least in its philosophical version. Stating that there is an art form related to each of the senses itself contains some problems. Within the aesthetic discourse, there seems to be no agreement on this point unless one introduces the so-called "minor" arts, such as cooking and perfumery (cf. Nancy 1996: 11). As for touch, which becomes an important sense in Nancy's discussion, "it does not open onto any kind of art" (Nancy 1996: 11).

A theory that aspires to say something about art in general must be able to transcend the division of the arts, but if the concepts used within such a theory of art are differentiated in accordance with the differentiation of the senses and the subsequent differentiation of the arts, then a problem arises. The aesthetic discourse seems to operate on two different levels at the same time, a level of art in general, and a level of the arts in their differentiated understanding. Such a division between two different layers of aesthetic discourse is the theme of Theodor W. Adorno's essay "Die Kunst und die Künste" ("The Art and the Arts"). Adorno's essay discusses whether there is such a thing as Art, here understood as art in the singular, and often capitalized so as to underline this very singularity. The concept of "Art" is clearly fundamental to philosophical aesthetics, and it questions the very foundation of such a discussion. As a general or generalized concept, it also seems to partake in a discussion resembling the medieval discussion of general concepts, that is, the discussion of whether there can be such a thing as general concepts, and if so, what these would be or refer to. Art in the singular should most certainly be seen as emanating from a conception of the arts, and it thus seems like a concept arrived at by a process of induction. However, the question then arises: how can one get from arts to Art?

One proposed solution to this problem is the Wagnerian project of the *Gesamtkunstwerk* (the "Total Work of Art), a project discussed as well by Philippe Lacoue-Labarthe. Here it makes sense to follow the early Nietzschean interpretation. However, instead of claiming a birth of tragedy, it makes more sense to see it as a re-birth of dimensions from the ancient tragedy. Such an interpretation of the Nietzsche-Wagner relation is found in Lacoue-Labarthe's book *Musica Ficta (Figures of Wagner)*, where Nietzsche is understood as a renaissance philosopher, understood here in the literal sense of the word as a philosopher of the re-birth (*re-naissance*), and where the renaissance dimension of opera is underlined. Lacoue-Labarthe also claims that opera is the modern art form par excellence. What is interesting about this claim from our perspective is that the *Gesamtkunstwerk* attempts to bring together the different art forms that were differentiated somewhere at the end of the Greek period of philosophy. In the project of the total work of art, we find an art form that speaks to several senses at the same time, a project that is also claimed to continue with film.

Another possible solution to the "problem" of the differentiation of the arts is related to synaesthetic experiences, the latter understood as attempts to (re-)integrate the different senses and thereby close the differentiation of the senses that Nancy claims are the foundation of the pluralization of art. However, synaesthesia does not necessarily re-integrate the different art forms any more than does the *Gesamt-kunstwerk*. Perhaps it is more to be seen as challenging the borders between the different art forms, and thus in a more general sense fringes or frays these borders, as Adorno argues in his essay (cf. Adorno GS 10: 432). Such a fringing or fraying still requires a notion of the singular art forms, but in the process, the boundaries between the art forms are questioned.

What the total work of art shows us is also a version of the story of art that is strongly related to the question of the senses, or perhaps even more strongly to the question of why the arts (and by extension the senses) came to divide themselves. Here one sees a kind of Heideggerian motif, where there is a beginning and an end of the period of philosophy or metaphysics, combined with a Hegelian theory of the end of art. This theme is also present in Nancy's discussion, by which the question of the senses is viewed as coexisting with philosophy and its history, and in terms of the important alterations in the question of the plurality both of the arts and the senses, both at the beginning and the end of the project known in Heideggerian as "metaphysics". Nancy clearly refers to this understanding, as well as to the Hegelian interpretation of "the end of art". While these two strains of Nancy's thinking are not conflated, there seems little doubt that they both colour his interpretation.

Nancy's question that makes up the title for the essay is a timely one. It is also a question with a history, a fact that Nancy acknowledges as he pursues his argument. It was not always the case that there were several arts. At one time there was not even a concept of art comparable to the present situation. To write "comparable to the present situation" might in itself be problematic, since it might easily be argued that one characteristic of the present situation is that the differentiation of art from its "others" is becoming increasingly more difficult.

Nancy's essay takes its point of departure in the understanding of the Muses. The concept of the Muses, Nancy writes, is related to a plurality; there are always several Muses. Aesthetic thinking, or the thinking of and around the aesthetic, is thereby always already related to plurality, to multiplicity or to heterogeneity. Consequently, we also find this

25

related to the art forms, which are more or less understood as the materialization of the Muses, or at least as to their attributes. In the same sense as there are Muses only in the plural, art exists only in the plural, as "arts". At the same time we have, as Adorno points out in his title, a term for "art" in the singular. What does this term refer to? And where could we then find this "art"? It seems like art should be something that is common or homogeneous within the heterogeneity, that is, a dimension that transcends the singular art forms and thus says something about art in general. An aesthetic discourse that has this point of departure would then also be related to a more general or abstract discourse that transcends the divisions or differentiations of the individual art forms. Art transcends the arts. But we are still faced with the existence of a given multiplicity. How does this relate to art, or, as Nancy asks, "why are there several arts and not just one?"

According to Nancy, the question of the multiplicity of the arts can be avoided in two ways. The first one is a manner that only accepts or confirms a given plurality of arts.

> One is content to affirm that plurality is a given to the arts. To tell the truth, one does not even affirm it; one observes it – and who would not be forced to make this observation? (Nancy 1996: 2)

This version then often leads to a hierarchization of the arts, a hierarchization that has taken different forms throughout history. However, Nancy argues that the theories which derive from these various hierarchizations fail to pose "the ontological" question of the unity within this plurality. "Either the unity is presupposed as a vague unity of subsumption – 'art' in general – or else one receives the plurality without interrogating its own order, the *singular plural* of art, of the arts" (Nancy 1996: 2). Here we see one of Nancy's key arguments: the given plurality of the arts, as well as the concept of art, raises the question of what he calls "the singular plural", and it is to this rather paradoxical conception that the aesthetic discourse has to respond. Such a response would be compelled to discuss the theme of Nancy's essay, as well as the language used within the aesthetic discourse. Is it simply due to the language we use that this at all constitutes a problem? Addressing this question requires not only an exploration into the problem of language, but also addressing the paradox of the singular plural. The question of the relation between art and the arts is intimately tied to the language of the aesthetic discourse. For Nancy, "the ontological question" of arts requires us to question this very language. Thus, Nancy's project is clearly a project of conceptual criticism, of criticising the conceptual framework of the aesthetic discourse.

The second way to avoid this problem is so to speak the opposite of the first. Here one presupposes that there is art, or an essence of the arts. According to Nancy, this is the "philosophical" response to the problem (Nancy 1996: 3). Here, too, the conceptual seems to hide a problem more than reveal it. At least this follows from the Adornian critique of the concept of "essence". One might, of course, presuppose that there is such a thing as "art". However, this does not pose a solution to any problem, but rather a new question, the question of what one means with this concept, and how one could arrive at such a concept. More importantly, this question evolves into the question of the relation between the arts and the art, or more precisely, between the different art works and the general concept of art. If, as Nancy claims, there is a "singular plural" of art, then this concept needs to be philosophically worked out, and this would seem to be the task for contemporary aesthetics. That it is a contemporary question is also shown by the discussion of the historical situation that has led to this problem at all. The historical discussion here seems in a way to follow the very history of aesthetics, at least aesthetics understood in the modern sense of the word.

The historical discussion about the relation between unity and plurality in relation to the art(s) points to a division within romanticism. It is only since the Romantic period, that "we have been saying 'art' in the singular and without any other specification", Nancy writes (1996: 4). Before this, he argues, in the time of Kant and Diderot, there is instead the concept of the fine arts, the "beaux-arts", a concept often distinguished from "belles-lettres", and clearly part of a completely different understanding of arts. The discussion along the lines of the history of these concepts and their relation points to a period of the history of the arts and of aesthetics where the plurality of the arts is taken for granted, a period which begins with the decline of classical Greek thought and ending, at least in one sense – perhaps the modern sense – of the word, with the Wagnerian project of reconfiguring the plurality into a unity. This time span might also be called the time of "art as we know it" (or, perhaps, knew it). It is the time of art. A comparable interpretation is found in Nancy's discussion of sense, when, in *The Sense of the World*, he writes that "sense makes sense only in the space of philosophy as it ends by opening up the world" (Nancy 1997: 50). Thus, the argument would be that "sense" and "philosophy" are contemporaneous, and that with a certain end of philosophy there would also be an end of sense, and, similarly, that there would be a possible common or simultaneous birth or origin of these two concepts. For Nancy, this origin is related to Plato's thinking, where sense is related to "the Good". Via this discussion, Nancy also points to a necessary historicity of sense, and not least with the references to Hegel and Heidegger, both on the "end of art" and the end or closure of metaphysics. This historicity, however, also needs to be stressed in relation to the modern, or at least a certain notion of the modern, and this is what Nancy highlights when he writes that "art" in the singular is a recent concept, a concept whose use begins with the Romantic period.

Nancy moves further back in time, towards antiquity, and what could be called the origin of the entire discussion, and he points out how one then comes to the relation between arts and technics, in the sense of the Greek *tekhnē*.[1] This discussion throughout history not only shows that there have been different conceptions of art, and a particular conception that evolves from plurality to unity, but also that the earlier use of the concept of arts was not limited to what we now call art. Art, or *ars* as it was known in Latin, was a broader concept including technics, or what the Greeks called *tekhnē*. This relation is not as explicit today. Nancy claims that a title such as "Art and technics" today is understood as showing a problem, and not as a tautology, as he claims it is.

> Art and technics are so distinct for us that the title "art and technics", which has been the theme of more than one essay and more than one exhibition, is necessarily understood as the assertion of a problem and not as a tautology. (Nancy 1996: 5)

Of course, Nancy will not remove the distinction between art and technics of today, but he points to the similarities found here, also in a historical-theoretical context. This context can then again be used in thinking the aesthethic today. Nancy uses history to find examples and to discuss earlier positions and theories, but he is all the time contemporary and actualising. It is a philosophy or a philosophical discourse for today that is his project.

One feature of both arts and technics that can be agreed upon, and that confirms some of the affinity, even if on an almost mystical level, is how they both are in opposition to nature, or as Nancy writes, "what we still sometimes call 'nature'" (1996: 5). According to Greek thinking, art (in accordance with the concept *tekhnē*) has obtained two referents. Art has divided itself, and it is this division that is the theme for Nancy's essay. Nancy relates this division to a thinking of genus and species, that also parallels the division between the concepts of the individual and the universal found in medieval philosophy.

> Why did art divide itself? And why did it divide itself in such a way that on the one side, the side of "art", the unity of the presumed genus seems at least indifferent to and at most rebellious against the plurality of the presumed species, while on the other side, that of "technics", the unity of the genus – and we need not demonstrate this – is immediately understood as effectuated in a plurality of species that are multiplied indefinitely? (Nancy 1996: 5f)

But as Nancy shows with reference to the Muses, the question of why the art divided themselves is perhaps wrongly raised. Perhaps the arts never had such a unity that is presupposed in the "philosophical" thinking. At an ontological level, art is perhaps necessarily related to a multiplicity, as the terminology of the *singular plural* seems to describe. Still there are differences here. At the level of arts, or aesthetics, the division between arts and technics can be understood as a double thinking about both the product and the production. This is an opposition – if it is an opposition at all – which Nancy relates to Greek thinking, where he establishes a relation between *poiesis and tekhnē*. This division does not divide art in relation to the many ways a work can be established, but in relation to two different poles that both strive towards a unity, the product and the production. The division proposed here would then divide the product from the process or mode of production. And this division clearly has consequences for aesthetics today as well. As Nancy argues:

> The work has been divided, not according to the multiplicity of the ways in which it is put to work, but according to two poles, each of which tends towards unity: the product and the production, or, in other terms, the finite operation and the infinite operation. (Nancy 1996: 6)

Within, or between, these two domains, the diversity of the works and the modes of work come to the fore. There arises a relation between two different domains, and this relation is at the same time, he claims, a tension. This tension is between arts and technics, between product and production, and it oscillates, he writes, between repulsion and attraction (cf. Nancy 1996: 6f). The tension between product and production, which is also related to the relation between the finite and the infinite, establishes something between the two poles, where the extremes become important. The two extremes, or poles, refuse to acknowledge each other, and this is the reason for the tension between art and technics. We find this division again as a tension between the artistic and the artificial. In another vocabulary, this difference could also be seen as the difference between production and reception, and thus in a sense between two severely different relations to the work of art, the artist's point of view versus the aesthetician's point of view.

Arts and senses

For Nancy, perhaps, the most important moment in the division between the arts is related to a differentiation between the senses. The differentiation between the arts seems to follow a differentiation between the senses, in a manner comparable to how the various art forms are related to the different senses:

> This difference seems to propose itself right away as the difference between the senses. Nothing, it seems, any longer makes sense other than this: the difference between the arts has to do with the difference between the senses. (Nancy 1996: 9)

Here Nancy follows up the dense argumentation from *The Sense of the World*, explicitly playing on the double reference of the term *sense*. Nancy follows Hegel in his use of this term and claims that one can transform

31

the question about the differences between the arts to the question of the differences between the senses:

> At this point, the question of the difference between the arts ought to be transformed into the question of the difference between the senses. Perhaps in fact they are the same question. (Nancy 1996: 10)

Art, or the aesthetic, is related to sensation and to the sensible. Art is for the senses, as indicated by the Greek term *aisthesis,* and this term is an explicit reference for Nancy.

In Nancy's text we find that several established oppositions disappear. The aesthetic, which he sees explicitly as a theory of the senses, or of sensation, removes the division between the empirical and the transcendental, or between perception and act, as well as other more or less classical oppositions.

In the interplay between art(s) and sensation, we also find the interplay between sensation and meaning. The arts to a certain degree remove sensation from signification, Nancy writes. The world is no longer (necessarily) related to signification. The sensation establishes something external to signification, and this something is again related to what Nancy calls "the sense of the world". In the arts one find a suspension of signification:

> Art disengages the senses from signification, or rather, it disengages the world from signification, and that is what we call "the senses" when we give to the (sensible, sensuous) senses the sense of being external to signification. But it is what one might just as correctly name the "sense of the world". The sense of the world as suspension of signification – but we now understand that such a "suspension" is touch itself. Here being-in-the-world touches on its sense, is touched by it, touches itself as sense. (Nancy 1996: 22)

Nancy differentiates between *sense* in two meanings, one sensible and one intelligible, but these are closely related. It is in this relation that both of these dimensions come forward and become meaningful or possible to experience at all:

> (Sensuous) sense senses only if it is oriented to an object and if it valorizes it in a meaningful, informative, or operational context; reciprocally, (intelligible) sense makes sense only if it is, as one says, "perceived" and the "intuitive or perceptive relation to *intelligible sense* has always included, in finite being in general, an irreducible receptivity". (Sensuous) sense makes (intelligible) sense; it is indeed nothing but that, the intellection of its receptivity as such. (Intelligible) sense is sensed/senses itself; it is indeed nothing but that, the receptivity of its intelligibility. (Nancy 1996: 28)[2]

Continuing the discussion about the singularity and multiplicity of the arts and of the singularity and the multiplicity of the senses, Nancy claims that sensation is related both to the singular and to a multiplicity, both to the unique and the plural, and he claims this by way of a chiasmus: "So sense is multiply unique, and uniquely multiple" (Nancy 1996: 31). It is within this span that the aesthetic discourse takes place, and this is why Nancy's question about the "ontological" dimension of the arts and of sensation becomes important for this discourse. The question about differentiation thus becomes fundamental. Nancy also relates this to phenomenology, and here, too, the relation between product and production becomes important.

Nancy argues that there is a strong relation between the plurality of the arts, the necessary differentiation such a plurality implies and a differentiation of the senses. Thus, the question arises as to the relation between art and sensation, the arts and the senses, and, perhaps, Art and Sense. Nancy claims that "the plurality of the arts is as essentially irreducible as the unity of art is absolute" (Nancy 1996: 9), but this implies a tension here between art and arts, a tension perhaps irresolvable. Nevertheless, given the historicity to which I have alluded above, it might still be possible to present this tension. Nancy makes clear that the question of differentiation in relation to art is also a question of differentiation of the senses. This also seems to mean that the question in a way becomes more "empirical"; it becomes related to the sensuous, and to the ways that we might make sense of the sensuous. Perhaps, Nancy writes, the question of the difference between the arts is the same question as the question of the difference between the senses (cf. Nancy 1996: 10). Even with the "perhaps", there is still an alteration at stake here (perhaps minor), from the question of the differentiation of the arts/senses to the question of the difference between the arts/senses. To point to such an alteration – a minor one on first sight – just highlights the complexity Nancy wants to show in raising the question(s) in the first place:

> The relation between the two differences, therefore, that between the arts and that between the senses, does not let itself be treated lightly. Their identity and their difference contain no less than the structure and the stakes of the *sense* and/or the *senses* of what is called, perhaps too quickly, "art". (Nancy 1996: 10)

Thus, these questions, which perhaps are a single question, also question the very notion of art. And, as should be clear by now, we must question the very possibility of making sense of art. Hence, the question is not a question of sense alone, nor a question of art alone. It is a question that necessarily opens up the whole complex of art, sensation, and meaning, as well as both production and reception of (the) art(s).

Touch

Nancy's questions of the relation between art and sensation open a whole complex of questions. This is not least clear from his discussion of touch, which he, referring to a long tradition, understands as the "paradigm or even essence of the senses in general" even if "it does not open onto any kind of art" (Nancy 1996: 11). Touch shows itself to be of importance by the fact "that art in general cannot not *touch*, in all the senses of the word" (Nancy 1996: 11).[3] Nancy refers to Lucretius' statement that touch is "the sense of the body in its entirety", and continues: "Touch is nothing other than the touch or stroke of sense altogether and of all the senses" (Nancy 1996: 17). Touch is thus both a sensuous dimension of relation to the world, and a kind of bodily "perception". As Nancy writes: "Touch *forms one body* with sensing, or it makes of the sensing faculties a body – it is but the *corpus* of the senses" (Nancy 1996: 17). Touch here clearly also functions as metaphor, or, perhaps, quasi-metaphor, for the kind of feeling related to the act of sensing. Perhaps it would be better to say that "feeling" is the metaphorical concept here, since it seems as well to allude to a certain kind of tactility, whereas it clearly also designates a more "spiritual" entity. However, this whole question of metaphoricity might perhaps be bypassed, in that Nancy so clearly writes about how touch, as the "paradigm of the senses in general", also removes other important dualisms:

> But what does art do if not finally touch upon and touch by means of the principal heterogeneity of "sensing"? In this heterogeneity in principle that resolves itself into a heterogeneity *of the* principle, art touches on the sense of touch itself: in other words, it touches at once on the "self-touching" inherent in touch and on the "interruption" that is no less inherent in it. In another lexicon, one might say: it touches on the immanence and the transcendence of touch. Or in still other terms: it touches on the trans-

immanence of being-in-the-world. Art does not deal with the "world" understood as simple exteriority, milieu, or nature. It deals with being-in-the-world in its very springing forth. (Nancy 1996: 18)

The different wordings Nancy employs are clearly meant to show different ways of approaching the very question. I will not follow the more Heideggerian reading here, however, but would like to stress that Nancy is describing how the duality he locates in the touch at the same time breaks down, or deconstructs, several of the classical dichotomies related not only to sensation and art, but metaphysics as well. The heterogeneity of touch both self-touches and interrupts touch. It simultaneously touches both the immanence and transcendence of touch, and it breaks down the opposition between an exterior and an interior. This last dimension is not found in this wording, but seems as well to be how one should understand touch in the duality of touching with the hand, touching the exterior, on the one hand, and being touched, touched in the interior, on the other.

Touch thus makes contact between what used to be called the body and the soul, in a manner comparable to how sense might do the same in its double reference. Touch thus functions at borders or at thresholds, and exists primarily in a status of the in-between. It is double. However, as the paradigm of sense, it also reveals how sensation works. "Touch is nothing other than the touch or stroke of sense altogether and of all the senses" (Nancy 1996: 17). For Nancy, touch is not synonymous with tactility. One can touch also at a distance. There is a heterogeneity of touch. "Touch is proximate distance. It makes one sense what makes one sense (what it *is* to sense): the proximity of the distant, the approximation of the intimate" (Nancy 1996: 17). Thus, touch is both the paradigm, or the model, of sensing as such, it shows the sense of sense and is at the same time also a kind of general sense, showing how one might sense with the other senses, or how the other senses might sense.

Touch shows how one might become touched by sensation.

In approaching the plurality of the arts, perception, or the senses, become forces. Here another dimension of touch comes to the fore; forcing the senses means that the senses in a way become aware of the act of sensation, as well as the act of perception. Nancy refers to this as the act when a sense touches itself:

> Art forces a sense to touch itself, to be this sense that it is. But in this way, it does not become simply what we call "a sense", for example, sight or hearing: by leaving behind the integration of the "lived", it also becomes something else, another instance of unity, which exposes another world, not a "visual" or "sonorous" world but a "pictorial" or "musical" one. It makes of the "sonorous" or "auditory" region, for example, a world composed of equivalents, pitches, scales, harmonic relations, melodic sequences, tonalities, rhythms, timbres, and so forth – a world one of whose faces, the written and calculated one, has nothing to do with sound and another of whose faces is taken up in the always unpredictable quality of a singular "interpretation" or "execution". (Nancy 1996: 21)

In this act, the "force of the Muses" (Nancy 1996: 22) is at stake. It is a force that at once both separates and unifies, it alters or metamorphoses something that was once a unity of signification and representation into something else. This something else is not "a detached part but the touch of another unity – which is no longer the unity of signification" (Nancy 1996: 22). It thus alters the very foundation of what is commonly understood as a work of art, where "signification" and "representation" are two of the key terms, at least within modern aesthetics. Signification, according to Nancy, is suspended, and in this touch between unities, "meaning's extremities" is touched as well. Thus the suspension of signification, and by extension a kind of signification beyond signification, leads to the extremities of meaning, or perhaps beyond meaning.

Here the discussion of touch, perhaps paradoxically, seems to be somewhat parallel to how Nancy, in *The Sense of the World*, discusses music, of which destiny he writes "is not without a very intimate and complex relationship with the destiny of sense" (Nancy 1997: 84):

> Indeed, regulated, rhythmical sonority can take on, at least to our Occidental *sense*, the value of a threshold between sensibility and signification. One could say that music has signified for us significance itself, and even beyond significance the sublime access (say, in the mode of negative theology) to a pure presentation of sense. But in order for this to be the case, it was necessary that it be understood as "an art beyond signification". The threshold of such a "beyond" is the critical point par excellence of any approach to sense: one can always pass on anew to an ineffable (but sonorous, audible, vocal, evocative) "oversignification", but one can also keep to the threshold as to the in-significant opening of sense. (Nancy 1997: 84f)

Evoking music here might not be that surprising. It follows a long tradition within Western aesthetics in seeing music as non-referential, and thus as, in a profound sense, unavailable for language. This should not be taken to mean that the other arts are necessarily closer to language, but this tradition is nevertheless a strong one. One does not have to subscribe to the idea of the ineffable dimension of music. One might simply state that music is beyond signification. Nancy invokes Lacoue-Labarthe, who argues that music is "an art (of the) beyond (of) signification, which is to say (of the) beyond (of) representation" (Lacoue-Labarthe 1994: 144). In this way, Nancy can claim, in relation to touch, that there are two different unities, one of signification and representation, and another where signification has been suspended, and that these two meet, or touch each other (cf. Nancy 1996: 22). If signification is suspended, it seems to follow from Lacoue-Labarthe's statement that so would representation. Lacoue-Labarthe's argument is here related to Adorno and to Adorno's reading of Arnold Schoenberg's opera *Moses und Aron*, and it is fundamentally a question of the possibility or impossibility of presentation or representation. Lacoue-Labarthe also uses another concept to designate what Nancy calls suspension, caesura, which he takes from Hölderlin:

> For Adorno, as for Schönberg, music in its very intention would, in short, come under the horizon of what Benjamin called "pure language", which is perhaps not without a relation to what Hölderlin, on the subject of the caesura, called "pure speech". [...] Ultimate paradox: the naked word – the language of signification itself – comes to tell of the impossible beyond of signification, something that Benjamin would not have denied. (Lacoue-Labarthe 1994: 144f)

This is not the place to discuss Lacoue-Labarthe's reading of Adorno and Schoenberg.[4] Nevertheless, Lacoue-Labarthe's discussion of music reveals dimensions of music and touch similar to those of Nancy. Hence, touch for Nancy is not solely a question of tactility, it is also a question of "tact", in the sense of rhythm, caesura, interruption, syncopation, or suspension.

Exposure

Touch is also intimately related to the body, and one could thereby think that we are back to our point of departure, with Eagleton. To a certain degree, I am, but that raises the question of the body. In his text "Corpus", Nancy claims that "there is no such thing as *the* body. There is no body" (Nancy 1993a: 207). At the same time, Nancy argues that touch, in a way because of the absence of *the* body, is related to the, or a, limit.

> The gesture of the limit, the gesture at the limit, is touch – or rather: touching is the thought of the limit. To touch is to be at the limit, touching is *being* at the limit – and this is indeed being itself, absolute being. If there is

something rather than nothing, it is because there is this limit made body, these bodies made limit, and exposed by their limits. Absolutely. Thought must touch on this. (Nancy 1993a: 206)

The body is exposure, and as exposure it could be thought to express something. But this is only partly true. The naked body, Nancy writes, "gives no sign and reveals nothing, nothing other than this: that there is nothing to reveal, that everything is there, exposed, the texture of the skin, which says no more than the texture of the voice" (Nancy 1993a: 204f). Here, too, there seems to be a relation between touch, or at least a certain notion of tactility, and sound, here related to the voice and not to music. The voice is an exposure in a manner comparable to the exposure of the naked body. And just as touching, when taken in its multiple meanings, removes the dualism of exterior and interior, so does the voice, so much so that there is a long tradition of seeing the voice as an exteriorization of the interior, or of the soul becoming sensible.[5] The discussion of the limit also becomes a discussion of what Nancy calls "the threshold". Being at the threshold is at the same time to occupy a position that is at the limit, or in-between traditional dualisms. The threshold is neither inside nor outside. Discussing laughter in terms of Derrida, Nancy in his "Elliptical Sense", also discusses the limit. Here it becomes clear that this discussion is also related to the very concept of exposition.

It [the laughter] is beyond all opposition of serious and non-serious, of pain and pleasure. Or rather, it is at the juncture of these oppositions, at the limit which they share and which itself is only the limit of each one of these terms, the limit of their signification, the limit to which these significations, as such, are exposed. One could say, in another language, that such a limit, as the place where pain and pleasure partake each of the other, is a place of the sublime. I prefer to say, in a less aesthetic language, that it is a place of exposition. (Nancy 1992: 41)

The threshold, which I see as another concept for the limit, would thus be similar, if not completely identical, to "a place of the sublime". However, it is especially clear that Nancy sees a similarity between "a place of the sublime" and "a place of exposition". The difference between these two designations is only, and this "only" seems to be what Nancy is alluding to, a question of which language one poses it in. "A place of exposition" would be just another way of saying "a place of the sublime". And this place is in a profound sense a non-place, a limit or a threshold, neither outside nor inside. Related to Nancy's discussion in "On the Threshold", from *The Muses*, it would seem that this place is "nothing other than place itself" (Nancy 1996: 57). This "place itself" would thus be, and here the concept of exposition comes to the fore, very much a dimension of being, if not *the* dimension of being. We are exposed, and this exposition is our position when we are towards something, in our context, when we are towards the work of art.

Nancy argues that both the body and the voice are important in establishing (if that is the word) a community. Such a community is primarily found in his focus upon the notion of sharing, of sharing what is common. In the case of bodies, what is common is a certain dimension of space, even if two bodies can never occupy the same space, they are in proximity, a proximity dependent upon touch or the possibility of being touched. This, too, would be a result of the total exposure of the naked body, an exposure at the same time necessarily also showing vulnerability. What we share is being bodies, and thus touching and being touched. We also share language, and language in sharing is a common language, a necessary dimension of both community and communication. The sharing of language is communicability, the very possibility of community. But this is so, so to speak, at a certain distance. Nancy discusses a voice that "is not language, and what is more, this voice remains without vocabulary, without vocalization, and without vocalics" (Nancy 1993a: 201). This discussion is where one can find the relation to how Nancy also discusses music, as sound without or beyond signification, as indicating signification. Here he seems close to Giorgio Agamben's discussions of the voice in, for example, *Language and Death*, where Agamben writes about the voice as "mere sound" or "pure voice".

> The voice, taken in this way, will then show itself as a pure intention to signify, as pure meaning, in which something is given to be understood before a determinate event of meaning is produced. (Agamben 1991: 33)

He relates this to the medieval discussion of *flatus vocis*, which, he writes, "is not meant [...] as mere sound, but in the sense of the voice as an intention to signify and as a pure indication that language is taking place" (Agamben 1991: 34). This taking place of language, beyond or before meaning, and as such as a showing the fact of language, would in Nancy's terms constitute a sharing of communicability, in other words, the ability, or possibility, of a common language, sharable and as such, a necessary dimension of community. According to Agamben, there is a negativity in this argument, at least in its medieval version. But within modernity, or a version of modernity, it is not nothingness that is signified, but rather signification as such that is shown. It is a self-demonstration of the absolute that "does not show or signify other than itself" (Agamben 1991: 103). This, then, would be somewhat comparable to how Nancy describes the voice as not language and as without vocabulary, vocalization, and vocalics.

Touching is intimately related to our skin. This is also one of the important dimensions of Nancy's argument. When we touch, we touch a surface, and the most important "things" are on this surface. They are skin deep, as one might also put it.[6] Here the skin functions as a surface, as the surface making touching possible. This is the empirical touch, the facticity of touch, touching in the most literal, corporal sense of the word. However, we might be touched in another sense as well, as when we are touched within. This is not, at least at first sight, the same as touch at a surface. Here we are no longer skin deep, but deep in another sense. Touch might still refer to the body, but it is the interior of the body, the depth of the body. It is also a depth that, at least metaphorically, moves beyond the body. We are touched in our souls. This touch, a second version of touch, is at the same time an alteration of the feelings. We feel, and we feel touched. This is how we describe the alterations of our interior; the way the exterior alters our interior. The way our body in a sense moves beyond itself, and establishes contact with the soul. The soul, here, must be understood as our feelings, our ways of thinking, the way our mind responds to being touched. Thus, there is in the acts of touching and of being touched a certain sense of communication: a communication that alters our very being. The skin thus functions in a manner comparable to an interface, as when we are caressed and there is a movement of the touch from our skin to our soul. Here touching functions as a paradigm of being together; the experience we have when being touched is the experience of being exposed, exposed to the touch of the other. In thus being exposed, we are touched, and we are no longer the same. Touching, and the accompanied feeling, alters us, we are no longer the same, we become different.

A similar process is at stake in our encounter with a work of art. Here, too, we are touched. We touch the work of art – remember that touching here is not the same as tactility, every sense touches, even if it touches at a distance – and this touch at the same time touches us. We are exposed to the work of art, and the work of art alters us, our "soul", as the receptive organ, the organ with the ability to be touched. Thus, the sensation and perception of the work of art, our very encounter with the work of art, touches us, and consequently alters us. This is not even an act of making sense, in the sense of making meaning. We are altered without meaning, at least without meaning in the sense of intellectual sense. The encounter with the work of art is more than an intellectual act; it is more than simply, or not so simply, interpreting the artwork to have it deliver some sense of meaning.

Thus, our encounter with the work of art, removes the doubleness that Susan Sontag raised in the conclusion to her "Against Interpretation" from 1964. Sontag argued for an alteration in the response to the work of art, seeing to substitute hermeneutics with an erotics of art (cf. Sontag 2001: 14). Such an erotics seems to be inevitably present if we follow Nancy's argument. When we are touched by the work of art, this is, is a profound sense, a kind of eroticism. The work of art touches us, and in this touch we are altered in our soul, even without any meaning in the so-called "intellectual" sense, and this, as I understand it, would be the meaning found after the act of hermeneutics that Sontag would substitute.

However, given Nancy's argument, it does not seem to be the case that these two ways of responding to the work of art exclude each other. In my view, it does not even seem to be the case that we have to choose between them, and perhaps it is not even possible to choose. Being touched by a work of art is not something we can choose. It is beyond our capacity to choose to be touched. On the other hand, what we can choose is a certain attitude of exposure, an exposure making it possible to be touched. This act of exposure, and the subsequent experience of being touched, also shows that this very exposure is not as such a passive pose. This is also why I would claim that it is in a sense possible to choose this kind of attitude. The very possibility of being affected, of being touched, is there as a modulation of our attention, and this attention is in a sense beyond the dualism of activity and passivity. Nancy claims that "affect presupposes itself", and that "in this, it behaves like a subject, but as a passive or passible actuality of being-subject-*to*" (Nancy 1997: 129). It would thus seem to be closer to a passivity than to an activity, but that is not the main point. More important is the very ability to become affected – what Nancy calls our "affectability" – that lies at the bottom of this possible process. We have the possibility to freely choose to inhabit this ability; we can allow ourselves to be exposed to the possibility of getting touched. As Nancy writes:

Affectability constitutes the pres-ence of sensible presence, not as a pure virtuality, but as a being-in-itself-always-already-touched, touched by the possibility of being touched. For this, it is necessary for being-passible in itself to have already offered some part of itself – but here, the part counts for the whole – to something outside of itself (or to some part of itself set apart from itself). (Nancy 1997: 128f)

We expose ourselves, and thus allow ourselves to be struck by the work of art. This is the attitude that allows us to be touched by the work of art, in our body and our mind. We might shiver, we might tremble before the sublime. We might get goose bumps from the experience, the hair on our body stands. These are alterations of our skin, but alterations which are an integrated part of our experience. The skin shows itself to be an interface, or perhaps rather a threshold, a boundary that separates our bodies from the rest of the world, but that at the same time communicates between the world and our innermost selves. Such experiences, comparable to how psychoanalysis describes "oceanic fantasies", might be very different, but they share something. As Daniel Schwarz writes in his book *Listening Subjects: Music, Psychoanalysis, Culture*, there is a common feeling that "the boundary separating the body from the external world seems dissolved or crossed in some way" (Schwarz 1997: 7). Schwarz discusses this feeling by employing a vocabulary taken from psychoanalysis, and he claims that this feeling is a fantasy. However, this does not challenge the experience we obtain when our skin communicates, and we are touched. The skin becomes a threshold, at once separating – being a boundary, as Schwartz writes – and at the same time dissolving. The skin is not dissolved in a physical sense, of course, but there is a dissolving process that establishes the very fact that we are touched.

The skin as threshold also says something more generally about the threshold, another concept highlighted by Nancy in his "On the Threshold" (from *The Muses*). Related to how we experience viewing a painting, Nancy discusses the threshold, a threshold that is the place where we view the painting without being able to enter it, but where we are still in contact with it. We are thus at the threshold, "neither inside nor outside – and perhaps we are, ourselves, the threshold, just as our eye conforms to the place of the canvas and weaves itself into its fabric" (Nancy 1996: 57). Here Nancy is discussing Caravaggio's *The Death of the Virgin* (1695–6), a painting also showing other thresholds. It is a painting showing life and death, and thus in a profound sense staging what Nancy calls "the threshold of existence" (Nancy 1996: 61). Nancy primarily discusses this other threshold, a threshold in a way beyond sense, but still a threshold saying something about existence. And the experience of existence, as Nancy argues in *The Birth to Presence*, is one of being exposed, of being able to be touched. "Experience is just this, being born to the presence of sense, a presence itself nascent, and only nascent" (Nancy 1993a: 4). The representation that is Caravaggio's painting does not show this presence of sense. Comparable to how birth "as such" has no sense, neither does death. However, the threshold makes sense, it tells us something, alters our being, moves us. We thus find as well a relation between feeling and motion, what Nancy describes, in "The Sublime Offering", as "(e)motion" (Nancy 1993b: 44).[7]

The attitude that allows us to become touched, the exposure towards the work of art, is thus in a sense what makes aesthetic experience possible. We are touched by the work of art, but this process of being touched presupposes a certain receptivity. "To be touched is sublime because it is to be exposed and to be offered", Nancy writes (1993b: 50). In offering ourselves over to the possibility of getting touched, we thus take upon us an attitude of receptivity. I would be tempted to call this receptivity an aesthetic attitude, an attitude exposing the sensing body, exposing the senses, and thus allowing it to become touched. Claiming that this is an aesthetic attitude might at the same time also show that one of the fundamental oppositions of aesthetics is anaesthesia, the numbing of the senses. Thus, the inability to be touched might be the result of anaesthesia, of having senses that have been numbed and thus not being open, exposed towards the outer. At the other end, being open towards the work of art or the aesthetic might also be seen as being open towards something that makes us lose ourselves. We lose touch with our bodies, existing on the limit, on the threshold.

1   The term "technics" is how the English translation of Nancy renders *la technique*. The term is chosen to indicate that it is not simply a question of technical skills or technology, but "the whole order of *tekhnē*" (Nancy 1996: 104, note 4, translator's note). A similar manner of translation is found as well in Bernard Stiegler's *Technics and Time, 1: The Fault of Epimetheus* (Stanford: Stanford University Press, 1998). Nancy refers to this book, and discusses some of the same questions, albeit from a different perspective.

2   The quote within this quote is from Derrida's *Khōra*, where Derrida discusses Kant: "The Kantian moment has some privilege here, but even before the *intuitus derivatius* or pure sensibility has been determined as recepticity, the intuitive or perceived relation to *intelligible sense* has always included, in finite being in general, an irreducible receptivity." (Derrida 1995: 111)

3   The importance of touch in relation to Nancy's writings is also the theme of Jacques Derrida's *Le toucher, Jean-Luc Nancy* (Paris: Galilée, 2000).

4   For more on Schoenberg's opera, an interpretation of it, and a presentation of the readings of Adorno and Lacoue-Labarthe, I refer to my doctoral dissertation *Arnold Schoenberg's* Moses und Aron: *Music, Language, and Representation* (Trondheim: Norwegian University of Science and Technology, 2002).

5   A discussion of the voice from another, somewhat similar perspective might be found in Jonathan Rée's *I See A Voice: Language, Deafness and the Senses – A Philosophical History* (London: Harper Collins, 1999). Rée's discussion of the different ways of making the deaf learn language points to the importance of the different senses here. He shows how both the senses of vision and of tactility have been essential in such a pedagogical project. In showing *why* it was seen as important that the deaf would learn to speak – and not "simply" to have a sign-language – he points to the important relation that was understood to exist between the voice and the soul. Learning to speak was a manner of saving the soul, since those who have no spoken language – which is also an important interpretation of the infant, *infans*, the ones who do not have language – do not have access to salvation. The discussion of infancy and language is also found in Giorgio Agamben's *Infancy and History: Essays on the Destruction of Experience* (London: Verso, 1993).

6   For more on the "Skin deep", as well as on perception, sensation and art, see Mieke Bal's *Quoting Caravaggio: Contemporary Art, Preposterous History* (Chicago: University of Chicago Press, 1999). Bal provides some fascinating examples of the discussion of representation of skin and the "depth of surface, reaching skin-deep" (p. 27), primarily via discussions of different versions of the baroque.

7   This term can also be discussed in relation to Wim Wenders' book *Emotion Pictures* (reprinted in Wim Wenders: *On Film: Essays and Conversations*. London: Faber and Faber, 2001), where the relation between motion and emotion is highlighted.

Literature

Adorno, Theodor W. (1997 [1971ff.]): *Gesammelte Schriften*. Frankfurt am Main: Suhrkamp.

Agamben, Giorgio (1991 [1982]): *Language and Death: The Place of Negativity*. Minneapolis: University of Minnesota Press.

Agamben, Giorgio (1993 [1978]): *Infancy and History: Essays on the Destruction of Experience*. London: Verso.

Bal, Mieke (1999): *Quoting Caravaggio: Contemporary Art, Preposterous History*. Chicago: University of Chicago Press.

Derrida, Jacques (1995 [1993]): *On the Name*. Stanford: Stanford University Press.

Derrida, Jacques (2000): *Le toucher, Jean-Luc Nancy*. Paris: Galilée.

Eagleton, Terry (1992 [1990]): *The Ideology of the Aesthetic*. Oxford: Blackwell.

Lacoue-Labarthe, Philippe (1994 [1991]): *Musica Ficta (Figures of Wagner)*. Stanford: Stanford University Press.

Nancy, Jean-Luc (1992): "Elliptical Sense", in David Wood (ed.): *Derrida: A Critical Reader*. Oxford: Blackwell, pp. 36-51.

Nancy, Jean-Luc (1993a): *The Birth to Presence*. Stanford: Stanford University Press.

Nancy, Jean-Luc (1993b [1988]): "The Sublime Offering", in Jean-François Courtine et al.: *Of the Sublime: Presence in Question*. Albany: State University of New York Press, pp. 25-54.

Nancy, Jean-Luc (1996 [1994]): *The Muses*. Stanford: Stanford University Press.

Nancy, Jean-Luc (1997 [1993]): *The Sense of the World*. Minneapolis: University of Minnesota Press.

Rée, Jonathan (1999): *I See a Voice: Language, Deafness and the Senses – A Philosophical History*. London: Harper Collins.

Schwarz, David (1997): *Listening Subjects: Music, Psychoanalysis, Culture*. Durham: Duke University Press.

Sontag, Susan (2001 [1966]): *Against Interpretation and Other Essays*. New York: Picador.

Steinskog, Erik (2002): *Arnold Schoenberg's Moses und Aron: Music, Language, and Representation*. Dr. art. dissertation, Trondheim: Norwegian University of Science and Technology (NTNU), Faculty of Arts.

Stiegler, Bernard (1998 [1994]): *Technics and Time, 1: The Fault of Epimetheus*. Stanford: Stanford University Press.

Wenders, Wim (2001): *On Film: Essays and Conversations*. London: Faber and Faber.

Challenging Modernism in Sloterdijk's Spheres

Michael Penzold

"Spheres are shared spaces which are established by living together within them. They are the first product of human cooperation; they are the immaterial and yet most real result of an original work being done only by resonances. It is not division of labour that has propelled the process of civilization but the sharing of spheres; this is the original vote of the community in and about itself."[1]

Spaces

IN – UP TO now – two bulky volumes, the German philosopher and literary critic Peter Sloterdijk writes in some detail about spheres as philosophical phenomena: their aesthetic aspects are considered, they are analyzed as political and psychological symbols, they are considered as a kind of hyper-forms behind the logical generation of evidence and even as a basic framework of theological argument. Sloterdijk dwells on the cultural metamorphosis of "spheres", describing the metamorphosis of forms behind thoughts and – vice versa – intellectual conditions of forms in general.[2] Not being a work of historical science, *Sphären I* (published in 1998) and *Sphären II* (1999) deal with analyzing modernism on the background of a more general theory of "spheres".

And "spheres" are – most generally speaking – nothing else but spaces that science (e.g. physics) is unable to describe. They are spaces, extensive imaginations, that people share and that have a share in people's lives. They are the natural surrounding of human beings seen not only from the outside as a very sophisticated and intelligent kind of animal, but seen from the inside, as intellectual and to some degree imaginative and emotional beings. And human beings are not autonomous rulers and masters within them, but the spheres of the single person are occupied by others, polycentric and in constant movement.

For human beings, consciousness of these spaces is essential, because their "primary productivity" consists in "working" for their place in spaces that are surreal and which obey their own logic, "working" for their "billeting on peculiar, surreal space-relationships/constellations."[3]

As Sloterdijk is one of the most prominent critics of the thesis of the autonomous, atomistic and self-confirming subject proposed by modern thinkers, the idea of the subject as sharing spaces, as the restless remainder of a lost unity, is essential for him. What makes Sloterdijk write books about "spheres" is the idea that the subject itself has been left behind by the other half of the couple, the other half that never stops trying to lay claim to the subject.[4] Moreover, this restlessness is the stylistically and intellectually characteristic feature of Sloterdijk's texts: in cascades of reformulations and joyful puns, the books seem to create "spheres" of their own.

Sloterdijk's rather artificial, almost effusive style and the rich material he deals with – and sometimes almost wrestles with – makes it difficult to systematize his arguments, but on a more abstract level, his thought can be surveyed.[5] Sloterdijk's texts are "spatially" conceived. They intermingle, open up for new aspects of the basic concern with each chapter, and the numerous "excursions" are like funnels in a complicated underground system, connecting even more rooms, caves and other textual "spaces" with his main speculations on spheres.

Another thesis that sets the books in full swing is that the spaces which form the subject interface with other spaces, spaces from the outside. But these spaces are usually seen as challenges or even menaces, and that is why we need spheres: they are parts of the subject's physical and intellectual immune system.

Microspheres

Sloterdijk's project is divided into three parts. He distinguishes spheres in their dominant and most basic forms of appearance as microspherical "Blasen" (bubbles, blisters, blabs, bladders, but also "to blow"), macrospherical "Globen" (globes) and "Schäume" (foams, froths, scums, lathers): these are the three ontological modes of representation of spheres.

In the "microspherical" part of the book, Sloterdijk deals with a theory of intimacy, a collection of evidence showing that all human sciences have given hints to a "topological surrealism" because it has never been possible to talk about human beings without taking into account their rather opalescent "poetics of the inhabited intrinsic space."[6]

How do we know that there is something like intrinsic space and why it is so important to write and read books about it?

The answer to this question can be found only through a recapitulation of Sloterdijk's view on the inherent living conditions of a human being. The human being, as an "open" being, is always exposed to influences and spatial claims from the outside and has to distinguish threats from help. It is easy to experience that human beings have no center of their own: the child that follows a soap-bubble on its way through the air or the person who eats an extraordinarily palatable sweet are for a short period eccentric, more part of a very special spatial constellation than a "self". But it is even more than that: the person who eats the sweet "fuses" with an object as unpretentious as a piece of chocolate or a soap-bubble. Intrinsic spaces unite and the heroic subject is gone.[7]

Spatial "intruders" are even necessary to the development of a mature person.[8] The establishment of a uniform identity does not correspond to the natural potential of man.

In his microspherical speculations, Sloterdijk searches for the main symbols of the human being's spatial openness.

The first symbol is the heart as the main metaphor for life and emotion in Western literary tradition. The rhythm of the heart which surrounds the unborn child is the basic biological fact behind the symbol's universality. In various excursions in literature, art and religion, Sloterdijk shows, that – even after birth – the heart, in its proper destination, has always been the heart of the other, a medium of communication rather than the center of a system of blood circulation. In the history of religions, this interpretation of the heart culminates in the Eucharist and in Christ's spiritual self-communication through bread and wine. Then there is the "interfacial intimate sphere", a more artificial and more complex means of establishing non-physical spaces. The "opening of the faces" – "Gesichtsöffnung" (Sloterdijk, vol. I, p. 166) – is, more than the use of tools or the hand, the main characteristic of human beings. The openness of the faces – and not necessarily the fitness of the body[9] – leads to the establishment of human culture, and the strength of interfaciality is that it is based on joy between the faces, as mutual as in sexuality, which, by the way, Sloterdijk does not take into consideration as an intimate and spheropoetic relation between human beings.

The third important ground on which intimate spaces can develop is magnetism. However antiquated and esoteric this notion may sound at first glance, magnetism sums up all interpersonal reciprocal interactions which transgress space and time and a material world as a basis for interpersonal relations. Magnetism is a word for the idea that people are connected with each other and that the discussion of the ways they communicate beyond time and space has always been of interest. Discussing magnetism, Sloterdijk has in mind how the human being's interest in universal and non-technical communication goes beyond the invention of telecommunications and the modern media. Sloterdijk shows that modernism in that sense seems more of a reduction and not of the realization of human potentials. As the exorbitant success of *Harry Potter* has shown, magnetism and magic are still on the agenda, even if interpersonal spaces seem to have shrunk to a disobliging universal intimacy by the extensive use of mobile telephones.

For Sloterdijk, birth becomes an example of the dynamics of microspherical evolution. The argument that spheres – as much security and certainty as they may convey – are always exposed to an intrinsic dynamics of self-destruction or transmutation is one of the strongest critical elements in Sloterdijk's project. Therefore, "spheres" are fugitive matter, but as we all fade away, we learn a lot about ourselves by scrutinizing the conditions for our "spheres".

Over a long period of time, the child's security in the womb of the pregnant woman has been a kind of paradigm of the dyadic situation, and the prenatal shaping of basic possibilities of experience in the person's later life. Pregnancy has been idealized without taking into account developments of the "child" during its prenatal existence, and forgetting, that the establishment of this first bipolar sphere in which the person is involved, is bound to be destroyed by birth. The intrinsic processes, that leads to the sphere's establishment can at the same time explain the collapse of this sphere in the process of birth.

For Sloterdijk, the necessary destruction of this first sphere is not only paradigmatic in relation to other spheres, it is first of all the period of a harmonious living together with the symbolic representations of the afterbirth in one's later life: nobody is ever alone, nobody is born alone, there is always the placenta with you.[10] The afterbirth in a more abstract form is the "nobject", that determines the existence of each human being, it is looked after and re-established in different ways. It is "the ur-companion" ("der Urbegleiter", vol. I, p. 347) that is at the same time the "with" and the "also" (vol. I, p. 360) in later life. It is nameless, could never be named and it is without perceptible appearance (vol. I, p. 362), it is the first resort in relation to which we place ourselves within our first sphere and later on in an originally sphereless world and thereby helps us to form and to establish our Ego (vol. I, p. 360–61). And it is the first experience of a medium, it is the reason why we are "open" towards the world around us, the "afterbirth" being the unshaped condition of realizing our environment as being "around" us.[11]

For Sloterdijk "life-trees", the symbol of the tree or even angels, clouds, twins, doubles and even beds are ontological and symbolical representations of the first "with-nobjekt" ("Mit-Nobjekt", vol. I, p. 366),[12] which shares the space we could call "soul".

Sloterdijk's explanations leave the reader with the impression that the book that is pursuing a special psychological theory of literature that focuses on the very artistic possibilities of literature.

And indeed, it is sound and language Sloterdijk writes about in the last parts of *Sphären I: Blasen*.

The role language and sound plays in Sloterdijk's thinking can most adequately be sketched by recapitulating the basic thought in "spheres" in Sloterdijk's own words:

> In the beginning, the accompanied animals, the human beings, are surrounded by something, that can never be seen as a thing. They are – first of all – the invisibly supplemented ones, the corresponding beings, the ones who are embraced, and, in case of disorder, the ones who are left behind by all good company. Therefore, to ask what the human being is in a philosophical way primarily means: to analyze couples, obvious and not so obvious

ones, those in which one lives together with sociable partners, and those that establish unions with problematic and unattainable others. Only the ideologia perennis, that floats on the mainstream of individualistic abstraction, speaks of an unaccompanied individual.[13]

Language and sound are the main manifestations of the others, and a simple reflection makes this idea into a well-founded suspicion. The absolutely largest part of acoustic stimulus and information is filtered out, leaving only an almost marginal percentage that is apt to cause resonances (vol. I, p. 489).

To find the "other" means to draw the logical consequences of spherical interaction: Sloterdijk can speak of "pre-natal acoustic prejudices" (vol. I, p. 518), that are the predispositions for the subsequent development of selective mechanisms in the noisy and therefore menacing world around the self. For Sloterdijk, becoming human being seems to be closely connected to the speech-act of being welcomed, greeted, saluted (vol. I, p. 515). It is indeed not a very new finding that the unborn child has a special relation to the mother's voice, but Sloterdijk inserts this insight into his framework of the structurally open human being. He not only draws the consequences in the framework of developmental psychology, he also claims that we have to deal with ontological and logical consequences of this notion as well.

The "sonosphere" (vol. I, p. 530) is therefore the most important sphere with regard to sociability and therefore also concerning religion. Religion is closely connected with the call-and-response-relation between mother and child: "Religion survives as a reminiscence of the time, when calling still helped."[14] As opposed to Lacan, Sloterdijk emphasizes the structural role of acousticity in the development of the child (vol. I, p. 547).[15]

And as the God of the Bible often manifests Himself in acoustical phenomena and therefore corresponds in a more universal way to the first spheres in which the human being is placed, Sloterdijk's "spheres" are also theological phenomena, or at least stipulations to religious belief. It is therefore not surprising that Augustine's description of God as the one who is "interior intimo meo" (vol. I, p. 569),[16] and as the one who is at the same time absolutely different and farthest away from me fascinates Sloterdijk. Speaking about God as a basic element of a sphere closest to me, and as a representative of a larger, all-comprising cosmological sphere Sloterdijk opens up for "macrospherology", the second volume of his "Sphären"-project.

One of the basic points of the first volume of Sloterdijk's "spheres" is:

> that each inspiration (or: animation) is a media-event – and that all psychic disturbances are distortions of partnership, one could even say media – diseases. The fixation to the objects is in itself the logical matrix of neurosis.[17]

Seen in themselves, "spheres" are conditions for mediality, the whole life being determined by media-events. Seen in this way, Sloterdijk's project is a diagnostic essay on our media society. In the microspherical part of the project, we have seen the single person's dependence on media. The macrospherical considerations will show us how spheres keep human beings together.

Macrospheres

All the fascinating and at times surprising and almost puzzling acrobatics of language and style with which Sloterdijk confronts the reader makes the reader forget, that the argumentation about spheres is intended to recall the preformative conditions of man's search for truth and evidence. Macrospheres are the social and historical equivalents of microspheres.

The second volume *Sphären II: Globen* is not only about the globe, the ball, the sphere as a symbol in arts, literature, science and theology.

It is more of an essay about how people thought and think in a spherical way. The globe as well as the bubble protect human beings from an antispherical "outside", that remorselessly annihilates the basic conditions of life – be they material or non-material. Human beings have always been fascinated by balls and spherical visions and interact with them in a special way. For the German medieval theologist Nicolaus von Kues, this special relation to the sphere is the distinguishing feature between animal and man: "Nulla enim bestia globum et eius motus ad terminum producit" (No animal can set a globe in motion and move it towards its final destination. vol. II, Globen, p. 48, note 13).

Human beings not only produce and move globes, they think in global dimensions, and here it is first of all mathematics that has started the globalization of humanity: "The mathematical globalization precedes the terrestrial one by more than two thousand years."[18] Being the most fascinating geometrical object for mathematicians the globe is at the same time the symbol of evidence and logics.

Evidence

The beginning of Western thinking is the beginning of considering evidence as a spherical phenomenon: Thinking has to kindle its own light, the light of a different coherence, in which finally everything depends on the highest principle, on the Good and its emanations. This is how mathematics starts its secession from reality; this is how evidence is established as an immanent system of self-references; thinking becomes enraptured with its own possibilities. In the final analysis, however, all logical operations are only a description of one big circle, all 'light' comes from the one, logical beginning (vol. II, p. 509–510).

At this point, the reader may think that globes are only the consciously conceived variations of the bubble. In fact, the sphere is a far more binding and socially relevant matter than the bubble. The sphere is an extraordinarily distinct kind of world apart, and evidence is the way in which this other world is realized in the material world (vol. II, p. 508). For Sloterdijk, this is where globalization as a scientific phenomenon emerges: "Globalization begins as the geometrization of the immeasurable."[19]

And indeed, one of the first object thinkers tried to "measure" with the help of the sphere is God. But as soon as God is identified with the sphere, He has to be described as the sphere that excels all other spheres in its dimension and in its spherical feature. In hermetic philosophy, one can find definitions of God where "God is the infinite sphere, that has its center everywhere and its circumference nowhere", or: "God must be considered as a sphere, which has as many circumferences as points" (vol. II, p. 538–539).[20] This would be mere spherical speculation if there were not monotheism's fundamental decision to constitute the dyadic situation together with the Absolute (vol. II, p.536). How can we even imagine, let alone enter a spherical connection with a sphere that cannot even be imagined as something that is at the same time nowhere and everywhere. How can someone be placed in relation to something "absolutely decentralized"? Sloterdijk calls this way of conceiving about God the "infinitistic turn" ("infinitistische Wende", vol. II, p. 551) of human thinking about God. Thus, the immunizing sphere "God" explodes, loses its protective function from the menaces from the outside world.

Sloterdijk even goes so far as to find the roots of modernism in this infinitistic notion of God (vol. II, p. 553). He criticizes the view that the basic intellectual decisions towards modernity were initiated in the era of the Enlightenment. Already the notion of God as a "meta-globe" is the beginning of the destruction of the old European theological macrosphere (vol. II, p. 550).[21] On the other hand, this implosion of the theological sphere releases the philosophical energy for the movement of the free subject and thereby also of the aesthetics of the genius (vol. II, p. 559).

Antispheres

With no new lasting macrosphere being established, man is left alone in space. The modern subject lives in a manner structurally similar to the rejected sinners in Dante's hell. In Sloterdijk's terms it is the place of sphereless existence:

Dante's hell has the opposite shape of a sphere – it looks like a giant funnel, that emits a typhoon of sighs (vol. II, p. 599), noise that reminds one of the fatal voices of the sirens, fatal others. The situation of the antispherical being is rather desperate:

> Each convict is part of his own environment, that is shaped by penetrating negations. Calling this environment a "world" would be a malicious exaggeration, because the permanent presence of the confinement is a parody of existence of a clearing, space – granting universe. Only the refractory, offensive and glutinous character is left of something that – in the "openness" – was called the world. That is why the sinners retain their bodies, as far as they link the soul with the particular future.[22]

It is easy to guess that this is Sloterdijk's description of today's human beings, their obsessive individualism. Their spheres are reduced to economic relations and consumption, they are reduced to an "antisphärische[n] Außen", an "antispherical outside" (vol. II, p. 617): "The tradition of all dead climates weigh on the mood of the living like a nightmare."[23]

The political problem of the future is therefore simply the *"Neuprojektion von Solidaritätsräumen"*, the "new projection of spaces of solidarity" (vol. II, p. 1013), politics being the *"Kunst des atmosphärisch Möglichen"*, the "art of the atmospherically possible" (vol. II, p. 1013). In Sloterdijk's thinking, this is connected with the clearing of the intellectual dust stirred up by postmodern media, of antispherical narrowness produced by reducing the human being to a consumer.

the rivalry of offensives of disillusionment and defending of illusions. The economy of Enlightenment: the free market of insults and the free choice of the attending illusionist.[24]

These are the characteristics of the era, in which Sloterdijk writes his "spheres". He even speaks of a war of immune systems (vol. II, p. 590). In this perspective, he can even talk about a "menschengemachte [...] Klimakatastrophe", a "man-made climate disaster" (vol. II, p. 591). He draws direct connections between the global climate change and the lack of spheres in the lives of human beings.

Before we follow Sloterdijk lament on the living conditions of our time, it is important to have a look at his ideas about why everything was bound to go wrong. The globe as the symbol of the world has traditionally been accompanied by another globe which is the symbol of the universe. The latter one being a kind of representation of the afterbirth helped the thinker to avoid concentrating only on terrestrial phenomena, but with the emergence of geography as a science, this second globe began to disappear as a critical corrective. The "home" of living man became a "place", a point on the map projected onto a globe. At the beginning of the geographical definition of the world, finding oneself in a geographically definable position was enough for the human being. At the same time began the global movement of capital, the movement itself being the reason for the augmentation of capital.

> Money and the globe belong together, because the typical movement of money – return of investment – makes up the principle of surrounding the globe. [...] In modern times, money, as real and as speculative funds, subjects human beings to the domination to a traffic considered absolute. What dominates the circulation, seizes hold of the whole.[25]

The philosophy of today is a kind of "Chancen-Ontologie", an ontology of opportunities (vol. II, p. 856), and as an effect of this, the ability to distinguish between good luck and logic consequence is vanishing, first of all in the elite of the society, which is

> a society of people having become in a somnambular way rich, famous and privileged, people who will never completely understand what carried them to the top.[26]

And who is to explain them that it is their quality of professionals and not – as the fact is – mere luck, that made them the persons they are and always wanted to be? In Sloterdijk's opinion, it is the armies of consultants that are inundating the global elite society. The magic formula with which these professionals work is the "spell" of innovation, in fact nothing but a hidden promise of salvation. The consultants combine technological advantage and ambitious pursuit of personal advantage. They are the first professionals to "mercantilize" differences in knowledge, while traditional universities are degraded to shabby schools with almost no intellectual radiation (vol. II, p. 872).

Almost like a moralist, Sloterdijk complains about the modern economy of the greedy, who only invest to make personal profits and in an extremely profitable way (vol. II, p. 774).

Human beings have shrunk, not grown, as idealism and the idealistic way of creating spheres has decayed. That is what Sloterdijk's argument is all about, – a rather courageous statement at a time where commercial optimism is on the agenda, even if there is no reason for being optimistic.

This criticism would not necessarily require the long excursions into micro- and macrospherology if there were no hope of reestablishing a kind of global sphere. To prepare the reader to guess what Sloterdijk might soon be up to in the as yet unpublished third volume of *Sphären*, it is necessary to return to the role of geography in the process of the dissolution of the traditional spheres.

The one who lives today, after Magellan, feels compelled to "project" even his hometown as one point perceived from outside. The transformation of the Old World into an aggregate of positions reflects the new reality of the globe, as it presents itself after the surrounding of the Earth. The position is that place in the imaginary world, where the natives see themselves as those seen from outside; there, those who have been surrounded return to themselves.[27]

The globe as a sphere has been reinterpreted as a system of positions referring, to an infinite amount of geographical points, and therefore it must be considered as something antispherical: the points simply do not matter, they cannot replace the spheres, as they only quantify your positions and do not place the single human being in relation to the other. The points do not matter, they are representatives of the outside, a world without a center and limits, even if the human beings still do as if they lived in couples and were parts of spheres (vol. II, p. 824). Positions are former homes that have been lost, to which one can never really return. You can only touch the point in a new way (vol. II, p. 864).[28]

The Western world has reacted to this change in the views of the world by a "Gegenrevolution der Mobilität", a counter-revolution of mobility (vol. I, p. 277). It is the restless mobility of a psychotic being (vol. I, p. 335), dependent on a regular system of voyages back and forth, and in the end, space in itself is no longer a matter of concern. The system of trains and telegraphs is only the first step of the evaporation of space in modern times (vol. II, p. 835). Even heaven as a physical phenomenon cannot be saved from the rational disenchantment. What looked like a vault is now seen as a menacing abyss (vol. II, p. 831).

How can we vulnerable human beings live without being swallowed by this abyss?

Depression as a crisis of extension

The first answer is, that people become depressive because they simply have no space: they are reduced and compressed to a vulnerable degree close to self-extinction. The spherical shape, the circle, is in the eyes of a depressive person the shape of a menacing encirclement, even the symbol of the state of siege (vol. II, p. 613). Phenomena like trivial literature or the mass media as a whole can simulate spherical impressions, where the speed of change and the foaming variety of images distracts the human being. The "Selbstapplausmühle für das Auch-nicht-so-Besondere", the "mill of self-applause for the not-so-special-either" (vol. II, p. 787) works brilliantly and its value for the single person can be considerable, but in the end, it is just a constant reformulation of nothing, and still a depressive phenomenon (ibid.). Trivial culture is a culture without space-creating qualities, but on the other hand, it is the end of the fatally imperial and power-based ideologies and theories, which must ultimately be compared with Satan sitting in Dante's hell:

> Satan is in possession of the full panoramic view. [...] His amphiscopia comprises the whole panorama of the lost. That is why, for him, theory and self-torture have become the same thing. [...] The negation of the spherical union creates the antispherical isolation all around all that characterizes the depressive position.[29]

The centrist perspective, amphiscopia and all-comprising theories or ideologies can no longer solve the problem of modernity, as the trivial culture no longer allows a "radiocratic" (Sloterdijk and Heinrichs, p. 224) reign of diabolic comprehensiveness of a closed system (vol. II, p. 619). But on the other hand, trivial culture can't cure depression either.

For the future, Sloterdijk sees only the possibility of a global air-conditioning to adapt the world to the spherical needs of human beings.

The new leading science is metereology:

only recently, through the rise of metereology as the paragonal science of chaos rationalism, has the atmosphere of the earth finally been understood as the only remaining equivalent ethereal shells.[30]

Sloterdijk can even speak of the future as an era of climate technology, which recognizes, that society and the world as a whole are artificial instances, politics will change into climatical technology (Sloterdijk and Heinrichs, p. 245). Sloterdijk uses the term "climate" in a more than metereological way. For him, forms and design are matters of interest. First of all architecture seems to be important for him (Sloterdijk and Heinrichs, p. 254).

Spheropoetics – spherodesign

On the other hand, many of the more important elements of the spheres-project seems to be open-ended following the publication of the second volume. The first volume "grew" out of a huge amount of examples from literature and fine arts, and although the second volume – *Globen* – provides some hints at literature, the project lacks such a theory: It is never clear, what function literature has in the "Sphären"-project as a whole.

For Sloterdijk, the modern author has lost the authority to express "commands". Neither the public or society, nor truth is represented in the literary work of art. The reader on the other hand no longer makes up his mind. He just buys the book and does whatever he wants to do with it:

> Is not the reader himself the human being, who is happy to be able to continue without taking any decision? He feels free as long as he understands that someone, who seems to be in command is in most cases only someone who is quoting something. And indeed – is freedom anything else but the insight into the difference between a command and a quotation?[31]

Does Sloterdijk himself want that kind of reader?

If Sloterdijk wants to avoid getting lost in a more trivial sphere of commentary on design, he must develop a kind of theory of texts within his spherical project, and cannot just be content with the few remarks on the modern author and his products. It might be trivial to require self-reference in a text, but to a great extent, the spheres Sloterdijk describes "vault" out of textual universes, and, moreover, sound, rhythm and dialogue are central items in the first volume.

This shift of interest and these deficits seem to be the reason why we have to wait such a long time for the third volume: the question why there should be texts about spheres does not seem to have been sol-ved... yet. Sloterdijk seems to have come to a dead-end, because he no longer inquires as to the role of sound and language as a major sphero-poetic medium. He also seems to have forgotten the question of why we need texts to learn something about spheres, texts like his text in the "spheres"-project.

On the other hand, we can learn from Sloterdijk's speech on the history of imagination, called *Tau von den Bermudas* (*Dew from the Bermoothes*),[32] that imagination has not yet reached its end. Here he deals mostly with examples from literature. Considering this speech as an anticipation of the third volume on spheres, there is hope that the "foams" of the third volume can wash away our doubts about the self-reflective qualities of Sloterdijk's spherical and spheropoetic texts.

1 "Sphären [...] sind geteilte Räume, die durch gemeinsames Einwohnen in ihnen aufgespannt werden. Sie sind das erste Produkt menschlicher Kooperationen; sie bilden das unstoffliche und doch allerrealste Resultat einer Ur-Arbeit, die nur in Resonanzen vor sich geht. Nicht die Arbeitsteilung hat den Prozeß der Zivilisation vorangetrieben, sondern die Sphärenteilung; sie ist die Urabstimmung der Gemeinschaft in sich selbst über sich selbst." Sloterdijk, Peter: *Sphären. Makrosphärologie, Band II. Globen*, Frankfurt am Main: Suhrkamp 1999 (vol. 2, p. 1011). This and all subsequent translations from the German are by the author.

2 In Sloterdijk, Peter: *Sphären. Mikrosphärologie, Band I. Blasen*, Frankfurt am Main: Suhrkamp 1998, Sloterdijk suggests that to live, to think and to shape spheres are almost the same things (vol. 1, p. 12).

3 "In bezug auf Wesen, die auf menschlich ekstatische Art *am Leben* sind, stellt sich die Ortsfrage von Grund auf anders, weil die primäre Produktivität der Menschenwesen darin besteht, an ihrer Einquartierung in eigensinnigen, surrealen Raumverhältnissen zu arbeiten" (vol. I, p. 83).

4 "Die Individuen, die sogenannten Unteilbaren, sind Subjekte nur insofern, als sie Teilhaber einer geteilten und zugeteilten Subjektivität sind. [...] Jedes Subjekt ist der unruhige Rest eines Paares, dessen entzogene Hälfte nicht aufhört, den Zurückgebliebenen in Anspruch zu nehmen" (vol. I, p. 85). "Was bleibt vom Traum der humanen Autonomie, wenn das Subjekt sich als durchdringlicher Hohlkörper erfahren hat?" (vol. I, p. 94).

5 Sloterdijk has been attacked by the German academic philosophers because of his style. See Sloterdijk and Heinrichs, *Die Sonne und der Tod*, p. 27.

6 "Die Theorie des Intimen, die mit der folgenden Mikrosphären-Analyse in Gang gebracht wird, ist dem Versuch gewidmet, zu zeigen, daß alle Wissenschaften vom Menschen immer schon Beiträge zu einem topologischen Surrealismus gesammelt haben, weil es zu keiner Zeit möglich war, von den Menschen zu reden, ohne es mit den irrlichternden Poetiken des bewohnten Innenraums zu tun zu bekommen" (vol. I, p. 90).

7 Sloterdijk writes about the "Durchschlagenwerden meines Leibesinnern durch die Präsenz eines Geschmacks, [...] der mich aus dem Weg räumt [...]. Das schlichteste Genußmittel ist geeignet, mich davon zu überzeugen, daß ein einverleibtes Objekt, weit davon entfernt, eindeutig unter meine Hoheit zu geraten, von mir Besitz ergreifen und mir sein Thema diktieren kann" (vol. I, p. 93).

8 "Formative Invasionen und interessierte Hingaben an bereichernde Eindringlinge" (formative invasions and interested devotion to enriching intruders) are Sloterdijk's words for the process of continous exchange between spatial concepts and human beings that participate in them (vol. I, p. 96).

9 Sloterdijk is sceptical towards "fitness" as a human strategy of living. He has the vision of a "blossoming" mankind, creativity, variation and singularity are the strategies of survival, he envisages (vol. I, p. 173).

10 "Alle Geburten sind Zwillingsgeburten; niemand kommt unbegleitet und ohne Anhang zur Welt" (All births are twin-births; nobody comes to the world unaccompanied and without appendage; vol. I, p. 419).

11 "Die Offenheit der Welt ist das Geschenk des Doubles als Membran" (The openness of the world is the doubles gift as a membrane; vol. I, p. 450).

12 *Passim.* A *nobjekt* is defined thusly: "Nobjekte sind Dinge, Medien oder Personen, die für Subjekte die Funktion des lebenden Genius oder des intimen Ergänzers wahrnehmen" (Nobjekts are things, media or persons that fulfil the task of the living genius or the intimate supplement; ibid.).

13 Vol. I, p. 487: "Im Anfang werden die begleiteten Tiere, die Menschen, von etwas umgeben, was nie als Ding erscheinen kann. Sie sind zunächst die unsichtbar Ergänzten, die Entsprechenden, die Umfaßten und, im Fall der Unordnung, die von allen guten Begleitern Verlassenen. Darum heißt philosophisch nach dem Menschen zu fragen an erster Stelle: Paar-Ordnungen untersuchen, offensichtliche und nicht so leicht sichtbare, solche, die mit umgänglichen Partnern gelebt werden, und solche, die Allianzen mit problematischen und unerreichbaren Anderen stiften. Vom unbegleiteten Einzelnen spricht weiter nur die Ideologia perennis, die sich im Hauptstrom der individualistischen Abstraktion treiben läßt." "Von allen guten Begleitern Verlassene": This is an allusion to the German idiom "von allen guten Geistern verlassen sein" (to be left alone by all good spirits), i.e. to go mad.

14 "Religion überlebt als Erinnerung an die Zeit, als das Rufen noch geholfen hat" (vol. I, p. 537).

15 There is a rather polemic "Exkurs" against Lacanian thinking, which Sloterdijk considers as being a victim of an "Urpsychose – Dogmatismus". This polemic is only one of Sloterdijk's many appendices which are at the same time marginal essays which serve to place his project in the actual debate. The discussion of Lacan is not a matter of argument in the main thinking line of the books about spheres, while Sloterdijk considers Lacan as one of his main teachers (Sloterdijk and Heinrichs, *Die Sonne und der Tod*, p. 20).

16 Sloterdijk quotes *Confessiones* III, 6, 11: "Tu autem eras interior intimo meo et superior summo meo" (You have been closer to me than my closest friend and higher above me than the highest place above me).

17 "...daß jede Beseelung ein Medienereignis ist – und daß alle seelischen Störungen Teilhabeverzerrungen sind, man könnte sagen Medienkrankheiten. Die Fixierung an die Objekte ist selbst die logische Matrix der Neurose" (vol. I, p. 305).

18 "Die mathematische Globalisierung geht der terrestrischen um mehr als zweitausend Jahre voraus." (vol. II, p. 48). In Sloterdijk and Heinrichs, *Die Sonne und der Tod*, p. 238, three stages of globalization are mentioned: metaphysical-cosmological, terrestrial and electronic. *Globen* may also be read as a historical theory about globalization as a mental, social and political phenomenon.

19 "Die Globalisierung beginnt als Geometrisierung des Unermeßlichen" (vol. II, p. 47).

20 Theosophy is therefore the most consistent to think God as the absolute sphere: "Theosophie ist die Denkform, die alles auf Gott setzt und der Welt nur den Stellenwert einer komplexen Falte im Inneren des Absoluten zugesteht" (Theosophy is the way of thinking that sets all upon God and that concedes to the world only the value as a complex fold in the interior of the absolute; vol. II, p. 537).

21 Sloterdijk compares the unfolding of European theology to a time bomb. Rational mysticism destroys the "cave qualities" of God (vol. II, p. 558).

22 "Jeder Verdammte steckt in seinem eigenen Um, das sich aus penetranten Verneinungen formt. Dieses Um-Feld eine Welt zu nennen, wäre eine boshafte Übertreibung, denn die ewige Gegenwart des Beengenden parodiert das Gegebensein eines gelichteten, raumgewährenden Universums. Von dem, was im Offenen die Welt hieß, bleibt hier nur der widerständige, verletzende und klebrige Charakter zurück. Deswegen behalten die Delinquenten ihre Körper, sofern diese die Voraussetzungen sind für die Fixierung einer Seele an die Tortur" (vol. II, p. 609).

23 "Die Tradition aller toten Klimata lastet wie ein Alp auf den Stimmungen der Lebenden" (vol. II, p. 1010).

24 "Das Gegeneinander von Desillusionierungsoffensiven und Illusionsverteidigungen. Aufklärungswirtschaft: der freie Markt der Kränkungen und die freie Wahl des behandelnden Illusionisten" (vol. II, p. 590).

25 "Geld und Globus gehören zusammen, weil die typische Geldbewegung – return of investment – das Prinzip der Weltumrundung bildet. [...] In der Moderne stellt das Geld, als reelles und spekulatives Kapital, die Menschen unter die Herrschaft des absolut gesetzten Verkehrs. Was den Kreislauf beherrscht, bringt das Ganze an sich" (vol. II, p. 56).

26 "Eine Gesellschaft aus nachtwandlerisch Reichgewordenen, Berühmten und Begünstigten, die nie recht begreifen werden, was sie nach oben getragen hat" (vol. II, p. 859).

27 "Wer im Heute lebt, nach Magellan, sieht sich genötigt, auch die Heimatstadt als einen von außen wahrgenommenen Punkt zu projizieren. Die Verwandlung der Alten Welt in ein Aggregat von Standorten reflektiert die neue Globus-Wirklichkeit, wie sie sich nach der Erdumrundung darstellt. Der Standort ist jener Ort in der vorgestellten Welt, an dem sich die Einheimischen als von außen Erfaßte erfassen; an ihm kommen die Umrundeten auf sich zurück" (vol. II, p. 826). The ship as a kind of sphere is mentioned by Sloterdijk is mentioning Sloterdijk and Heinrichs, *Die Sonne und der Tod*, p. 241. In terms of the history of sphere, this idea could explain why maritime navigation had such wide-ranging philosophical consequence, as Sloterdijk asserts. The transatlantic longing being the turning-point in the development of human imagination: See Sloterdijk's *Tau von den Bermudas. Über einige Regime der Einbildungskraft*, pp. 27–40.

28 Even television is prefigured in the era of navigation. In Sloterdijk's thinking, the technical solution sometimes seems to be a rather delayed answer to a basic need of humans, that at the same time reduces that need to a rather trivial method.

29 "Der Satan besitzt die volle Rundumsicht. [...] Seine Amphiskopie erfaßt das ganze Panorama des Verlorenen. Darum sind bei ihm Theorie und Selbstfolter dasselbe geworden. [...] Die Negation der sphärischen Union erzeugt eben die antisphärische Ringsum-Isolierung, welche die depressive Stellung charakterisiert" (vol. II, p. 618).

30 "erst in jüngster Zeit wird durch den Aufstieg der Metereologie zur Muster-wissenschaft des Chaosrationalismus die Erdatmosphäre endlich als das einzige verb-liebene Äquivalent der Ätherschalen begriffen" (vol. II, p. 829).

31 "Ist nicht der Leser *per se* der Mensch, der froh ist, ohne Entscheidung weiter-zukommen? Er fühlt sich frei in dem Maß, wie er begreift, daß jemand, der zu befehlen scheint, meistens nur jemand ist, der Zitat vorbringt. Und wirklich – ist Freiheit etwas anderes als die Einsicht in den Unterschied zwischen einem Befehl und einem Zitat?" (vol. II, p. 695).

32 *Tau von den Bermudas*, p. 38; an allusion to Shakespeare's *The Tempest*, Act I, Scene 3, lines 228–229.

Literature

Sloterdijk, Peter (1998): *Sphären. Mikrosphärologie, Band I. Blasen*, Frankfurt am Main: Suhrkamp.

Sloterdijk, Peter (1999): *Sphären. Makrosphärologie, Band II. Globen*, Frankfurt am Main: Suhrkamp.

Sloterdijk, Peter and Heinrichs, Hans-Jürgen (2001): *Die Sonne und der Tod. Dialogische Untersuchungen*, Frankfurt am Main: Suhrkamp.

Sloterdijk, Peter (2001): Tau von den Bermudas. *Über einige Regime der Einbildungskraft*, Frankfurt am Main: Suhrkamp.

Orpheus as Socrates Practising Music

On the Synaesthetic Origin of Literary Philosophy

Mischa Sloth Carlsen

> "Death is like a mirror in which I allegedly achieve narcissistic self-communion; it is the event in which I am constituted as a self."
>
> *Simon Critchley*

THE ORIGINAL MYTH about Orpheus and Eurydice has been lost. This lack of an original source not only signifies the almost mythical hearth of its composition, but also reveals its intrinsic aesthetic impact as a literary philosophy: sense does not exist in advance. Rather, sense is suggested by the senses in the event of the work of art. The traditional version of the myth presently available to its audience is but a patchwork of fragments from several different literary and philosophical contexts of ancient Greece and Rome. Particularly in Vergil (70–19 B.C.) and Ovid (43 B.C.–18 A.D.), who have had the chance to consult multiple previous sources, we obtain the most comprehensive version of the myth *in toto*. The classical version has inspired various artists, among them Rainer Maria Rilke (1875–1926), whose modern poetical interpretations are precious illuminations of its poetico-philosophical potentialities.

According to the source material, the two mythological personae Orpheus and Eurydice lived one generation prior to Homer (circa 700 B.C.), the father of the epos. In his fourth *Pythian Ode*, also known as "Orphic Argonautica", Pindar (520–440 B.C.) mentions Orpheus among the heroes that return from the Argonaut expedition. Moreover, Pindar tells us that Orpheus' song saved the boat and its crew from foundering; his song surpassed the song of the sirens, for which reason he is also appointed as, "that minstrel of the lyre, the father of song, the famous Orpheus" (Pindar 1915: 217). The sovereign power of his song and lyre has become the emblem of the philosophical capacities of a poetical art which is at once able to awaken both an aesthetic effect and a philosophical reflection, not least because of his character as magician and prophet and his specific techniques of instituting mysteries. His mystical and prophetic aspects have made an imprint on occidental art due to the particular ways in which they appreciate the imagination as more than pure fancy: the imagination is viewed as a capacity to reflect subjective potentials within the sense performed by the virtual reality of the senses which constitute the artistic event.

Here I shall examine Orpheus and Eurydice as metapoetical personae. I will endeavor to draw out the characteristic qualities of Orpheus as a literary philosopher who – though from the absolute opposite angle – mirrors Socrates (469–399 B.C.) and the Socratic destiny known from his apology. In their situations, Orpheus and Socrates share two crucial aspects. First, they are both sentenced to death as the consequence of their respective aesthetic action and philosophical statement, so that their encounters with death are their individual sources of sense. Second, Dionysus has an old score to pay each of them. Orpheus' resemblance to Socrates helps elucidate why the myth about Orpheus and Eurydice (hereafter: the Orphean myth) becomes the emblem of an occidental horizon of literary philosophy by means of its two main motifs: Orpheus' *creation* in the Underworld versus the *disjecta membra poetae* when he has been dismembered by resentful Dionysian maenads. Hereby I intend to discuss how the German romantic, progressive universal poetry defined by Friedrich Schlegel (1772–1829) can be said to incarnate these Orphean motifs in his theory of *wit* (*Witz*) and *irony*, thus discovering the Socratic qualities of the Orphean myth by which it becomes a literary philosophy based on aesthetic premises.

The two main philosophers whose continuation of this literary philosophy I wish to discuss both take their respective points of departure in a post-romantic context: the Frenchman Maurice Blanchot (1907) and the German vitalist Friedrich Nietzsche (1844–1900). They both reflect upon the poetico-philosophical potentialities of the subject who is abandoned to the incarnate human condition. That is, I will throw light on how Blanchot develops an art phenomenology based on two aspects of artistic inspiration, from which the work of art originates. The potentialities of this art phenomenology can be further specified by Nietzsche. Nietzsche claims that Dionysos had been expelled by Socrates; hence, the return of Dionysus would procure the experience of the origin of sense. On this basis, I will argue that in a post-romantic modern perspective, the Orphean synaesthesia between the visual and the auditory suggests a phenomenological nexus of sense and senses. This argument raises a general problem regarding the Orphean myth as the origin of literary philosophy: How should we understand the imaginative power of Orpheus' musicality – which constitutes this synaesthesia – as a question of the dialectics of senses? And, as his song indicates the origin of poetical art in the human sensorium, how should we conceive the sense of this dialectics in the reflex of the incarnate human condition? Finally, how can we define the philosophical qualities that stem from the origin of the work of art by the synaesthetic dialectics?

From myth to metapoetical personae

Let us first summarize the plot as we know of the myth from Ovid's *Metamorphoses*, Vergil's *Georgics*, and Rilke's poem "Orpheus. Eurydike. Hermes": Shortly after the wedding of Orpheus and Eurydice, Eurydice is bitten by a snake and dies from the poison. Orpheus suffers deeply from the sorrow caused by the loss and sets off on a journey down into the Underworld in order to bring her back to the living. By means of his elegiac song which expresses his complaint, he manages to enchant Persephone, queen of the Underworld, who persuades her husband Hades to let go of Eurydice. Hades now allows Orpheus to reclaim his dead wife provided that Orpheus does not look back at her until they have completely left the Underworld, which Hermes, the messenger of gods, will control as he is to accompany them. As they are about to exit, the ecstatic Orpheus is struck by impatience and forgets Hades' prohibition. He looks back at Eurydice, who is apparently struggling with her long and heavy winding sheet. He looks straight into the sheer nothingness of her gaze, for which reason she vanishes immediately into the abyss, accompanied by Hermes. Orpheus now implores Charon, the ferryman of souls, to sail him back into the Underworld a second time, but in vain. Returned to the earthly life, it is said that Orpheus' music charms everything – the forest, the animals, even the stones. Later he gets attacked by resentful maenads, Dionysian women, who stone him to death, because they find that he has deserted the female sex and Dionysus. They scatter his body all over the country, but his head and lyre are thrown into the river Hebrus, where they are carried along by the stream. The lyre plays an elegy, and the river bank echoes the constant calling from his head, "Eurydice!". The head flows ashore on the island Lesbos, where Apollo saves it from a poisonous snake and metamorphoses Orpheus' gaping mouth into a stone. His shadow goes into the Underworld where it can be definitively reunited with Eurydice. Elsewhere it is told that the Orphean head flows ashore near Lesbos at

75

the port of Smyrna – exactly where Homer is born a generation later – and that the lyre ascends up into the northern firmament to become a constellation as an eternal memory and promise of the power of art.

Orpheus parential background in the Hesiodian theogony is unclear and imprecise. He is said to come from Thracia, and his name is of oriental origin. Often, such as in Plato (427–347 B.C.), Orpheus is described as a son of Oiagros, who is a Thracian river god (Plato 1991: 119). Elsewhere he is described as a son of Apollo, the god of the sun. Usually, his mother is Calliope, the muse of elegy. The two significances of Orpheus' paternal origin, which become intrinsic aspects of his intelligence, could therefore both be an Oiagrian "profundity of mind" and an Apollonian "clarity of thought". Yet, there is a common feature to be drawn: an ability to throw light on life's interior and more profound sources of meaning, which Orpheus shows by the reference of aesthetic experience. Oiagros protects Orpheus' head and lyre in the stream. And Apollo plays a significant part as Orpheus' spiritual father. Orpheus is a worshipper of Apollo's cult, plays the Apollonian lyre, and makes use of the Apollonian catharsis in his rituals. For this reason, destiny has also made Orpheus a mortal enemy of Dionysus who is antagonistically related to Apollo. His maternal origin indicates one very specific feature of the Orphean intelligence which is expressed by the art form. Like the other muses, Calliope is a natural deity and the daughter of Mnemosyne, the goddess of memory, and Zeus, the king of Olympia (who is also Apollo's father). A muse is "one who remembers". Reflecting that Orpheus' connection to the goddess of memory goes through his elegiac mother, we understand the values of his song. The elegy is a song or poem of complaint that is usually written on the occasion of someone else's death. Orpheus' urge to descend into the Underworld and reawaken the departed Eurydice with his elegy is exactly the sorrow and memory of her significance.

The source material is even less clear as to the identity of Eurydice.

Mostly she serves as an accessory for Orpheus – as an *unknown quantity*. Her most striking and precisely described feature will be her beauty, which conquers all. The interesting quality about her character is the impact of her name, which is of Greek origin. Two roots appear in the etymology of the transcribed Greek version of *Eurydike*: *eurys* which means "far and wide" and *dike* which means "custom", "right", or "justice" just as in the Greek god of justice, Dike. Dike is related to the verb *deiknymi* which means "I show"; this signifies how Eurydice refers to an existing law in the light of which justice is exercised. Thus, Eurydice is to mean "the custom/right/justice exercised far and wide" – that is to say, Eurydice is the justice exercised by Hades and Persephone, the performance of death amidst life. The significance of her name becomes a *quality* as soon as Orpheus initiates his descent into the Underworld. Justice is done when Hades and Persephone show mercy towards the convincing elegy of Orpheus. Justice is also done when he transgresses law by looking into her gaze. She is an unknown quantity whose justifying qualities one can only "relate to", without a definite knowledge of them. She also affirms the limit of law by her existence in the Orphean sensorium. By all these means she renders a paradox as she indicates the peculiar *law of imagination*. Thus, she urges him to transgress rational laws of nature by the desire of his senses in order to bring her back to the living. Moreover, her gaze harbors the unavoidable state of sublime art which allows the Orphean subject to see the interior other nature of imagination; here the actual difference between life and death affirms the significance of experienced life mirrored in the work of art.

In this way, Orpheus and Eurydice become metapoetical personae complementing one another. He performs all the known and identifiable features. She presents the determining justice exercised by the unknown death matrix of life, and she can be identified only as the affirmation that determines the expressive tension of known and unknown qualities. However unknown, Eurydice is now to be known as the imagined per-

sona "you" immanent in any reflective work of art. As the subject per-
sona "I", Orpheus is able to institute her within the all-embracing
imagination of the senses and thereby as more than pure fancy: as an
existing other of the senses that reflects himself, performing the "you"
of a philosophical dialogue. They personify the acting parts of the art
phenomenon – the Orphean powers – that derive from the fundamental law of imagination which appears to be based on a paradox: that the
law must be transgressed before imagination can emerge. The Orphean
work of art is an all-embracing imaginary fusion of fantasy and reality
that happens singularly in the sensorium, most veritably *at the risk of
one's life*. The sensorium hereby provides the sphere for the experience
of death, which affirms life at the closure of the imaginary act. Thus,
the Orphean powers not only form the mythical hearth of the originating occidental literature, but they also highlight the philosophical
impact of Orpheus' dialogical character which is forever doomed to
search for its own significance by the encounter with the other.

Poetry practicing philosophy – death and Dionysus

The metapoetical personae and the inference of the particular Orphean
powers have revealed a myth due to an aesthetico-philosophical centaur: from one perspective the senses evoked by the Orphean instrument institute an imaginary sphere of aesthetic experience; from another perspective, the Orphean subject inquires into the philosophical
sense by the dialectics of self-reflection. In order to approach the immanent potentials of this centaur, it is particularly relevant to consult
those classical sources that express a critique of Orpheus' character, not
least because their critical hints and remarks draw attention to the sharp
edge of the potentials for a subsequent occidental literary philosophy.
Two central motifs form the principles of the myth: first the *creation* of
the Orphean originating work of art at the returning *ascent* from the
preceding *descent* into the Underworld; and second the *disjecta membra*

poetae, the fateful dismemberment of the Orphean body carried out by the maenads in order to do justice to his excessive oblivion. The crux of the matter is how we interpret Orpheus' offence when he looks back at Eurydice during the ascent.

Several voices of the classical tradition have questioned whether Orpheus even loved Eurydice enough to bring her back to the living. In a sequence in which Admetus moans for the death of Alcestis who has chosen to die for him to save him from being killed, Euripides (485–406 B.C.) makes a subtle allusion to the view that Orpheus should have reached further by his sovereign creating power:

> If I had the voice and music of Orpheus so that I could charm Demeter's daughter or her husband with song and fetch you from Hades, I would have gone down to the Underworld, and neither Pluto's hound nor Charon the ferryman of souls standing at the oar would have kept me from bringing you back into light alive. (Euripides 1994: 195)

The love that Orpheus shares, however, is not the love of the gods, but rather the human desire of spirit and senses which implies both an infinite potential and a finite limit. For this reason, Orpheus is only able to fetch her from Hades and bring her back into the light alive during an infinite event which ultimately dissolves and vanishes into the finite sphere of human destiny. Thus, Orpheus is no hero. Rather he is the first literary example of the human anti-hero who is forever sentenced to the mercy of senses and to experiencing their own sense. He experiences the power of Dionysus whose tribute is the ecstasy of desire on the one hand and the dismembering and multiplying experience of finality on the other. The Dionysian power challenges the Apollonian clarity of thought that Orpheus sees in Eurydice's gaze by multiplying the insight of this truth into his own life.

Conceivably because of Orpheus' imagination, which is his most refined talent, Orpheus' most relentless critic Plato distances himself sharply from him through Faidros' speech in *Symposium*:

> But Orpheus, son of Oiagros, they sent back from the Place of the Dead emptyhanded, showing him an appearance of the wife he'd come for but not giving her, because they thought he was soft due to being a musician, and didn't dare die for the sake of Eros as Alcestis had, but contrived to go [*sic*] the Place of the Dead alive without having accomplished his mission. For this reason, then, they punished him and caused his death at the hands of women. (Plato 1991: 119)

This lack of trust in Orpheus could be due to the fact that he challenges any rational principle and idea by pointing out the very premises and laws of art and imagination whereby the human being – alias poet – may momentarily transgress the law that separates life and death by the reflex of alterity. Yet, even elsewhere in the oeuvre of Plato – in the end of the *Apology of Socrates* – Socrates considers the significance of his death sentence. Socrates sees the outstanding profit of death and eternity that follows by the sense of the irony of destiny, i.e., in meeting the progenitors of poetic art at the destination of death: "Would that journey be worthless? And again, to meet Orpheus and Musaeus, Hesiod and Homer – how much would any of you give?" (Plato 1984: 103). At this point, Socrates reflects the anticipation of the death sentence of all humankind, and all these poets know the importance of death for their literary life, the dark nothingness that affirms the light of origin and genesis within any creation. Socrates is accused of impiety against the gods of Athens, i.e., against the one and only accepted image of truth about origin and eternal life which is autocratically decided by the Athenian authorities. Since Socrates believes in demons and relates existentially to the eternal life of the Underworld and its significance for his present trial, there is evidently another way to approach the question, if one listens to the ambiguity and play of language and sense. By virtue of his pseudonym, Socrates, Plato ironically expresses a consideration of the particular premises and potentialities immanent in the counterpart of religion and philosophy accepted by the law of Athens: in the artistic imagination. This would highlight Friedrich Nietzsche's witty remark that Plato was originally a tragic poet who had to burn his writings in order to become a scholar of Socrates (Nietzsche 1988: 92; 1956: 87). Thus poetry, it appears, is Plato's own demon – the centaurian counterpart of philosophy in his mind. Socrates acknowledges another sense-generating power other than the gods of Athens, as he identifies himself with another kind of philosophy other than the one based on propositional language. His religion is a philosophy which mirrors poetry's discovery of the significance of death that makes thought possible. And poetry answers religion by its own intrinsic and non-authoritarian origin in the human life of the modern subject. This origin mirrors philosophy by its ubiquitous sense-generating dialectics of dialogue.

Hence, the aesthetico-philosophical centaur could be further characterized as a connection between the Orphean imagination and the Socratic propositional principles. Nietzsche also indicates this connection, but from the opposite perspective seen through the situation of Socrates. Nietzsche calls Socrates "the new Orpheus who, though destined to be torn to pieces by the maenads of Athenian judgment, succeeded in putting the overmastering god [Dionysus] to flight" (Nietzsche 1988: 88; 1956: 82). According to Nietzsche, Socrates expells Dionysus from the Attic tragedy. As Euripides invents the spectator on stage, Dionysus is replaced with the philosophically doubling reflection of Socrates that – against aesthetics – functions as a repressive accomplice of the remaining Apollo. Socrates resembles Orpheus in the sense that he adopts Apollo's proverb written on the portal of the Delphic oracle: *Know thyself!* Searching for this Apollonian truth, the Socratic subject –

similar to Orpheus – gets nothing but a brief vision of the veil that covers the shadowy abyss of life and thereby a returning gaze that reflects himself. In reply, the Dionysian principle makes its entry disguised as the Athenian judgment doing justice to the repressive crime. This pattern, says Nietzsche, has irreversibly become a condition within the aesthetic structure of occidental poetry which finds justice only through the rebirth of Dionysus as Socrates practicing music (Nietzsche 1988: 102).[1] With this cure, Apollo and Dionysus will again be able to coope-rate within their generating and antagonistically doubling unity. Never-theless, from the perspective of the arts, the idea of Socrates practicing music thus mirrors the challenge for the modern, Orphean artistic imagination from the paradigm of modern literary philosophy from Nietzsche onwards.

A post-romantic potentiality

The preconditions for the concept of a modern literary philosophy are presented by the discoveries in Friedrich Schlegel's *progressive universal poetry*. Schlegel defines his progressive universal poetry as a union of natural poetry and art poetry in one organon – a symphilosophy – which constitutes a mirror of the world. As he writes in the famous Athenaeum fragment number 116, the progressive universal poetry presents an infinite becoming of mirrors: "And, however, it is also – more than any other – able to drift on the wings of poetical reflection right between the represented and the representing, free of any real or ideal interest, and to multiply the reflection just like in an endless series of mirrors" (Schlegel 1988, vol. 2: 114–115, my transl.). The reflective activity of progressive universal poetry is carried out using the concepts of *wit* and *irony*. The coupling of these two concepts forms the core of a literary philosophy that hereby implements the afore-mentioned two crucial motifs in the Orphean myth, *creation* and *disjecta membra poetae*.

Schlegel defines occurrances of romantic wit as the "proverbs of educated people" (Schlegel 1988, vol 2: 107). It thus resembles the English wit in being a clever remark which presents a new perspective. Wit is as a sudden idea (Einfall) that occurs like a glimpse of knowledge. The operation of wit is clearly illustrated by the identity between the two rhyming words *Witz* and *Blitz* (lightning) of the German language. Thus, wit is a visionary heuristics of thought consisting of heterogenous elements that altogether renders a sudden experience of certainty. Philippe Lacoue-Labarthe and Jean-Luc Nancy view a similarity between the romantic wit and the Kantian endeavor to solve the enigma of image formation by understanding it as a transcendental schematism. In Immanuel Kant (1724–1804), the scheme constitutes the universal image *a priori* that presents itself between the categories of understanding and the phenomena intuited in time and space. The scheme itself is not a synthesis *sensu stricto*, but rather its representation. As a transcendental product of imagination, the schema is a pictogram that presents the information of congruent concepts and senses which thereby *indicates* the synthesis of the subject (Kant 1990: 190). Lacoue-Labarthe and Nancy thus comment upon the similarity between romantic wit and Kantian schematism:

> *Witz* very precisely represents an *a priori* synthesis in the Kantian sense, but one that is removed from Kant's limiting conditions and critical procedures and that involves the synthesis not only of an object but of a subject as well (or at least the synthesis of the power of the producer-subject). In this respect, *Witz*, in short, is the solution of the enigma of transcendental schematism (Lacoue-Labarthe & Nancy 1978: 75; 1988: 53).

In other words, wit is a symphilosophical variant of the transcendental scheme that points toward the synthesis of sense experienced by the senses. It has become a fundamental, infinite principle of, at once, *creation* and *recognition* concerning both the arts and philosophy –

thanks to the free, productive imagination of the modern subject whose source of sense is abandoned to the human condition.

As the counterpart of wit, Schlegel introduces the operation of irony. Irony separates heterogenous elements of a certainty by questioning it. Schlegel defines irony as the form of the paradox, a function that belongs to philosophy (Schlegel 1988, vol.1: 242–243). Furthermore, the romantic irony refers to the concept of Socratic irony, by which the subject puts a distance from him-/herself by mirroring an idea by its reversion. It also refers to the philosophy of Johann Gottlieb Fichte (1762–1814) who attempts to situate the foundation of all thinking in the self-reflexivity of the subject; that is to say the I (Ich) is assumed by a reflection of what differs from it (nicht-Ich), the other. In its romantic incarnation, irony is thus the skepticism by which the subject reverts and questions the sense of his/her certainty in order to reflect upon its actual significance by reference to a larger, temporal perspective of existence. Having mentioned above that wit renders a sudden experience of certainty, we may now add the nuance that this act of experience is obtained by the operation of irony. Because of irony, the perspective of experience is formed by the dialogue which links the wit of every singular fragment to that of other fragments in "a chain or garland of fragments" – just like a poetic event is linked to other events in the form of narrative (Schlegel 1988, vol. 2: 111).[2] About this perspective, we may also quote the contemporary philosopher Simon Critchley's remark regarding the operation of irony: "Irony is the expression of the double bind at the heart of the human condition. It is the recognition of the simultaneous necessity and impossibility of complete communication" (Critchley 1997: 114). The human condition, to which the subject is abandoned, thus implies a double premise for any possible sense-giving significance which will always remain sheer becoming. This premise is a cyclopic eye of the sensorium between synthesis *and* antithesis, certainty *and* skepticism, answer *and* question caused by the existential premise of life *and* death; the doublebind thus stresses the importance of the copula understood as the oscillating movement of language. Irony is the means by which we are reminded of the trace of death in the face of creation itself.

The stage is now set for a focus on how the oscillation between wit and irony seems to incarnate the essential operation of the Orphean myth between *creation* and *disjecta membra poetae*. Hereby we can draw out the principles of a literary philosophy that juxtaposes the poet with the philosopher, Orpheus with Socrates. Wit is evidently the sudden certainty, the event that presents the glimpse of Orpheus' creation, Eurydice, the you – i.e., we recognize the power of imagination on its own premises of self-reflection. However, the recognition itself forms the copula of the oscillation by which the doubling action occurs, when Orpheus sees Eurydice's gaze before the abyss. The view of Eurydice is the recognition by which Orpheus anticipates his own destiny. Recognition not only views the life of creation, but also irony's questioning the enigma of death, to which life itself is an answer. By means of the senses, the recognition expresses the ironic aspect of the Orphean myth, as the elegiac powers of the ecstatic moment mirror the elegy sung by the head of the dead Orpheus, as it is carried along by the stream of the river Hebrus. This metaphor on irony's way of reflecting the death premise of life is a most incarnate example of the poet's capacity to create eternal life on the purely immanent suggestions of the human condition. Most witfully, Orpheus' floating head signifies the profoundly ironical condition of the human mind.

The sensorium thus harbors an impact of wit and irony by two reverse activities between which the stroke of recognition forms the nodal point and the vertigo of the copula: Orpheus both sees an eternal vision of his memorized, imagined you and the truth of his own transitory nature. Hence, the recognition reflects the image of the self by the creation of the other's face. Moreover, the sight of creation reveals its other origin by the musical reflex between the creation and the limit of life's forthcoming destruction. Recognition must therefore be understood as the constitution of the *image* of senses formed by the disparity of sense, which is suggested by the uniting *music* of senses. What the age of antiquity was not yet ready to conceive about the Orphean capacities can now be understood in a post-romantic modern context: the *transcendentally* conceived romantic wit and irony must be radicalized; they must be conceived *immanently* on the basis of subjective experience. In a modern, post-romantic context, the subject recognizes the power of the *immanent* operations of wit *and* irony. These operations procure a dialectics of sense and senses which experiences and profits aesthetically by the bare human condition. From the perspective of modernity, we now see how Orpheus sacrifices his life to testify the Socratic power of art in the double-edged mercy of the human condition.

The synaesthetic origin of literary philosophy

Let us assume that the functioning of the copula – which forms a nexus of the Orphean motifs of creation *and* disjecta membra poetae that are incarnated by the romantic motifs of wit *and* irony – anticipates Maurice Blanchot's art phenomenology. Blanchot's project is inspired by Schlegel's as well as Nietzsche's. Blanchot contributes with an emphasis on art's *immanent phenomenological* premises that are presented by the two Orphean motifs and their creating power. Most importantly for our purposes, he provides us with the key to understanding Dionysus' significance – as to Nietzsche interpretation of it – for the creating, poetical subject: the Dionysian power is the key that opens the origin of literary philosophy.

Blanchot introduces his own incarnation of the described Orphean and romantic motifs as two aspects of the work of art itself. He speaks of two movements: *the first night* versus *the other night* that reveal two characteristics of the phenomenon of poetic *inspiration*. Blanchot defines the first night as the disappearance of everything, the approaching absence, the silence, the welcome. It is the construction of the day, as the day reaches out towards the unlimited sphere of night, in which the whole is completed; here, the apparition of death is expected: "Then day is the whole of the day and the night, the great promise of the dialectic" (Blanchot 1995: 220/1982: 167).

In the other night, what has disappeared presents itself, whilst death remains hidden as the suspension of that which presents the event and on which the night borders. The other night is neither welcoming nor inapproachable, neither open nor closed; it simply remains one still outside which one – when in the light of day – keeps believing could be reached: "But in the night it is what one never joins; it is repetition that will not leave off, satiety that has nothing, the sparkle of something baseless and without depth" (Blanchot 1995: 220/1982: 168).

The two aspects of inspiration further clarify the definitions of wit and irony, respectively understood as the desire for a synthesis of heterogenous elements versus the experience of what borders on the exterior of the world, mirrored by the work of art. Hereby, the limit is experienced and recognized as *that* which – despite the promise of a dialectic – may never be sublated by the synthesis, as *that* which provides the disjunctive matrix of the synthesis being the reason why dialogue remains an infinite series of mirrors in an eternally desiring dialectical movement. Thus, the poem qua fragment is but a singularly inspired event of an eternal chain or garland of dialectics. Inspiration manifests itself as a point in the vertigo of Orpheus' "gaze" while meeting the profoundly obscure nothingness of Eurydice's "reflecting gaze". Hereby, inspiration manifests itself as the "appearance" of Eurydice when art opens; and here, the other night is art's most beautiful, unknown quantity, desired and expected, the justice exercised far and wide, though *dressed up* in art's own winding sheet:

> When Orpheus descends toward Eurydice, art is the power by which night opens. Because of art's strength, night welcomes him; it becomes welcoming intimacy, the harmony and accord of the first night. But it is toward Eurydice that Orpheus has descended. For him Eurydice is the furthest that art can reach. Under a name that hides her and and a veil that covers her, she is the profoundly obscure point toward which art and desire, death and night seem to tend. She is the instant when the essence of night approaches as the *other* night (Blanchot 1995: 225/1982: 171).

This instant is the *conditio sine qua non* of writing, in which the poet, due to his desire, reaches the true face of inspiration at the origin of the work of art. In the instant, the paradoxical law of imagination must necessarily be "obeyed": it is what must be transgressed before imagination can emerge. Art's own significance emerges in this instant. Death itself cannot show its true face; however, it hides in the shadow of Eurydice, in the abyss behind her reflecting gaze and behind her vanishing figure. Her hiding is the aspect which qualifies her as the unknown quantity of poetical thinking that stands in the light of one's own true and proximate death, as its distancing veil. In this instant, one's own death becomes presence as absence. During the encounter, the poetical subject experiences a voice from the sphere of silence which is different from the subject itself by virtue of its exterior, while the intended work is being lost in the profundity of mind: "To encounter Orpheus is to encounter this voice which is not mine, this death which becomes song, but which is not my death, even though I must disappear in it more profoundly" (Blanchot 1995: 204/1982: 156). Thus, in the vanishing presence of Eurydice's death that veils the point of his own, he hears the reflex of his own unknown event of dying.

The inspiration – which happens at the origin of the work of art during the transition from the first to the other night – is thus the axis of an oscillation between two senses: *sight* and *hearing*, which constitute a vital act of sense by the synaesthetic unity of *imagery* and *music*. The sight constitutes a spiritual vision of all the invisible and disappeared things, with which the subject – while in the light of day – desires to synthesize. As its counterpart, hearing operates as the antithetic gesture of bodily suggestions. Hearing at once destructs and unites the constitution of sense by experiencing the reflex of the disjunctive element that is immanent in the synthesis. The visibility of the spiritual constitution is revealed as the projection of day and world in the encounter with the other – a projection behind which alterity itself only makes its imprint as the act of withdrawal. Everything which was previously a spiritual imagery reveals itself as a sensation, in which Orpheus experiences the proximity of the other qua the voice of silence. Conversely, the voice of the silence returns the Orphean voice at the spur of the moment when his song ceases. Hence, the synaesthesia of sight and hearing generates sense through the most originally *presen*-ting material of poetry. Sense originates from the oscillation of sounds and images: poetry itself.

If the synaesthesia of senses is able to suggest a philosophical point of view and hereby to generate sense, how, then, must this relation of senses and sense be understood as an impact? And how do we avoid a fallacy of reduction whereby sense is regarded as truer than the plurality of senses? An answer to these questions could be found in Nietzsche's vitalist considerations of the sense qualities attributed to the movement between the senses sight and hearing. In *The Birth of Tragedy*, Nietzsche presents his view regarding the intrigues of Apollo and Dionysus in occidental aesthetics and philosophy. As mentioned previously, the problem arose as an irreversible condition after Dionysus had been put to flight and replaced by Socrates and the Socratic *dialectical* principle. Dionysus' one and only rescue in modern aesthetics and thinking is to be reborn as Socrates practicing music.

According to Nietzsche, the original *oneness* (das ur-Eine) of the visual and auditory senses is personified by Apollo and Dionysus, whose simultaneous desires often urge each other to an open conflict. The oneness, therefore, is the tension of their antagonism. Apollo and Dionysus each represent a set of sensory qualities. Apollo is associated with plasticity, visual art, the dream, the high illusion (Schein) of imagination, the majestic aspect of art, and thereby *principium individuationis*. In contrast, Dionysus is associated with musicality, with the non-visual and auditory qualities of music, the joyous ecstasy, the innermost foundation of nature, and thereby *dismemberment of principium individuationis* through the revelation of oneness. Apollo and Dionysus thus complement one another as the image of the self versus the harmony and tension of self and alterity. Apollo presents the temple of spirit and its illusion about infinite truth. This is synthesized in the concepts of subjective identity, of self-recognition, and the idea of objectivity all included by "the Delphic oracle, that seat of 'objective' art" (Nietzsche 1988: 43/1956: 37). Through the dismemberment, stone by stone, Dionysus refers to the oneness in his way of pointing toward the original foundation of the Apollonian "edifice": the subjectivity that precedes the narcissistic image of the self seen as an object. The crucial aspect of the relation between these two sets of sensory qualities that urge each other to conflict is their common and mutual potential: the will. It is thus a will to the sense of the senses which is the intrinsic power of life that conquers life's death sentence. Whereas the Apollonian qualities provide an image of will's presentation, the Dionysian provides will itself as a presentation of the Ding an Sich through music.

By means of his ecstatically dismembering power, Dionysus indicates how Apollo qua the deity of music, worshipped by Orpheus, had "originally" built up the clarity of his thought, i.e., music's union of heterogenous elements. This very union leaves behind a disjunctive remainder that prevents the possibility of an absolute sublation by the synthesis of senses, for which reason sense will always be a tension of experienced plurality. Orpheus' descent into and ascent from the Under-world can thus be regarded as a will to express the absolute diversity of the manifold that the human condition presents into a vision of sounds suggested by the loss of sense. It is a will to expression by means of his synaesthetic instrument, the poem. The oneness of will thus consists in two reverse desires and their mutual, dialectical movement. This dialectic is initiated as a will to synthesis. It peaks at the recognition of the impossibility of synthesis. It is then followed by an experience of the dual human condition as the fundamental premise of oneness, which is the original source of the will to synthesis. The dialectics within this oneness affords two archpoetical principles of a way of thinking which are at once new and archaic, because the antique myth has found a new, post-romantic, phenomenological origin of its qualities. It can now be said to originate out of an event that constitutes the modern occidental Orphean subject amidst an aesthetico-philosophical work of art through the poetical instant.

Conclusion: Orpheus as the new Socrates

This argument has taken its point of departure in the myth of Orpheus and Eurydice and its metapoetical and Socratic qualities. I have analyzed the origin of a literary philosophy and how I understand it as an em-blem of the possibilities of philosophical aesthetics from its incarnation in German romanticism onwards. In Schlegel's romanticism, the two reciprocal Orphean motifs, *creation* and *disjecta membra poetae*, are metamorphosed into the motifs of the fragment, *wit* and *irony*, which Blanchot radicalizes into two aspects of artistic inspiration, *the first night* and *the other night*. In this respect, Blanchot stresses the importance of the work of art as an intended phenomenon which presents itself qua a synaesthesia of sight and hearing through imagery and music – i.e. in the immanent act of experiencing human life. The two Orphean motifs hereby end up presenting their development into a post-romantic literary

91

philosophy as they express the dialectical event of a philosophical dialogue at the heart of aesthetics. Because of the Nietzschean *will*, dialogue never ceases to move by the pattern of desire for synthesis *vis-à-vis* the indispensable dismemberment, which sees a tension of oneness in life's manifold character and questions its certainty. By this tension, we can grasp the significance of the copula that forms the pair of Orphean motifs and its foundation of a literary philosophy. The synaesthetic phenomenon of the Orphean work of art can thus be perceived by an epoché of Apollonian and Dionysian qualities that constitute the basis of a philosophy of the human sensorium on archpoetical premises.

In this way, the synaesthetic tension of will becomes a rescue to the subject who is abandoned to the incarnate human condition, as it points toward the nexus of senses and sense. The nexus creates the Orphean music that suggests the image by which the subject mirrors him-/herself and recognizes his/her own power. The ancient dual principle of sense represented by the reciprocity of Apollo and Dionysus, for which Nietzsche instituted a search, has discovered a new foundation for its reactualization in the late modernity of occidental art. The dismembering Dionysus can now be reborn as the musical oneness of Socratic dialectics. Just as Nietzsche regarded the Socrates of Athens as the new Orpheus, we may now regard Orpheus as the new Socrates: a Socratic Orpheus who mirrors the temple of spirit while practicing music.

1 Nietzsche's emblematic example of the philosopher practicing music is the Wagnerian opera (Nietzsche 1988: 102).

2 Schlegel associates the dialogue with the epistolary principle, by which the I imagines his/her absent you and thereby reflects him-/herself (Schlegel 1988, vol. 2: 100). We can compare this to the kind of meeting between Orpheus and Eurydice, which throws light on how "The novels are the Socratic dialogues of our time", as Schlegel writes (Schlegel 1988, vol. 1: 240).

Literature

Blanchot, Maurice (1995). *L'espace littéraire*. Paris: Éditions Gallimard.

Blanchot, Maurice (1982). *The Space of Literature*, transl. Ann Smock. Lincoln/London: The University of Nebraska Press.

Critchley, Simon (1997). *Very Little... Almost Nothing: Death, Philosophy, Literature*. London/New York: Routledge.

Euripides (1994). *Alcestis*, in *Cyclops – Alcestis – Medea*, transl. David Kovacs. Cambridge, Mass./London: Harvard University Press.

Hjortsø, Leo (1987). *Græske guder og helte*. Copenhagen: Politikens Forlag.

Kant, Immanuel (1990). *Kritik der reinen Vernunft*. Frankfurt a.M: Suhrkamp Verlag.

Lacoue-Labarthe, Philippe & Nancy, Jean-Luc (1978). *L'absolu littéraire: Théorie de la littérature du romantisme allemand*. Paris: Éditions du Seuil (reprinted as *The Literary Absolute: The Theory of Literature in German Romanticism*. Albany: State University of New York, 1988).

Nietzsche, Friedrich (1988). *Geburt der Tragödie*, in *Die Geburt der Tragödie u.a.*, Kritische Studienausgabe, Giorgio Colli & Mazzino Montinari (eds.). München: dtv/de Gruyter.

Nietzsche, Friedrich (1956). *The Birth of Tragedy & The Genealogy of Morals*, transl. Francis Golffing. New York: Anchor Books, Doubleday.

Ovid [Publius Ovidius Naso] (1986). *Metamorphoses*, transl. A.D. Melville. Oxford: Oxford University Press.

Pindar (1915). *Pythian Odes IV*, in *The Odes of Pindar*, transl. Sir John Sandys. London: William Heinemann/New York: The Macmillian Co.

Plato (1984). *Apology of Socrates*, in *The Dialogues of Plato*, vol. 1, transl. R.E. Allen. New Haven/London: Yale University Press.

Plato (1991). *Symposium*, in *The Dialogues of Plato*, vol. 2, transl. R.E. Allen. New Haven/London: Yale University Press.

Rilke, Rainer Maria (1987). "Orpheus. Eurydike. Hermes", in *Werke I–VI*, vol. 1. Frankfurt a.M.: Insel Verlag.

Schlegel, Friedrich (1988). *Kritische Fragmente*, in Friedrich Schlegel. Ernst Behler & Hans Eichner (eds.). *Kritische Schriften und Fragmente [1794–1797]*, vol. 1, Paderborn: Verlag Verdinand Schöningh.

Schlegel, Friedrich (1988). *Athenäums-Fragmente*, in Friedrich Schlegel. Ernst Behler & Hans Eichner (eds.). *Kritische Schriften und Fragmente [1798–1801]*, vol. 2. Paderborn: Verlag Verdinand Schöningh.

Tortzen, Christian Gorm (1999). "Orfeus", in Jørn Lund et al. (eds.). *Den store danske encyklopædi*, vol. 14. Copenhagen: Danmarks Nationalleksikon.

Vergil [Publius Vergilius Maro] (1999). *Georgics*, in *Eclogues, Georgics, Aeneid I–VI*, transl. Fairclough, H. Rushton. Cambridge Massachusetts/London: Harvard University Press.

Warden, John (1985). "Introduction", in Warden, John (ed.). *Orpheus: The Metamorphoses of a Myth*. Toronto/Buffalo/London: University of Toronto Press.

Wissowa, Georg et al. (eds. (1907). "Eurydike", in *Paulys Real-Enzyclopädie der Classischen Altertumswissenschaft*, vol. 11. Stuttgart: J.B. Metzlersche Buchhandlung.

Wissowa, Georg et al. (eds. (1939). "Orpheus", in *Paulys Real-Enzyclopädie der Classischen Altertumswissenschaft*, vol. 35. Stuttgart: J.B. Metzlersche Buchhandlung.

Suspicion in the Ear

The Phonemic Reading of Garrett Stewart in a Scandinavian Context

Per Bäckström

THIS ARTICLE DISCUSSES the hypothesized hierarchy of the senses. It focuses upon the relation between the eye and the ear in the reading process, with special emphasis on aesthetics. When we are making sense with our senses, it is usually presupposed that the eye plays the dominant role, and when the gaze is analyzed, the eye is considered in isolation from the other senses. Similarly, the other senses are viewed in isolation when they are discussed. However, I find it unlikely that we – taken either as human beings or as animals – use our senses in such a restricted way. Rather, we activate our senses, making them cooperate as mutually supplementary organs, to help us collect information about reality and about the world.

As an example of this commonly given priority of the eye, let me refer to the media theoretician Marshall McLuhan, whose book, *The Medium is the Massage: An Inventory of Effects* (1967) discusses the historical transition from a priority of the ear to the dominance of the eye. This transition takes place through the invention of the alphabet and is further accelerated by the technology of printing:

The dominant organ of sensory and social orientation in pre-alphabet societies was the ear – "hearing was believing." The phonetic alphabet forced the magical world of the ear to yield to the neutral world of the eye. Man was given an eye for the ear.

Western history was shaped for some three thousand years by the introduction of the phonetic alephbet, a medium that depends solely on the eye for comprehension. The alphabet is a construct of fragmented bits and parts which have no semantic meaning in themselves, and which must be strung together in a line, bead-like, and in a prescribed order. Its use fostered and encouraged the habit of perceiving all environment in visual and spatial terms – particularly in terms of a space and of a time that are uniform,

> c,o,n,t,i,n,u,o,u,s

and

> c-o-n-n-e-c-t-e-d.

The line, the continuum

> – this sentence is a prime example –

became the organizing principle of life. "As we begin, so shall we go." "Rationality" and logic came to depend on the presentation of connected and sequential facts or concepts.[1]

As far as I can see, this is an accurate description of how the child learns to read; the focus changes from the sound to the written letter, then to the word, and finally to the sentence. However, this point of view overlooks the fact that language is already a given for the child. To learn to read, the child must know how to speak. And to speak is not something one learns solely through the eye. It is learned by knowing how to use language. Disregarding the standard opinion, that one learns to speak by hearing the word while seeing its reference pointed out, I want to suggest, following Stanley Cavell (1979), that this process can be conceived as an acquisition of knowledge which involves the senses *in toto*, since it is the lived experience that is the foundation for the ability to learn language. I therefore object to the definition of reading as a transition from "the magical world of the ear to [...] the neutral world of the eye", since, apart from the fact that the world of the eye can be as magical as the world of the ear, the magic of the ear will certainly never cease to intrude upon the neutrality of the eye. Furthermore, I will try to demonstrate that it is the combination of these two senses that makes the world more magically complete than either of the senses could accomplish alone. Life is a whole before the "fragmented bits" are given sense by the senses; hence, life always interrupts a complete understanding of the world.

*

In language, and more specifically in written text, there exist two levels or strata that are important to our understanding of the reading process: the graphemic and the phonemic strata. These two layers will be the focus of this article. My aim is to propose a theory that can be used to discuss experimental poetry, such as "concretism" and other "sound-poetry", and to analyze the creative process from within the text itself, i.e. without having to involve the long since deceased author. The purpose of this exercise is to find a supplement to Michael Riffaterre's semiotics of poetry, which is directed towards mimetic poetry and thus not suitable to explaining experimental poetry.

This article is a preliminary attempt to transfer the theory of the American literary theorist Garrett Stewart to the Scandinavian language areas, and I will begin by introducing Stewart's ideas in *Reading Voices: Literature and the Phonotext*, published in 1990.[2] I will then discuss the possibility of transferring Stewart's theory to the Scandinavian language areas by trying it out on some chosen Swedish examples.

Presentation

Garrett Stewart's studies concerning the phonemic layers in language are part of his attempt to find the "hidden voices" of the text. His main question is, "Where do we read?" His answer is that we read noiselessly – to our inner ear – by sounding the text silently to ourselves. That this has not always been the case is illustrated by the church father St. Augustine's comment about the monk Ambrose's silent reading of the texts, something that was seen as deviant in the third century, when the common practice was to read texts aloud.[3]

Stewart's investigation is in line with Jacques Derrida's questioning of the predominant tendency to stress orality at the expense of writing. The common belief in the priority of orality can be exemplified by Hegel's criticism of religion, which he attacked by claiming that the introduction of the written word has locked it into a blind belief in the letter, where the dead word is put into the focus.[4] This view is also applied by critics to poetry that has been experienced as "difficult", which can be exemplified by Anders Olsson's and Daniel Birnbaum's rendering of a poetry-reading by Rilke:

> It was said that Rainer Maria Rilke was once able to read one of his Duino elegies in such an animated manner that the audience did not have any problems whatsoever in grasping the poems. The voice transformed the complex structure of the linguistic work of art into a totally transparent body. But when the same people returned to the same poem, now in written form, the experience of intelligibility disappeared. The transparency of the voice had been transformed into an irresolvable muddle of the letters.[5]

It is this kind of focusing on orality that Stewart opposes, because it is a token of what he calls "phonocentrism". The citation above is nevertheless of great value, as it exemplifies the difference between the "dead letters" and their articulation. What is important is how the letters are articulated, i.e. how the phonemes are pronounced. Stewart seeks to establish an understanding for a phonemic level in the reading of poetry and prose, because the graphemic level can sometimes be experienced as an obstacle to the understanding of texts. His theory therefore focuses on a level between the written and the oral, where he emphasizes the inner sound of the words.

Phonemes can be combined endlessly, and it is only in the word-separating act of writing them down that they are bound together as words, i.e. structured in a way that is supposed to prevent uncertainties at the moment of reading. However, because of the character of the speech act, there is always a possibility for errors and unintended drift word constructions, what Stewart calls "transsegmental drift". Stewart therefore proposes a definition of the phonemic reading as a process distinct from the established stylistics.

> Stylistics studies the language act; phonemic reading intersects the action of lingual formation itself, its increments and transformations: the former is directed at *parole* (the speech act) in progress, the latter at *langue* (the whole structural fund of a given language) in its continuous but shifting provision for utterance. Stylistics is concerned at most with phonological patterns, while phonemic reading takes up their morphological implications, the junctural overlaps and detachments that both make and undo words. [---] In phonemic reading, the lexical code remains perpetually in play (RV: 26–27).

Stewart thus views phonemic reading as a phenomenon analogous to the Freudian slip of the tongue – "the parapraxis" – and to the function of such slips of meaning in puns. Somehow, it is the structure of language itself that is read, in the sense of *la langue*. And as with a Freudian slip of the tongue, the phonemic reading is an activity close to a reading off of the subconscious itself. The slippage in the syntax, which is what is at stake here, can be described as an approach to the pre-linguistic order, as described by Jacques Lacan and Julia Kristeva.[6] In a phonemic reading, the text is read the way it could have looked before the textual flow was turned into words, words still sticking to each other. Stewart is of the opinion that:

> It is within the activity – and activation – of phonemic reading that the exemplary case of the transegmental drift comes into play: exemplary because exposing most often and most clearly that unstable partition between lexemes which the blank between graphemes would attempt to secure (RV: 28–29).

Of the two strata that comprise a literary text, the graphemic and the phonemic, the latter can give the text a slightly different appearance. The most typical example of this is the pun, which can function as a transformative factor in the production of language as such. The pun can work through word-amalgamations, as in the phrase: "alco*holi*days" (RV: 31), but also through a re-reading with what Stewart calls "transsegmental drift" between words. One example of the latter is to be found in Jim Jarmusch's film *Down by Law* (1986), where the jingle "I scream, you scream, we all scream, for ice-cream" is persistently repeated. However, a pun must not necessarily be intended as a pun from the beginning, it might as well be a classical "slip of the tongue", since the function behind the pun and the parapraxis is very similar.

The main question, then, is what these phonemic slidings are symptoms of? Freud referred to the subconscious, and Garrett Stewart describes his phonemic reading in a way that indicates – as mentioned before – that it is an attempt to read off a prelinguistic level, what Lacan and Kristeva call, respectively, the imaginary and the semiotic level. The phonemic reading therefore seems to be connected to the linguistic production of language in the transition from the semiotic to the symbolic level, from the flow of the subconscious to an articulated language.

At the same time, this is a process that can be trained into an at least partly conscious act, as illustrated by the significance of punning in the English language, and also by the way the transsegmental drift is used by poets and authors. Stewart's point here is that it is possible to detect the drift within the written text, irrespective of which level of consciousness the process belongs to.

Theoretical background

In his own words, Stewart formulates his theory in a tradition from American deconstructionism, with Geoffrey Hartman's microlinguistics as a main incentive, but with the addition of ideas from other theoreticians as well:

> Acknowledging in this manner a reading eccentric to writing may finally provide one of the most convincing ways to localize the no longer metaphysical but no less mythologized status of writing, as a crisis of the decentered subject, in the work of Blanchot, Barthes, Derrida, Lacan, Kristeva, Deleuze, and others. In a melodramatic (often little more than metaphoric) scenario, writing in this way becomes the imputed emptying out of identity always incident to inscription, a traumatic alterity (RV: 31).

The main theoretician whom Stewart wants to relate himself to, however, is Jacques Derrida. Stewart argues that it is possible to develop Derrida's ideas in the direction of the phonemic reading: a reading in between the lexemes. Derrida's use of puns and word-amalgamations in his writings also suggests a similarity with the process of transsegmental drift, as proposed by Stewart.[7] Stewart presents his own theory as a development of the views on text-production as expressed in the works of Roland Barthes and Julia Kristeva, since neither takes any interest in the phonemic level:

the understanding of a "text" is based on a model of production rather than communication. A text is seen to actualize its semiotic operations by the manifestation of "significance" through a linear and discursive succession of words: by the conversion, that is, of "genotext" into "phenotext," of some already sub-"textualized" (rather than intentionalist) "conception" into the surface phenomena of its lexical and syntactical realization. Working within the model of produced textuality as well, this book will consider that dimension of the phenotext which is regularly ignored [---] the "phonotext" (RV: 27–28).

Another important connection made by Stewart is the one to Michael Riffaterre, but here the connection takes the form of a critical dialogue. Riffaterre published his *Semiotics of Poetry* in 1978, where he develops his structuralist theory about the construction of poems. A poem, according to Riffaterre, is structured by a matrix; this can be a word, a phrase or a system of meaning. The matrix does not exist in the text itself, but makes its presence felt by its variations throughout the text, and where the first variation – "the model" – determines the form of the rest of the poem. However, the poem is determined in a double way: besides the variations of the matrix that structure the poem vertically, so to say, every line or phrase is also determined by one or more "hypograms". The hypogram is the textual references, that one might call – and with Riffaterre today – intertextuality. Concerning the relation to Stewart's critic, the most important is that Riffaterre decides that the structuring elements are absent in the text *per se*.

Stewart develops Riffaterre's semiotics of poetry with a claim that the phonemic reading can reveal hypograms and/or matrices of a poem, that is, the cliché or systems of meaning outside the text that are modified through it, and the intertexts to which that it refers to. At the same time he claims, contrary to Riffaterre, that these might be inherent in the text, hidden for a graphemic reading. Riffaterre regards the center of the text as situated outside itself, in a succession from Saussure. For this reason, Stewart criticizes Riffaterre for looking beyond the text more than behind it, as he puts it. Even if Riffaterre himself has not brought his theory to a syllabic or phonemic level, there is no reason not to do so, according to Stewart.

> Evident here is Riffaterre's tacit holding action against exactly the kind of phonemic reading which this chapter finds invited by the Shakespearean text – as the clear (if pulsing) signal of its literariness. The phonotext "produced" in this way, as we are to see, occupies a middle ground between the lexical/grammatical sine qua non of Riffaterre's method and the graphemic free association of an anagram. Between full semantic security and syllabic mayhem, then, lies the domain of phonemic reading (RV: 41).

Riffaterre has explicitly stated that he takes no interest in either the graphemic nor the phonemic level of language – despite the fact that Saussure did so – because the matrix belongs to the textual level of a text. And this is precisely what Stewart criticizes, since he believes that the theory of Riffaterre becomes all too static because it is incapable of explaining all aspects of the literary language. And this is especially devastating for a theory about the poetic language, where rhythm and sound are of vital importance, and where the phonemic level should by all means have the same significance. In the critique that Paul de Man has directed against Michael Riffaterre, de Man concludes that Riffaterre places too much emphasis on the description and too little on the inscription, which, for de Man, is connected to the rhetorical level. As an example Stewart discusses the following line in a poem of Mallarmé: "Avec ce seul objet dont le Néant s'honore" – a line which not even Riffaterre could read without commenting that the last words sound like: "néant sonore". According to Stewart, this is the only instance where Riffaterre transgresses his own lexematic reading (RV: 124).[8]

Raymond Roussel is a French poet whose work cannot be explained by the theory of Riffaterre, according to Stewart. Roussel's poems can be seen as an attack on "normal" poetry, because Roussel is extremely sensitive to the phonemic level of the language. He works wholly or partly with transformations of the "normal" language, where trans-segmental drift are one of the main methods.

> Rather than generating a Riffaterrean paragram, it spawns ultimately a sentence that is more like an anagram (or hypogram) of *itself* – but of itself as different, alienated at base, uprooted at the point of semantic implantation and narrative departure. Signifying force in Riffaterre's semiotics comes from a tension between what is literally said and what is repressed by that phrasing. Roussel's texts, by contrast, short-circuit such a signifying system by extruding everything as surface play (RV: 123–124).

As always in cases like this, Riffaterre's theory fails, i.e., when the poets dare to play with the hypograms and matrices directly, devices which he uses to explain the lyrical production.[9] Stewart has a relevant point in his critique of Riffaterre, especially as his own theory comes much closer to what I understand to be the vital factors for both everyday and poetical language production.

Stewart's exemplification

Before continuing my analysis of the relevance of Stewart's theory for an analysis of Scandinavian poetry, let me provide some examples of transsegmental drifts from Stewart's book. I have already discussed the function behind the punning process. The next level where trans-segmental drift are at work is the rhyming. That a rhyme can be enriched through lexematic amalgamation is a well-known fact. This can be used especially to obtain the kind of rhyme that is called "rime très riche", i.e. leximatically complete rhymes. Stewart exemplifies from Chaucer's poetry: "'liven *may*' with 'rose in *May*'" (RV: 68).[10]

However, the rhyming words may also be made to sound identical through word amalgamation, here again shown by an example from Chaucer: "'*for age*'/'*forage*'" (RV: 70). We are dealing with leximatically complete amalgamations in the rhymes, and Stewart's purpose is to show how such "rich" rhymes can be formed through transsegmental drift, i.e. how phonemes slide from one word to another to enrich the rhyme. This mechanism operates entirely at the level of sound, since the words are still intended to be read separately. In John Donne's poetry we read: "do*th us*/*thus*" (RV: 77). This seems to be a result of the aspect that poets are supposed to be more sensitive to the sounds in language than "ordinary" people. Stewart goes on to discuss drifting in the verses themselves, which for him is even closer to the deconstructive process of reading texts against the grain. Besides making sound repetitions which function as assonance and alliteration, i.e. reinforcement through repetitions of word clusters, the transsegmental drift can also make words transform, sometimes even in a way that contradicts the original meaning of the text. This part of Stewart's text, with his analysis of the restructuring of words in a text, is rather difficult to grasp, even though he provides the reader with extensive examples. The examples come mostly from the Anglo-Saxon languages, apart from some citations in French, i.e. two languages where one has developed a hightened sense for the existence of such mechanisms, due to the vast difference between the lexematic and phonematic levels in the languages. More than half the book consists of Stewart's discussion of this phenomenon in prose writings, something that in this context – a general analysis of poetry reading – is of minor interest. Furthermore, the discussion focuses mainly on James Joyce and Virginia Woolf, both of whom were highly aware of the effects of drifting between words and phonemical resemblances. This makes it difficult to transform Stewart's discussion into a general theory for understanding the creative process of the "normal" author.

I therefore confine myself to a single exemplification of Stewart's discussion, a long citation about W.B. Yeats' poem "The Lake Isle of Innisfree", before going on to analyze the relevance of Stewart's theory for the Scandinavian languages.

> Or when, in the thundering paratactic redundancy of "The Second Coming":
>
>> Things fall apart; the center cannot hold;
>> Mere anarchy is *loosed* upon the world,
>> The blood-dimmed tide is *loosed*, and everywhere
>> The ceremony of innocence is drowned
>
> With the emphatic repetition of the participle "loosed" attracting the preceding sibilant – to form on its trace the passive transform of the transitive verb *sluice*, for "to drench" or "to flood" – we audit a decentering of the enunciatory regime of script itself (RV: 183)

From this citation, it is easy to follow the traces backwards to the thinking and practice of American deconstructionism, with its "decentering of the … script", while it is also interesting to follow Stewart's thoughts to a rereading of Scandinavian poetry. The question is: is it possible?

Transegmental drift in Swedish poetry

Considering the above-mentioned character of the French and English languages, and the emphasis in these language areas on the discrepancy between the graphemic and phonemic levels of language, one might inquire as to the relevance of transsegmental readings for the Scandinavian languages, where there is a closer connection between the levels. I will try to address this question through a discussion of some Swedish examples in light of Stewart's theory. Because of the close relationship between the Scandinavian languages, these examples will be assumed to represent Scandinavian literature in general.

It is not very difficult to understand that transsegmental drifting also operate in Swedish punning: one can just think about Brödinstitutets ("The Bread Institute") slogan: "Socialstyrelsen rekommenderar sex till åtta brödskivor om dagen" ("The Social Authority recommends six to eight slices of bread each day"), where the number was soon expanded to "sextioåtta" – sixty-eight. As mentioned before, such a mechanism is common in punning and can be compared with the function of the Freudian slip of the tongue.

The next step in Stewart's theory is also easy to transfer: an enrichment of rhymes seems to be a plausible prime mover in poets' choices of words. However, this does not appear to be as common in Swedish as in English and French poetry, and the designation *rime très riche* suggests that it is in French that this process appears most often. Nevertheless, a few examples can illustrate that the possibility also exists in the Swedish language.[11] Consider some versus from the poem "Dagning" (Dawning) by Vilhelm Ekelund:

> Det luftar upp. Se dagningen är *nära*!
> Nu viker nattens onda drömmar bort.
> Så stånden upp att bringa dage*n* *ära*,[12]

Here the "n" in the third verse drifts – or rather reduplicates – from "dagen" to the following "ära", in a way that enriches the rhyme. In the long poem "Italia" by Carl Wilhelm Böttiger, there are two different examples of the mechanism, on one double-page spread with six eight-line stanzas:

> där strålar rikt kupolers *topp*,
> där skimrar luftig kolonnad,
> som drömmen nu bygg*t opp*.
> ...

jordfästa sig kring Tiberns *ström*. —
Månn' det är verklighet hon ser,
ITALIA, månn' en *dröm*?[13]

In the first stanza, the "t" slides over to the ending "opp" in a way similar to the previous example. The rhyme of the last stanza, though, works – besides with the oppositions "d" and "t" – by the swallowing up of the first "s" in "ström" in the word before – "Tiberns". It seems as if this way of writing or thinking, consciously or unconsciously, is a question of personal sensitivity, and not a shared poetical technique – it is part of the idiolect. Böttiger's poetry is usually rhymed, and a well-developed feeling for rhyming should naturally be of great benefit for a mechanism like this. Even though I have given only a cursory illustration, it should now be obvious that the occurrence of *rime très riche* is also found in Swedish poetry.[14]

When it comes to transsegmental drift in other parts of poems than in the end rhyme position, more extensive research is necessary to make it possible to transfer Stewart's theory to Scandinavian conditions. Despite this fact, I will try to illustrate this mechanism in a poem by Vilhelm Ekelund, recalling that it is not really possible to analyze a single poem in this way without a thorough study of the phenomenon of drifting in the Swedish language as such, and without a profound knowledge of the author whom one is investigating! My purpose here is only to show that the possibility to detect this mechanism is present in the Swedish language.

The following is a stanza from Vilhelm Ekelund's poem "Final":

Och så plötsligt —
där djupt nere
i den dunkla dagen —
årets mörkaste tid var inne…

Eros, Eros!

Villat har du

mina sinnen,

djupt och ängsligt

är min själ förvirrad,

svävar redlös

utan fäste...

som om plötsligt

i mig rörts en

lönlig punkt

sprang en skräcksyn

upp i själen,

tog min dova

och förstenat stumma smärta

sagohemsk livslevande gestalt — — [15]

The state of confusion in which the I of the poem is brought by Eros is reflected in the overall ambiguity of the stanza *per se*, with its use of dashes and *aposiopes* as an indication of overwhelming feelings. With the use of Stewart's theory, it might be possible to find another ambiguity in the poem, where the I is floating intoxicated – "svävar *redlös*". If we consider the content of the poem, there is a possibility for a swallowing up of the ending "r" in "svävar redlös", which could then be understood as if the I, in spite of its state of petrifaction, makes an attempt to resist the state of confusion in an imperative: "sväva redlös" – "float intoxicated", something that is rather an assent to the delusion of Eros than a surrender to melancholy.[16]

Experimental poetry

One of the main uses of Stewart's theory is as a means of interpreting sound poems, which are more often based on the functions of sound and rhythm than on a feeling of mimetic wholeness. A heightened consciousness about the phonemic levels of the language might therefore contribute to a better understanding of how the poems are constructed and structured. The closeness of the phonemic reading to a pre-linguistic order, and the segmentation of the flow of the subconscious into words, results in a circumscription of the creative process. This is especially interesting as concerns sound poems and other experimental poetry based on these kinds of mechanisms, in which the sounds determine where a word or a phoneme is placed in the poem rather than the actual "meaning" of the word.

Stewart has formulated functions which lead directly to word-amalgamations such as the Swedish poet Gunnar Ekelöf's phrasing "krossa bokstävlarna mellan tänderna" – from the Swedish words for "letters" and "devils".[17] Transformations in poems like Ekelöf's "Perpetuum mobile" might also find their explanation at the phonemic level. The poetical reworking of poems such as this one is executed quite calculatedly, and the transformation from "vanliga skalligheten" to "skamliga vanligheten" in the first stanza is easy, phonemically speaking, because it is basically an inversion. In the third stanza, it is evident that the transformations are both poetically and linguistically motivated, considering its inversions and replacements:

> Den gamla hemliga skadligheten
> Den gamla saliga flabbigheten
> Den gamla skadliga skabbigheten
> Den gamla skabbiga saligheten[18]

For example, the transformation from "skadliga" to "skabbiga" can be described as a rather simple phonemic slippage from "dl" to "bb". Other poems that draw on the same mechanisms, i.e., which function more or less as flows of words and sounds, could also be more readily analyzed in terms of a phonemic reading, than by a traditional close reading.

Conclusion

Many theories have great difficulties adapting to an explaining pure mechanisms of language in poetry. Garrett Stewart's analysis of trans-segmental drifting at a phonemic level touches on a central mechanism in the production of everyday and poetical language, especially as concerns experimental poems where the semantic and syntactic planes in the poem are of minor importance. The great value of Stewart's theory is that it brings this level to the fore, a level that might help explain the claims of some theoreticians that poetry is not translatable between different languages, because his theory makes it very clear how dependent poetry is on the specific language.

The phonemic reading is a helpful tool for the analysis of the creative process, but as with all such theories, it is also a powerful instrument in the analysis and interpretation of poetry as a whole. The principal analytical power of Stewart's approach lies in its application to the study of how experimental poetry is structured, i.e. the kind of poetry that can be located in an area somewhere between mimetic, syntactical and semantic complete poetry, and poetry that can be said to build on the total "destruction of syntax" – where in the latter case also the phonemic level is missing. Sound poetry might therefore be analyzed on the basis of the premises made by the poet in his/her choice of phrases and phonemes, in addition to the analysis of rhythm and musicality that constitute the formal elements which have heretofore been the focus of concentration.

The analysis of the phonemical level in poetry which I have demonstrated with the help of Stewart's theory demands a more thorough empirical study to be applicable *in toto* to sound poetry and other experimental Scandinavian poetry. This article is meant as a first step toward developing a theory that can extract from the text itself, if not the whole creative process, at least the phonemic considerations that the poet must have made.

1 McLuhan 2001: 44–45.

2 *Reading Voices* will hereafter be referred to as "RV".

3 One explanation of this habit of reading aloud is that Latin during the third century was not written with word-separating spaces.

4 Birnbaum & Olsson 1992: 129.

5 *Op cit.*, 126–127, my transl.

6 Here I refer to Lacan's divide between "the imaginary" and "the symbolic" and Kristeva's modification of his terms to "the semiotic", "the symbolic" and "the chora". The term "pre-linguistic" is more general, covering both the imaginary and the semiotic. Stewart himself refers to Kristeva, among others.

7 Derrida's terms "différance", "supplement" and "trace" are discussed and given relevance for the phonemic reading, because all three terms touch on the "rest" that remains when one compares the phonemic reading to the graphemic level. As a good example on this transsegmental drift, Stewart refers to the wordplay of Derrida in the title of his book *Signéponge/Signsponge*, where a double pun is the point of departure for the whole of Derrida's discussion, even though his goal is different from that of Stewart.

8 It seems like Riffaterre has become more observant of drifting on the lexematic level, but it is still not on the basic phonemic level which Stewart analyzes. See Riffaterre 1990.

9 Bäckström 2000.

10 This is one case of a major drawback in Stewart's book, namely his tendency to make very short citations out of context, which can make his account hard to read.

11 A truly representative investigation of the appearance of the process in Scandinavian languages, would of course call for a much more thorough exploration of the phenomenon.

12 "It's airing up. See, dawning is close! / Now evil dreams of the night turns away. / So stand up to honor the day". Ekelund 1980: 30. My italics and my (rough) translation.

13 "there the top of cupolas richly shimmer, / there shimmer an airy colonnade, / which the dream has built up now. [—] burying itself around the stream of the Tiber. — / Wonder if it's reality that she sees, / ITALY, wonder if it's a dream?". Böttiger 1895: 210–211. My italics and my (rough) translation.

14 A deepened study of the subject might make it possible to establish a pattern, comparing the conditions for poets who frequently use this kind of mechanism to obtain enriched rhymes, and those who do not.

15 "And then suddenly—/ deap down below / in the dusky daylight —/ it was time for the darkest time of the year… / Eros, Eros! / deluded has thou / my senses, / deep and anxious / is my soul confused, / floating intoxicated / without a grip… / as if suddenly / in me a secret point / was moved / burst a frightening sight / up in the soul, / took my stifled / and petrified dumb agony / as in a terrifying saga lifelike shape — —". Ekelund 1980: 203. My (rough) translation.

16 I am sure that one at a deeper study of the phenomenon could relate this to the author Ekelund, with his shifting between high and low expressions of feeling.

17 "sonatform denaturerad prosa". Ekelöf 1981: 13.

18 "The old secret woundindness / The old blessed guffawness / The old harmful scabbyness /The old scabby blessedness". "Perpetum Mobile" Ekelöf 1981: 39, my (rough) translation.

Literature

Birnbaum, Daniel and Olsson, Anders (1992). *Den andra födan. En essä om melankoli och kannibalism*, Stockholm: Albert Bonniers förlag.

Bäckström, Per (2000). "Michael Riffaterre och poesins semiotik. En kritisk läsning", *Norsk Litteraturvitenskapelig Tidsskrift* no. 2.

Böttiger, Carl Wilhelm (1895). *Valda dikter*, Stockholm: F. & G. Beijers Bokförlagsaktiebolag.

Cavell, Stanley (1979). *The Claim of Reason: Wittgenstein, Skepticism, Morality, and Tragedy*, Oxford: Clarendon Press.

Ekelund, Vilhelm (1980). *Dikter*, Stockholm: Albert Bonniers förlag.

Ekelöf, Gunnar (1981). *Grotesker*, Stockholm: Ordström.

McLuhan, Marshall and Fiore, Quentin (2001 [1967]). *The Medium is the Massage: An Inventory of Effects*, Corte Madera: Gingko Press.

Riffaterre, Michael (1978). *Semiotics of Poetry*, London: Methuen & Co., Ltd.

Riffaterre, Michael (1978). "Sylleptic Symbols: Rimbaud's 'Memoire'", in Christopher Prendergast (ed): *Nineteenth Century French Poetry*, Cambridge: Cambridge University Press.

Stewart, Garrett (1990). *Reading Voices: Literature and the Phonotext*, Berkeley: University of California Press.

In Rot getaucht

Elias Canettis *Die gerettete Zunge* and the color 'red' in modern art

Karen Hvidtfeldt Madsen

IN SEEKING THE limits of one branch of art compared to others, one meets numerous difficulties. Rhythm and sound seems connected to music, as color and form seems to be concrete and useful terms when one seeks to describe a work of visual art such as a sculpture or painting. The branches of art can be divided according to their use of basic dimensions where music and literature use time as their common medium, the visual arts and architecture are spatial and material. We sense the visual arts with our eyes. Perception may take its time, but a painting has no beginning and no end in the sense of a novel or a symphony; these latter forms of art have no actual physical representation.

Nevertheless in describing concrete works of art, one repeatedly experiences the activation of unexpected senses. The limits between the different branches of art are constantly transgressed. In the process of understanding a piece of visual art, it may very well be necessary to consider dynamics, and in the interpretation of literature or music, questions of form or color can be shown to be both interesting and important.

This article takes its point of departure in the first volume of Elias Canetti's autobiographical trilogy, *Die gerettete Zunge*, a volume which concentrates on his earliest memories of his childhood years. I wish to examine the relationship between memorized history and created fiction and the "intermedial" aspect, under here focusing especially on Canetti's characteristic use of the red color. I will demonstrate that the color red is dominant in Canetti's autobiography and central to an understanding of his work. Focusing on the redness of the novel, the crucial theme becomes creation of identity. Here a characteristic ambiguity appears, specifically connected to the theme of religion and Canetti's identity as a Jew. It is my aim to examine the history of the color red; briefly through the scientifically based theories of Newton, Goethe and Jung, and to demonstrate traces of a connection between being Jewish and the use of red in modern art. In this latter task, I will draw attention to the poetry of Sylvia Plath and to Krzysztof Kieslowski's film *Rouge* as two examples of artistic work, where the use of red as a dominant symbol is comparable and enlightening to the understanding of specific elements of Elias Canetti's work, and of modernity in general.

Developing the senses

Elias Canetti's autobiographical trilogy describes processes of development in at least five different ways.[1] Some of these techniques resemble traditional modes of development as seen in the *Bildungsroman*, while others are specifically related to the "intermedial" aspect and to the development of the senses.

In growing up, little Elias experiences a number of geographic changes. His life is a concrete journey from Bulgaria, where he was born, to Manchester in England where his school years start, continuing to Vienna and Zurich. During the next two volumes of the trilogy, his travels include Frankfurt and Berlin, although Vienna is an even steadier point of departure and return.

The narrative is also a description and interpretation of Elias Canetti's journey through life. Dominating the first volume is the death of his father and the domination of his mother. His father died unexpectedly when he is only 6 years old, while the family was living in England. His mother became a widow at age 27, with three sons of whom Elias was the oldest. His mother never remarried, and a major theme in the trilogy is the very intense, but also problematic relationship between the oldest son and his mother. Their relationship culminates when Elias, as a mature man, succeeds in liberating himself from his mother's strong domination, and eventually marries a woman of his own choice. For years he convinces his mother that he has absolutely no passion for the beautiful and intelligent Veza Canetti, in order to spare Veza his mother's hateful jealousy.

The mother's understanding of why Elias' father died develops as a subsidiary story throughout the trilogy. She experiences a lifelong feeling of guilt, because she feels that the compromising of their relationship was the cause of her husbands fatal heart attack. She never managed to feel at home in England in the same way as did her husband, and she had just returned from a health resort in Switzerland, where she was supposed to regain her health. She enjoyed being in Central Europe so much that the stay was prolonged several times, until Elias' father lost his patience and simply ordered her to return to England. At her return, she confessed that a doctor at the resort spent a great deal of time with her, and that she had enjoyed his company very much. The doctor had fallen in love with her and had offered her marriage, which she had refused. There had been no intimacy between them, but (much worse) they had discussed literature. And what Elias' father was most indignant about, was that she had spoken German with him; the language which for the Canettis was *their* language, the language of love, intimacy and privacy, mainly because the children were unable to understand it.

With the tragic death of his father as a starting point, the trilogy is also a journey through languages. Elias Canetti learned Bulgarian, Hebrew, English, Latin and French. And after the father's death, his mother taught him German, not only because she moved to Austria with her sons, where Elias was to attend school, but also because she needed him as a substitute for her husband. She teaches him this "secret language", and they enjoy long, intense conversations about various aspects of literature and drama. Thus, Canetti adopts German as the language of intellect, of his knowledge and love of art, and German becomes the language of his own authorship.

Canetti's trilogy, in its relationship to the human senses, reflects a development from talking to seeing. *Die gerettete Zunge. Geschichte einer Jugend* from 1977 points towards the tongue as a central object. The second volume: *Die Fackel im Ohr. Lebensgeschichte 1921–31*, from 1980 relates to the ear, and refers specifically to the influence of Karl Kraus on Elias Canetti during his twenties. The third and concluding volume *Das Augenspiel. Lebensgeschichte 1931–37* from 1985 relates to the sense of seeing. The concrete occasion is the irresistible eyes of the young Anna Mahler. At a general level, however, the memoirs of Canetti also point towards the sense of seeing as being important in a number of different ways. Canetti's medium clearly becomes language, he is gifted at learning foreign languages, and he understands his development towards his profession as a writer as being unavoidable. Several times, though, he stresses how sorry he is that he never learned to draw or paint, whereas his mother makes no secret of not liking the art of painting: "Sie sprach nie über Malerei, es war die eine Kunst, die sie kaum interessiert, von der sie nichts verstand." [2] (Canetti 1992: 205) In this way, the autobiography treats the visual dimension in ambiguous terms. Painting is something not done, not liked, but at the same time longed for and desired. As a final aspect of a process of development, the sense of seeing also refers to the dimension of "ein*sehen*", of understanding, which is the underlying ambition of the whole project of memorizing.

The earliest memories

As a starting point I wish to draw attention especially to the beginning of the first volume, *Die gerettete Zunge*, of which the first paragraph reads as follows:

Meine früheste Erinnerung ist in Rot getaucht. Auf dem Arm eines Mädchens komme ich zu einer Tür heraus, der Boden vor mir ist rot, und zur Linken geht eine Treppe hinunter, die ebenso rot ist. Gegenüber von uns, in selber Höhe, öffnet sich eine Tür und ein lächelnder Mann tritt heraus, der freundlich auf mich zugeht. Er tritt ganz nahe an mich heran, bleibt stehen und sagt zu mir: "Zeig die Zunge!" Ich strecke die Zunge heraus, er greift in seine Tasche, zieht ein Taschenmesser hervor, öffnet es und führt die Klinge ganz nahe an meine Zunge heran. Er sagt: "Jetzt schneiden wir ihm die Zunge ab." Ich wage es nicht die Zunge zurück-zuziehen, er kommt immer näher, gleich wird er sie mit der Klinge berühren. Im letzten Augenblick zieht er das Messer zurück, sagt: "Heute noch nicht, morgen." Er klappt das Messer wieder zu und steckt es in seine Tasche.

Jeden Morgen treten wir aus der Tür heraus auf den roten Flur, die Tür öffnet sich, und der lächelnde Mann erscheint. Ich weiß, was er sagen wird und warte auf seinen Befehl, die Zunge zu zeigen. Ich weiß, daß er sie mir abschneiden wird und fürchte mich jedesmal mehr. Der Tag beginnt damit, und es geschieht viele Male.[3] (Canetti 1992: 7)

The memory resembles a recurring nightmare. Not until years later did the young Canetti dare confront his mother with this memory. It is she, who is able to place the events at a pension in Karlsbad, where the family stayed during the summer when Canetti was two years old. They had brought a young babysitter from Bulgaria, and she fell in love with a young man living in a room right opposite them in the pension. Her daily walks with the child was at the same time the opportunity to meet with the boyfriend, which of course was a secret, and in some sense this story explains the threat to cut off the little boys tongue. The forbidden relationship was revealed when the girl was seen slipping into the young man's room during the night, and she was immediately sent back home. The threat to cut off the child's tongue was made to make sure that he would not tell, which he did not, the narrator tells us, until ten years later.

This earliest memory provided the title for the book. The tongue (which may or may not have been threatened in Canetti's early childhood) is first of all a metonymic figure. It points towards the ability to speak, the meaning of language-learning and language-changing so important in the life of Canetti. It also points towards the art of telling and the profession of becoming an author.

Yet underneath the author's portrait of himself as a writer, the books are also about his development of an identity in a broader sense. Not only do we observe the growth of a writer; a man and a Jew are also taking form. When it comes to these issues it seems that the sense of seeing shows the path toward a deeper level of the narrative.

Memory and the formation of identity

The difference between fiction and the writing of history is not definite. In the ninth chapter of his *Poetics*, Aristotle discussed the difference between the role of a poet versus that of the historian, concluding that one can not easily separate these two modes of writing. The poet describes what might have happened, whereas the historian tells what actually did happen. However, what matters is that if what "might have happened" really did happen, it would not make the writing of the poet any less poetic. Conversely, the historians work can be true *and* poetic at the same time, if history is told according to the artistic rules of either the comedy or the tragedy.

In *Temps et récit*, the French philosopher Paul Ricoeur continues this line of thinking by arguing that history cannot be told or understood if not told according to the rules of artistic expression. We understand

and remember the past ordered as comedies or tragedies.

In her study on the subject of childhood memories, the Danish literary scholar Lilian Munk Rösing points out that the difference between "authentic" memories and fictional memories is not as profound as it may seem on first sight. In both cases there exists a binding relationship between the author and the child. Whether the child is memorized or the child is a construction, whether fictive or a "real" story; the child is in any case an "inner" child. The child described is a model of a child found within the author.

Elias Canetti writes down his memoirs, but at the same time he creates a fictional narration. He creates himself by telling a story, one could say. He creates an identity. Thus, Canetti's work, while autobiographical, can be seen as a kind of fictional story. And although we are dealing with an autobiographical story, where the relationship between the author and narrator should be obvious, it is necessary to consider the role of narrator.

Turning back to the first paragraph of the narrative, one meets a very self-confident, if not omniscient, narrator. In the first scene he both relates *and* interprets the role of the child. What he in fact remembers is the red color, the knife and the fear. The actual time and place he learns from his mother, and the interpretation of what really happened is a grown man's reflection. Many years later he states that "the threat worked". Recalling the early memories he nevertheless admits that: "Als Kind hatte ich keinen Überblick" (Canetti 1992: 8).[4] He remembers "der Farbigkeit dieser frühen Jahre" (Canetti 1992: 9), and constantly confronts the child he imagines to have been with his actual self-image.

The second chapter, based on the early memories of the Bulgarian community, is constructed as a series of episodes marked by themes of power and oppression. We are told about the quite humiliating manner in which a poor relative is treated by the powerful grandfather (Canetti 1992: 12). We hear about the harassment of the local idiot by children in the neighbourhood (Canetti 1992: 13). The power of nature and animals fills the scary stories told by his mother about the wolves living outside the town (Canetti 1992: 14). The power of his inner nature (his own imagination) is revealed in his fear, when he is told scary stories by his babysitters (Canetti 1992: 15). And finally the power of language: his parent's habit of speaking German when they did not want to be understood by their son. He was deeply provoked by this private "grown-up-language".

In the episodes mentioned above, the narrative is experimentally moved closer to that of the imagined and remembered child. Words like "fühlen", "erscheinen mir", "gefielen mir", are used: words characterised by feelings rather than reflections. At the end of the chapter, however, the reflecting mode once again takes over: "Was genau vor sich ging, kann ich nicht sagen", the narrator states. He realizes that everything is translated in (at least) a double sense of the word. Not only translated in time, but also from Spanish and Bulgarian, which was his language of speech then, into German, which is the language of his narration. "Ich weiß nicht, zu welschem Zeitpunkt, bei welscher Gelegenheit dies oder jenes sich übersetzt hat" (Canetti 1992: 15–16). He claims that the memories are completely vivid, but "sie sind zum allergrößten Teil an Worte gebunden, die ich damals nicht kannte."[5] It is not a translation to be compared with a translation of a book, he declares, but a translation made automatically sometime and somewhere in the unconscious. At the same time he distances himself from the word "unconscious", he does not want to talk about the unconscious, and it is indeed a narration struggling to keep control, to stay on the conscious level. For instance the life of Elias Canetti is related as a chronological development, which is not the way the human memory is normally thought to function. The German filmmaker Edgar Reitz, who has devoted the major part of his working life to creating filmed representations of memorized history, puts it this way:

What we store in our memory is not ordered chronologically, nor is it retrievable in a logical form. When we exchange memories, even when we silently remember or write down from memory, then we notice that memory puts together the experiences which have been stored in our mind in a new manner. Memory does not remember, but rather memory is creative, it builds new connections. It works associatively, narratively like a poet, and this applies to all people. The actual past reality is never really achieved. (Birgel: 1986)

The human mind remembers in pictures rather than in words, which matches the fact that Canetti's memories seem independent of the, at the time, spoken and understood language.

Andreas Huyssen points out that:

The past is not simply there in memory, but it must be articulated to become memory. The fissure that opens up between experiencing an event and remembering it in representation is unavoidable. Rather than lamenting or ignoring it, this split should be understood as a powerful stimulant for cultural and artistic creativity. At the other end of the Proustian experience, with that famous madeleine, is the memory of childhood not the childhood itself. If it were otherwise, we would probably not have *A la Recherche du temps perdu*. The mode of memory is recherche rather than recuperation. The temporal status of any act of memory is always the present and not, as some naive epistemology might have it, the past itself, even though all memory in some ineradicable sense is dependent on some past event or experience. It is this tenuous fissure between past and present that constitutes memory, making it powerfully alive and distinct from the archive or any other mere system of storage and retrieval. (Huyssen 1995: 3)

In Canetti's writings, the gap between the past and the present is "in rot getaucht": bathed in red. In the following discussion, I will argue that the literary use of the color might be seen as an opening between the experienced history and the actual representation in the autobiography, and that it therefore deserves special attention in an interpretation.

The Color Red in *Die gerettete Zunge*

When one examines what Canetti actually remembers – in the tongue-scene, for instance – the most significant aspect is the color red. The actual meaning of what has happened is an interpretation by the grown-up narrator.

The red color predominates throughout the first volume. There is significant use of redness in the novel: Canetti remembers in red. Obvious as well is that the color combines various and often conflicting kinds of feelings, such as fear and love, or episodes which are both fascinating and repelling. The color red turns out to be a sign of ambiguity: an ambivalent condition at least as important as the symbol of the tongue. On the one hand I will argue that words and visibility can be seen as competing media. The "pictorial elements" in the narrative, the visibility, express something that was not expressible for Canetti in all his words. On the other hand, the senses here are obviously combined. The tongue and the visibility (the color red) are in many respects connected, and in the following section I will show that they are connected to the development of identity.

The color red appears in many forms in *Die gerettete Zunge*. In a horror story told by his mother about wolves, which become the animal that he fears the most during his childhood, the primary characteristic of the wolves in the story is the big red tongues. The story told is from his mother's childhood: During the winter, when the Danube froze, they travelled by sledge to Romania. One day it happened that they accidentally forgot to bring weapons of any kind, and they were saved from an attack by wolves only because another sledge happened to come to their rescue.

125

> Die Mutter hatte große Angst, sie schilderte die roten Zungen der Wölfen, die so nahe gekommen waren, daß sie noch in späteren Jahren von ihnen träumte.
>
> Ich bettelte oft um diese Geschichte, und sie erzählte sie gern. [6] (Canetti 1992: 14)

Hence fear and fascination are closely connected in this memory, where one also notes that the connection between the tongue and the color red still exists.

Another memory from his early childhood is about the Gypsies coming to the Bulgarian village every Friday. "Ich lebte in panischem Schrecken vor ihnen" (Canetti 1992: 18), [7] Canetti writes, inspired by the stories he had heard of Gypsies stealing children, and he imagined that they carried children with them in their big colored bundles and bags. "Der ganze Aufzug hatte etwas unheimlich Dichtes, so viele Menschen, die sich bei ihrer Fortbewegung nah beisammen hielten, bekam ich sonst nie zu Geschicht; und es war auch in dieser sehr farbigen Stadt das Farbigste. Die Lappen mit denen ihre Kleider zusammengeflickt waren, leuchteten in allen Farben, aber am meisten stach überall Rot hervor" (Canetti 1992: 19). [8] Again the feeling is obviously ambivalent: "Ich wollte sie sehen, ich war besessen von ihnen, aber kaum hatte ich sie gesehen, packte mich wider die Angst, daß sie es auf mich abgesehen hätten, und ich rannte schriend davon" (Canetti 1992: 19). [9] And again there is an indirect connection between the tongue and the color: the Gypsies came on Fridays because the Jewish population prepared especially good food that day. Here the connection is made to the tongue as the instrument of the sense of tasting.

The first song he remembers is sung by his grandmother in Bulgarian-Spanish and the words in German are: "Äpfelchen rote, die kommen von Stambol". [10] Stambol is the Turkish city Istanbul, and in the boy's mind the childish song is associated with the imagined blood of a local Turkish woman who was murdered by her husband because of jealousy. Thus, his first experience of love and death is at the same time connected with, on the one hand, the color red and, on the other, the Turkish culture as an early experience of the ambivalent connection between love and hate, between life and death (Canetti 1992: 24–25).

In the next part of the novel, in England, Canetti himself falls in love for the first time with a young girl called Mary, and the explicit reason for his feelings is her very red cheeks (Canetti 1992: 55). She becomes an obsession, he stops working in school, walks her home every day, and is allowed to kiss her on the cheek once a day until her mother finds out what is going on and confronts the school as well as Elias' parents about their son's behavior.

Again the narrator draws a connection between the little-Mary-story and the Turkish song about the apples (Canetti 1992: 57). And the motif of love and red cheeks is repeated, when, in 1913, he moves from England to Vienna after the death of his father. During the journey they meet an uncle, who has recently married a young Greek girl. Her cheeks are painted so red that Elias Canetti is once again overwhelmed with passion, and although his mother lectures him on the artificiality of women's use of cosmetics, he refuses to kiss her anywhere else. At the same time, feelings of passion and danger are expressed. The danger is underlined by the destiny of the uncle: "Er wußte nicht, der Ärmste, was ihm bevorstand, sie entpuppte sich bald als zähe und unstillbare Furie."[11] (Canetti 1992: 81)

Throughout the volume, one recognizes the color red in the themes of love and eroticism, and later on in the construction of Elias' identity as a man. Red is also often an indication of ambivalence and ambiguity. An especially difficult aspect concerns Canetti's identity as a Jew. As the family moves away from their hometown in Bulgaria and their respective families, the Jewish traditions seem to become less important.

Canetti does not think much about being a Jew, the narrator claims, before the year 1919 when, living in Zurich, he suddenly finds himself having problems at school. Anonymous schoolmates address abusive words at him, he loses former friends, and he is suddenly forced into a community with the other Jews in his school, who suffer the same kind of persecution. There is only one Jew in his classes besides Canetti himself. His name is Färber (the meaning of which is related to "color"), and he is described as a not very charming boy, and the only one in class with red hair (Canetti 1992: 243–245). Pork, which by accident he happens to eat once, is described as "ein rötliches Fleich" (Canetti 1992: 256). [12] Very likely these are the most central representations of red in the narrative. The ambivalence has to do with the question of identity or non-identity, and it is remarkable how the problems of being Jewish during the 20th century are discussed by Canetti in only very vague terms. In school his problems seems to solve themselves, as the young Elias realizes that the reason his friends are excluding him is that he raises his hand far too often in class. Being a brilliant student, he often knows the answer almost before the question has been put, he says: "Es war ja wirklich so, daß ich die Antwort parat hatte, bevor der Lehrer seine Frage noch ganz ausgesprochen hatte" (Canetti 1992: 248). [13] As soon as he realizes the problem and manages to maintain a lower profile during lessons, it seems that he comes back into his friends' good graces. Thus, his problems are interpreted exclusively as being the problems of a very gifted child, which might also very well be the case. Yet compared to the well-known fate of millions of Jews during this century, a fate resulting from the Jewish identity and not from their behaviour, it seems that Canetti treats the question of being Jewish in a somehow shallow manner.

Furthermore it seems natural to pay attention to the symbolic level of red in relation to the Jewish question. What is the connection between being Jewish and the color red? As there seems to be no further traces in *Die gerettete Zunge*, I wish to broaden my investigation, and involve other works of art as possible sources of enlightenment.

Sylvia Plath: Jewish identity and the use of colors

Another modern artist systematically using different colors in her work and seemingly interested in the theme of being Jewish is the American poet, Sylvia Plath (1932–63). In *Ariel*, a collection of poetry, written in the last months before her tragic suicide, one encounters the colors blue, black, white and red over and over again, red being the most dominant, and often the color appearing in the final stanza of a poem.

And in the well known, very rhythmical and compelling poem "Daddy", the fate of the Jews in World War II is a major theme:

An engine, an engine
Chuffing me off like a Jew.
A Jew to Dachau, Auschwitz, Belsen.
I began to talk like a Jew.
I think I might well be a Jew
(Plath 1966: 50)

In a BBC-reading, Plath introduced the poem by saying that it was:

spoken by a girl with an Electra complex. Her father died while she thought he was God. Her case is complicated by the fact that her father was also a Nazi and her mother very possibly part Jewish. In the daughter the two strains marry and paralyze each other – she has to act out the awful little allegory once over before she is free of it. (Plath 1981: 293)

But what makes the poem so very controversial is that Plath herself did not have any known Jewish relatives. Moreover the poem seems rather to be about the problems of a woman standing between a dead father and a young husband:

...
I was ten when they buried you.
At twenty I tried to die
And get back, back, back to you.
I thought even the bones would do.

But they pulled me out of the sack,
And they stuck me together with glue
And then I knew what to do.
I made a model of you,
A man in black with a Meinkampf look

And a love of the rack and the screw.
I said I do, I do.
...   (Plath 1966: 51)

Sylvia Plath did loose her father early, not as a ten-year-old, but when she was eight. Her father was part German, but he was not a Nazi, and her mother was not Jewish. Plath herself did try to commit suicide several times, and the verse "I said I do, I do" may be seen as a reference to her marriage with Ted Hughes. In stanza 15, father and husband are closely connected:

If I've killed one man, I've killed two –
The vampire who said he was you
And drank my blood for a year,
seven years if you want to know.
Daddy you can lie back now

Red is represented through the "blood" in stanza 15 and in stanza 12's "Bit my pretty red heart in two". Ted Hughes had recently left Sylvia Plath and their two small children, and was now living with another woman, who was Jewish. It seems that the Jewish theme in the poems becomes a symbolic representation of primarily female victimization, and that the question of being Jewish in Plath's poetry refers less to a concrete racial issue, than to a condition of modernity in general: the problems of establishing identity as a woman in a male-dominated society.[14]

The red color seems to indicate strength and the will to live, especially in connection with the power of the female sex. For instance, in "Lady Lazarus":

> Out of the ash
> I rise with my red hair
> And I eat men like air.
> (Plath 1966: 9)

In the concluding verses of the poem "Ariel" the red color appears again, this time also connected to the motif of death:

> And I
> Am the arrow,
>
> The dew that flies
> Suicidal, at one with the drive
> Into the red
>
> Eye, the cauldron of morning.
> (Plath 1966: 27)

"The arrow ... that flies" is a figure known from the only novel Plath wrote, *The Bell Jar*, the arrow representing the man and his possibility to enter society, whereas the woman remains a base of operations, she is at home, from where the man flies and to which he returns.[15] Sylvia

Plath could not accept these conditions of gender inequality, and in "Ariel" one sees that the identification of the "I" with the arrow points towards the freedom to fly into death: "suicidal". The speaker subject is driven towards death, but it is a "red death", perhaps pointing at a hope of rebirth, a conclusion also supported by the last word "morning". These final lines are definitely ambiguous, not least because of the homonyms "Eye" and "I", "morning" and "mourning", which provide two possible interpretations.

It is significant that the motif of the red color differentiates the poems written in 1962, such as "Lady Lazarus" and "Ariel", from poems such as "Words" and "Edge", written during the final weeks prior to her suicide in February 1963 (Plath 1966: 84, 85). In the latter poems, the red color is no longer represented. These poems seem to have been written when her vitality was already gone. Death being the only possibility left, the color red is no longer an option of choice. Like Canetti, she uses the colors to seek and express identity, but her poetry provides no answer to the question of Jewish identity. Red becomes a symbol of the strength of the female sex, and of the will to live – both forces appearing to be deeply ambivalent.

Theories of the color red

In the scientific approaches to color perception and symbolism, red is viewed as having several key characteristics.

Red tends to be the favorite color of small children, being physically the strongest and most prominent, and therefore one of the first colors capable of being registered by the human eye. Both Goethe and Newton reaches the conclusion that the color red has a dominant status among the colors. Isaac Newton understood colors as being associated with music. He composed a system of tones and colors in a spectrum of 7 colors, where each color referred to a particular frequency. On a major scale, red was associated with the keynote, the tonic, followed by orange, yellow, green, blue and violet at the top. Newton imagined a harmony between notes and colors, with red being a fundamental color. J. W. Goethe composed his theory of colors, chromatology, in 1810. In contrast to Newton, he reduced the number of primary colors to six and arranged the pairs of complimentary colors, pairing red and green, orange and blue, and yellow and violet. Goethe demonstrated how the human eye itself creates the other color in the pair if it is not all ready there. The fundamental contrast in Goethe's understanding is the relationship between light and darkness. Yellow is the color of light and blue is the color of dark, the relationship illustrated by a triangle, where the intensity of yellow and blue rises up towards purple or red – red therefore being the color of the highest energy and intensity.

Modern color research stresses the contrast between red and blue in terms of heat; the two colors influence the human body in opposite ways. A room painted red appears to be several degrees warmer than a blue one. Symbolically, red is often associated with love, but at the same time represents the color of blood and symbolizes war, and it is said that the Cherokee Indians use the same word for war and the color red. Thus, red is positive and negative at the same time. This ambivalence represented in the color red is founded in science and underlined by Jung in his psychology of colors. Red is said to signal energy, but this is ambiguous energy: both hate and love. Red thus means danger and prohibition, but also love and warmth.

Rouge

Having established a connection between the use of the color red as a symbol of ambiguity, let us examine another relevant interpretation of modernity and the color red: the late polish filmmaker Krzysztof Kieslowski's film *Rouge* (1994). *Rouge* is the final of three in Kieslowski's film trilogy: *Trois couleurs*. In the trilogy *Bleu*, *Blanc* and *Rouge*, each film represents one of the three colors in the French flag and similarly symbolizes the concepts "freedom", "equality", and "fraternity" – three values fundamental to modern Western culture. In *Rouge*, the meaning of the color red and the ambivalent relationship between people living in modernity are in many ways clearly explicated, and there are a number of other similarities between Canetti's *Die gerettete Zunge* and Kieslowski's *Rouge*.

The story of *Rouge* is based primarily on the relationship between the young model, Valentine, and the retired judge, Joseph Kern. It takes place in Geneva, which is a city of many languages, as in Canetti's oeuvre. As with Canetti, Kieslowski's trilogy also includes the aspect of travelling: Switzerland is the central point of view in *Rouge*, with Poland, France and England as lines of action. Comparing Canetti and Kieslowski, it becomes obvious how much the means of transportation have changed throughout the 20th century, and the means of human communication no less. The modern communication is one of the main themes in *Rouge*; the film starts by visualizing the act of telecommunication, as the camera at full speed pretends to follow a long distance call through the cables. Judge Kern, the male protagonist, spends all his time spying on his neighbors by tapping their private telephone conversations. In a sense, he is omnipotent – he knows *everything* about everybody living close by, although he demonstrates at the same time the limits of communication in the modern world: he knows everything, but lives in complete isolation. The condition of isolation ends as he meets the beautiful young model, Valentine. She makes him want to breathe and live again. In return, he makes her understand the position of human existence in modernity. At the beginning of the film, Valentine has a naive belief in the good. Her encounter with Josef Kern convinces her that the world is dualistic – that good and evil go together like the game of heads or tails quoted in the film. His excuse for spying is that it brings him nearer to the truth about people, than he ever felt to be as a judge. However, he also realizes that no one is entitled to judge a fellow human being; a belief that one knows the truth is equivalent to vanity. Valentine's task is to understand and accept this ambivalent condition of the world. Kern is given the *will* to live; Valentine becomes the *possibility* to live, as she is finally seen as one of the few people who miraculously survives a terrible shipwreck. Her success in developing as an individual in modernity must be understood as the reason for her fortune.

In certain respects, Joseph Kern equals the Jewish God of the Old Testament, in being a judge and being omniscient. In *Rouge*, the constant red coloring of the narrative is a modification of the faith and belief in a God of this kind. Kieslowski seems to conclude that the clue to being modern is to find oneself, not in a world without God and without truth, but in a world where this belief is given up. To stop longing for assumption of the truth is to stop living. But the recognition of modernity is understanding and accepting that presumably there is nothing to find, but that the searching by no means stops because of this conclusion.

The autobiographies of Canetti describe European cultural history – but they are also to be read as sophisticated examinations of identity. "Who am I?", is a constant underlying question of memories in general. Specifically focusing on the question of Jewish identity, one gets the impression that Canetti does not really find an answer. The crucial point by Canetti might be exactly the question of fraternity, discussed by Kieslowski in *Rouge*. What can brotherhood be said to mean in the modern age of individualism? Does one choose identity? Is it given from birth or from God? Kieslowski's dualistic approach seems more adequate than Canetti's apparent rejection of the religious subject all together.

Conclusion: When words are not enough…

Characteristic of modernity is the ongoing process of creating identity: an individual identity as a man or as a woman, as part of a specific culture, according to belief in or rejection of a religion.

These themes are crucial in *Die gerettete Zunge*. They are remarkably colored in red, and the red color is characteristic in other works of modern art dealing with similar themes.

Referring to Freud, the artist is special in terms of being able to understand and express what is hidden in the unconscious of "normal" people. What we are mainly unable to accept is what Lilian Munk Rösing refers to as "affective ambivalence", i.e., the existence of positive and negative feelings at the same time (Rösing 2001: 33). "In all accounts of childhood that I have analyzed, the affective ambivalence towards the mother appears as a motif, and the tolerance toward ambivalence as the individuals possibility of healing" (my transl.).[16] This statement precisely fits Canetti and his relationship with his mother. The color red could be seen as relating to this "affective ambivalence". Red is the dominant color of the womb, and it would therefore seem obvious that childhood and the question of love and longing for closeness to the mother, existing only in the foetal stage of life, is represented by the color red. The focus on the literary use of the color red shows an alternative route through the narration, telling a far more open and ambiguous story about the growing up of the little boy, Elias Canetti, than the superficial narrative, which is strongly controlled by a dominant narrator.

The trilogy shows a superior development from speech to sight, moving from a metonymic meaning of the "tongue" to a symbolic meaning of "red". The color red appears not as a solution or an answer, but as a possible opening, going not necessarily to the unconscious level of the author's mind, but certainly to a level of information beyond the spoken and written language. In *Die gerettete Zunge*, the opening threat against the tongue is at first a threat against the person, the writer to come. It is a deformation of his existence. His life is completely dominated by words, language and literature. To some extent, however, the book may be read as an exercise in understanding the limits of language: asking what the situation would have been if he actually had had no tongue?

It seems that feelings in general, and the ambivalent feelings characteristic of the modern period in particular, often need more than a single artistic dimension to be adequately examined and expressed. Both Plath and Canetti are very strongly attached to language as an expressive medium – the will to live and the act of expressing oneself as a writer are closely interwoven. The colors seem to appear on the edge of what it is possible to express in words, and the special attraction of the color red seems to be that this color is strong enough to contain ambivalent conditions.

Thus, red is a sign of ambivalent conditions, but not only connected to feelings. The red color refers to the relationship between Canetti and his mother, but also to the question of identity and being in the world as such. At the same time, red regressively points back towards the womb and the foetal condition, and progressively forwards towards *Erkenntnis*: recognition of the ambivalent condition of modernity. This seems to be the case in Elias Canetti, Sylvia Plath and by Krzysztof Kieslowski. The color red appears as both symptom and solution to the question which never finds a definite answer.

The intermediary mode, obvious in Canetti and Plath's use of colors in literature, might well be closely connected with the mode of modernity as a condition of life without definite answers to even the most crucial questions of existence. As pointed out in the beginning of the article, the visual forms of art exist in space and do not have concrete beginnings and endings in the same way as, for instance, literary or musical artworks:

a song, a novel, or a poem. The coloring of literature, as argued in this article, seems to stand in a meaningful connection to the modern condition of life: Through the colors and the activation of the visual senses in experiencing and interpreting literature, the unending character of the spatial branches of art seems to be transferred to the otherwise abstract and temporary medium of literature. The red color gives the literary work of art a possibility to express modernity which had otherwise been closed: through the red color the spatial dynamics of the unending ambivalence of modern life receives its literary form.

1 Elias Canetti (1905–1994); *Die gerettete Zunge. Geschichte einer Jugend* (1977), *Die Fackel im Ohr. Lebensgeschichte 1921–1931* (1980), *Das Augenspiel. Lebensgeschichte 1931–1937* (1985).

2 "She never used to speak about painting, it was the one art that barely interested her and that she didn't understand". (Elias Canetti. *The Tongue Set Free. Remembrance of a European Childhood*, transl. Joachim Neugroschel, New York: The Seabury Press, 1979, p.173. Hereafter TSF)

3 "My earliest memory is dipped in red. I come out of a door on the arm of a maid, the floor in front of me is red, and to the left a staircase goes down, equally red. Across from us, at the same height, a door opens, and a smiling man steps forth, walking towards me in a friendly way. He steps right up close to me, halts, and says: 'show me your tongue'. I stick out my tongue, he reaches into his pocket, pulls out a jackknife, opens it, and brings the blade all the way to my tongue. He says: 'Now we'll cut off his tongue'. I don't dare pull back my tongue, he comes closer and closer, the blade will touch me any second. In the last moment, he pulls back the knife, saying: 'Not today, tomorrow'. He snaps the knife shut again and puts it back in his pocket.

   Every morning, we step out of the door and into the red hallway, the door opens, and the smiling man appears. I know what he's going to say and I wait for the command to show my tongue. I know he's going to cut it off, and I get more and more scared each time. That's how the day starts, and it happens very often." (TSF: 3)

4 "As a child, I had no real grasp of this variety", "the colorful time of those early years" (TSF: 3)

5 "I cannot say exactly how this happened. I don't know at what point in time, on what occasion, this or that translated itself the vast majority are tied to words that I did not know at that time." (TSF: 10)

6 "My mother had been terribly afraid; she described the red tongues of the wolves, which had come so close that she still dreamt about them in later years.

   I often begged her to tell me this story, and she enjoyed telling it to me." (TSF: 9)

7 "I lived in panic fear of them." (TSF: 12)

8 "I never otherwise saw so many people huddling so close together as they moved along; and in this very colorfull city, they were the most colorful sight. The rags they had pierced together for their clothing shone in all colors, but the one that stood out the sharpest was red." (TSF: 13)

9 "I wanted to see them, I was obsessed with them, but the instant I saw them I was again seized with fear that they were after me, and I ran away screaming." *(TSF: 13)*

10 "Little apples, red, red apples, those that come from Istanbul" (TSF: 17)

11 "He didn't know, the poor man, what lay ahead; she soon turned out to be a tenacious and insatiable fury" (TSF: 66).

12 "a reddish meat" (TSF: 216).

13 "I really did have the answer ready before the teacher had quite finished asking his question." (TSF: 210)

14 This implies a serious, and much discussed, ethical problem, especially because of the sexualising of the persecutions and the suggestion of masochistic pleasure following in the verses "Every woman adores a fascist / The boot in the face, the brute." (stanza 10)

15 *The Bell Jar* was first published in January 1963 (London: Faber and Faber) under the pseudonym of Victoria Lucas.

16 "I samtlige de barndomsskildringer, jeg har analyseret dukker den affektive ambivalens over for moderen op som et motiv, og tolerancen over for ambivalensen som personens mulighed for heling." (Rösing 2001: 34)

Literature

Birgel, Franz A. (1986). "You Can Go Home Again. An interview with Edgar Reitz", *Film Quarterly 4*.

Canetti, Elias (1992 [1979]). *Die gerettete Zunge. Geschichte einer Jugend,* Frankfurt a.M.: Fischer Taschenbuch Verlag.

Canetti, Elias (1980). *Die Fackel im Ohr. Lebensgeschichte 1921–1931*, Frankfurt a.M.: Fischer Taschenbuch Verlag.

Canetti, Elias (1985). *Das Augenspiel. Lebensgeschichte 1931–1937*, Frankfurt a.M.: Fischer Taschenbuch Verlag.

Elias Canetti (1979). *The Tongue Set Free. Remembrance of a European Childhood.* transl. Joachim Neugroschel, New York: The Seabury Press.

Fink, Hans Christian (1969). *Theorie der Farbe*, Köln: Verlag M. DuMont Buchverlag.

Hughes, Ted (1981). "Notes 1962", in *Collected Poems*, London: Faber and Faber.

Huyssen, Andreas (1995). *Twilight Memories*, London/New York: Routledge.

Plath, Sylvia (1968). *Ariel*, London: Faber and Faber.

Plath, Sylvia (1980). *The Bell Jar*, London: Faber and Faber.

Reiter, Brigitta (1989). *Noget om symbolfarver*, København: Det kongelige danske Kunstakademi.

Paul Ricoeur (1983–85). *Temps et Récit*, Paris: Seuil.

Rösing, Lilian Munk (2001). *At læse barnet. Litteratur og psykoanalyse.* København: Samleren.

The Tactile Image

A Veronican Approach to Pictorality in Michel Serres's Aesthetics of the Senses

Troels Degn Johansson

Tradition calls her Veronica, the saintly woman who wiped the crucified's saintly face, covered by a liquid mask, soaked in sweat and blood, and this name means, in the antique languages, the true icon, the authentic image. True, authentic because it is imprinted, impressionistic.[1]

Michel Serres, Les Cinq sens

Introduction

IMAGES – WHICH FOR obvious reasons are theorized as visual media, might paradoxically also to offer us help to understand further French philosopher Michel Serres's peculiar concept of general tactility (1977, 1985); a concept which is pivotal for the perception of his aesthetics of the senses. And although Serres's aesthetics is concerned with sensation rather than art – and only marginally with pictorial representation – it does in turn seem to enrich our understanding of images by making out an alternative approach to their conceptualization.

In his main philosophical treaty on aesthetics, *Les Cinq sens: Philosophie des corps mêlés - I* ("The Five Senses: Philosophy of Mingled Bodies, Vol. I," 1985),[2] Serres lays out the five senses in a general philosophical system by identifying tactility as the most fundamental sense as for the human soul and its experience of itself and its environment. Tactility should be understood as fundamental here in the sense that, for Serres, it makes out a conceptually "model sense" of the senses and of sensation as such, that is, a *sensus communis*, the Medieval concept of a distinct common sense by which each of the five senses could be understood in a common system, which anchors sensation in its totality and thus makes possible a general theoretical approach to sensation and the individual senses.

As Danish poet and critic Niels Lyngsø has demonstrated in his fine introduction to Serres's philosophy (1994), Serres's aesthetics should be understood as a continuation of his work on Lucretius's *De Rerum Natura* ("On the Nature of Things") and its theory of simulacra. Serres opens this work in *La Naissance de la physique dans le texte de Lucrèce* ("The Birth of Physics," 1975). For in *Les Cinq sens*, sensation is thought of precisely in terms of the mingling of subtle membranes, *simulacra*, which to Lucretius are emanating from all things, and which makes sensation a matter of proximity, contact, touch, rather than distance. For Serres, the human sensory apparatus (the skin, the tympanic membrane, sensory surfaces on the tongue and in the nose, the nervous system, etc.) is just one out of many sets of membranes in the world, and sensation – and even the thinking (of) – the world is in a sense just a "fold" (*pli*) among the world's membranes, that is, bodies mingling with each other and with the world. Hence the subtitle, "Philosophie des corps mêlés," a philosophy of mingled bodies.

In *Les Cinq sens*, Serres elaborates in detail as for how we are to understand sensation and the individual senses in terms of such folding and mingling of membranes. Interestingly, the aesthetics of Impressionism and especially French painter Pierre Bonnard's early work is analyzed carefully to demonstrate that general tactility may actually be thought of most clearly in what is supposed to be the visual domain. For Serres, Impressionism should be seen as a laboratory of, not only vision but also of the senses as such since this project in painting seeks to emphasize the physical impression of the world upon the canvas and the sensory apparatus. Serres's analysis of Bonnard makes him evoke a certain "Veronican motif"; St. Veronica, the saintly woman who, blinded by tears and agony, reached out for the face of Christ to wipe off sweat and blood on his face on his way to Golgotha. For Serres this motif may be said to lead to a notion of "tactile images," images "taken" by hands and fingers, as it were; not only in the literal sense but also, and more importantly in accordance with the concept of general tactility proposed by Serres; a tactility which encompasses all the individual senses and the senses in their totality.

This "Veronican approach" to images and sensation thus proposed by Serres, leads me finally to return to the realist apprehension of photographic representation that also fundamentally take photography and cinematography as a physical impression of the referential world and therefore also in some sense a "true image of reality." This goes especially for Barthes who in his beautiful book on photography directly has recourse to the shroud metaphor in order to develop his special realistic position. Taking thus photography and especially cinematography for an automatically and kinetically recorded and presented "membrane" or "film" of the world, a Serresean "tactile" approach to the film medium may seem obvious, perhaps even more so than painting. However, in this article I shall abstain from discussing such a possible theoretical approach to photography and cinema on a general level. Rather, I will seek to outline a concept of picture in Serres's philosophical aesthetics; a tactile image being a medium of (physical) impressions and emotions, of impressions of the physical world and their implications for sensation.

My article consists of four parts. After thus having presented the background for venturing into Serres and images, I shall start by making an introduction to Serres's aesthetics with recourse to Lucretius. Secondly I proceed by analyzing the first chapter of *Les Cinq sens, "Voiles"* (veils) which re-establishes the concept of general tactility; a concept which was originally addressed in Serres's work on Lucretius, and which in *Les Cinq sens* is seen as pivotal as concerns a fundamental connection between sensation, consciousness, and the soul. This leads me to discuss the significance attributed to the "tactile images" in the work of Bonnard and in respect of the metaphors of shroud and sudarium, that is a Veronican motif. The aim is thus to connect Serres's aesthetics of the senses with Barthes' radically realist position in image theory to outlin a concept of tactile pictures.

General Tactility and the Theory of Simulacra in Lucretius

Serres's philosophy of aesthetics is an aesthetic theory in the "classical" sense of the term, that is precisely, an aesthetics of the senses.[3] As mentioned above, Serres's starting point is in this, classical sense, Lucretius's *De Rerum Natura*, which first of all is an exposition on Nature, i.e. physics but which also contains elaborations that may be taken to be of aesthetic character. This goes especially for the "Fourth Book," in which Lucretius develops his theory of simulacra and its implications on sensation:

> I will begin to explain to you a matter that has important bearing these questions – namely, the existence of what we term images of things. Images are sort of membranes stripped from the surfaces of objects and float this way and that through the air. (Lucretius, 1975: vol. IV, v. 29–32; original line separation suspended)[4]

Both Serres and Lyngsø (1994: 315) stress that these membranes in no way should be taken for illusions, unreal entities but something that really exists in the world. This is true despite the fact that Serres assumes a direct connection between the idealism of Plato and the Epicurean philosophy of Nature, in which the Lucretean concept of simulacra is supposed to correspond with the Epicurean concept of idols and Democrito's *eidola*, i.e. small material images of things in the world that enter through the sensory apparatus. Whereas Plato's concept of idea (εἰδοζ) is eternal and independent of actual sensory experience, Serres still assumes that phenomena cannot be perceived as being discrete, separated from the realm of ideas. For, according to Lucretius, following Epicurean mathematics, geometric shapes should not be taken for empty and invariant but compact and filled with matter; matter that is still pertinent to geometry. Hence the so-called method of exhaustion that Democrito used to calculate the surface area of a circle; a method in which the latter is filled with less-complex geometrical shapes until its areal exhaustion (cf. Lyngsø, 315–6). In his book on *De Rerum Natura*, Serres thus ask us to

> Observe [...] the fluctuating confusion [*fouillis*], that separates and unites the edge and the adherence, the limited surface and the infinite extension of folds. This space is literally speaking and without recourse to metaphor, fluent. It is the mobile differentiation [*ecart*] from a fine fidelity. Here is simply the *genealogy of the simulacra*, the genealogy of these mobile idols that are emitted from the surfaces, the limited faces of the εἰδοζ, eidos. (Serres, 1977: 129, my inserts, translation mine)[5]

An important consequence of this "fluent," non-discrete intermittence between the idea and the material simulacrum that it emits is that Lucretius and Serres do not fundamentally distinguish between being and appearance, between the idea and the phenomenon. This leads

Serres to subscribe to the objectivity of the transcendental; that the truth of the objects, their true nature, lies immanent in the objects themselves (cf. Lyngsø, 1994: 107 ff., 314ff.).

Another crucial aspect in this perception is the *principle of fluency*, a flux that should thus be understood literally and which is difficult, if not impossible, to define entirely in terms of space or time. When Lucretius and Serres say that the simulacra emanate infinitesimally from the ideas, it means, first, that the simulacra are impossible to understand without the principle of flux, and secondly that the flux is because of an inherent quality of the world of ideas. Hence the eidetic genealogy of the simulacra referred to above.

Not only are the simulacra supposed to be emitted directly, genealogically, from the world of ideas; they also constitute the fidelity of the senses. With poetic accuracy, Lucretius argues that:

> So, I insist that you must acknowledge [that images move] at an extraordinary [speed].
> [....][6]
>
> [In the first place, all objects that are visible to us must necessarily discharge and scatter a continual stream] of particles that impinge on the eyes and provoke vision. Moreover, from certain things odors flow in a perpetual stream; cold emanates from rivers, heat from the sun, and spray from the waves of the sea – spray that erodes the walls skirting the shore.
>
> [...] So it is true that from all objects emanations flow away and are discharged in all directions on every side. These effluences stream away without any delay or interruption, since we constantly experience sensation, and we may at any time see, smell, and hear anything. (Lucretius: IV, line 215-229; original line separation suspended)

What is important to Serres here is that, since in Lucretius, sensation relies entirely on simulacra, those membranes that are emitted by all things, sensation must fundamentally be based on proximity, contact. In his analysis of *De Rerum*, he concludes that

> Finally, by the reception, the sensory apparatus comes into contact with this fine textile. In this sense, sight, smelling, hearing, etc., are only versions of feeling. *Sensation is generalized feeling, that is, tactility.* The world is no longer at a distance; it is quite near, tangible. (Serres 1977: 134, my italicization) [7]

For Serres, the understanding of sensation should be based on what he refers to as the principle of contact. As we shall se below, this principle and the concept of a general tactility becomes the starting point for *Les Cinq Sens* in its conceptualization of each of the five senses and of sensation in its totality. In Serres's *La naissaince de la physique*, however, because of the connection established in Lucretius's physics between sensation, simulacra, and the world of ideas, between the *eidola* and the *eidos*, tactility is moreover taken for the most important of the senses in respect of experiencing and knowing the world:

> As all philosophers passionately engaged with objective reality, Lucretius has a special sense of tactility rather than of vision […]. To know is not to see, it is to be in contact with things, directly […]. The objects exchange skin at a distance, they exchange kisses […]. This is a phenomenology of caress. (Serres 1977: 134) [8]

To Serres, experiencing and knowing the world means to feel and touch it, to partake in this exchange of kisses and caress. Unlike traditional philosophy, it does not mean unveiling it as in the philosophical figure of *aletheia*, the unveiling the truth. As Serres has it in *Les Cinq sens*,

> The world is filled with complex veils. [/] A tradition finds that truth should be unveiled; a thing or a set of things that are covered by a veil that should

be removed. [...] This seems puerile. [/] No, things are not veiled, just as little as woman is dancing behind her seven veils. For the dancer is herself a complex of tissues. (Serres 1985: 83–4)[9]

According to Serres, 'One must imagine that the real is covered in veils." (1987: 191) Still, 'the world is nothing but a bunch of clothes." (1985: 85)[10] To know the world is therefore not to unveil it. There is nothing there to unveil except for veils, membranes, simulacra. To experience and know the world, one should to slip into it as a piece of garment; one should form part of it as a veil among veils, a fold among folds. This leads us to another paradoxical consequence in Serres's reading of Lucretius, namely that by the end of the day, knowing and touching the world is just a particular way of being in it: 'experience (*connaissance*) is not different from being.' (Serres 1977: 134, translation mine)[11]

General Tactility, Consciousness, and the Soul

It goes without saying that experiencing and knowing the world in Serres is fundamentally a matter of aesthetics. This is so, not only because sensation is actually taken for an essential approach to Nature, i.e. the nature of things, but also since knowledge of the world, in order to be true, must be beautifully formulated. Thus, in *Le Tiers-Instruit* he concludes that "Beauty contains truth" (1991: 190, my translation), and in *Les Cinq Sens* he makes a Cartesian pun venturing to assert that "I think, therefore I am beautiful. The world is beautiful, therefore I think. Knowledge cannot exist without beauty." (1985: 212)[12] As Lyngsø notes, one could say that in Serres ontology and phenomenology meet in aesthetics (1994: 327).

Les Cinq sens is especially important here, partly of course because it makes out Serres's main contribution to the philosophy of aesthetics, and partly since stylistically it seems to form a dramatic turn in Serres's work. As Steven Conner notes in his exemplary introduction, "It is the book in which Serres begins to stretch his limbs, to burst into flames, the book in which he first makes his scandalous approach to things. In it he declares that the world exists." (1999)[13] Whereas *Les Cinq sens* should be taken for a direct return to Lucretius's theory of simulacra, one may argue that this declaration was already made in *La Naissance* ... However, what is significant in *Les Cinq sens* seems especially to be the "stretching of the limbs" and the "bursting into flames," that is, the evocation of a new style, or approach in Serres's work. At this stage, Serres seems to make something of an "existential choice" as a writer of philosophy; a philosopher that is writing as a body mingling with the world; a writing soul that sees beauty in the world and reproduces it before the reading body.

Thus, rather than pursuing the Lucretean exploration of the nature of the world, Serres dwells here especially on sensation and the soul as a site of experience and thought. Indeed, in *Les Cinq sens* the aesthetic notion of sensation is based on a perception of the Cartesian question of the location of the soul, a question whose answer for Serres lies in the contingencies of the body, its determination, and its sensory environment. This is anything but a philosophical inquiry on subjectivity in the traditional sense of the term, for in *Les Cinq sens*, the soul is just a fold in a world of linnet; a fold however in which consciousness awakes and knowledge takes place. Thus, unlike a Cartesian "puerile" attempt to unveil the soul, Serres takes the soul as something "profoundly superficial," something that is to be pointed, touched upon in the right, beautiful manner by writing or by any other creative act.

> It remains to draw or paint. Isolate, if possible, the secret little zones where the soul is always in residence, the corners or folds of contingency, isolate too, if possible the unstable zones where the soul knows how to play with another as though with a ball, mark out the spheres and slabs which become subjects only when face to face with objects, the dense and compact regions

which remain objects always, alone or facing those which objectify them, deserts lacking in soul, black; this drawing rarely marks off compact zones, for those explode, fuse and flee in narrow strips of color, forming hills, chimneys, passages, corridors, flames, zigzags and labyrinths, look at the changeable, wavelike and fugitive soul on the skin, on the surface, streaked, crowded, tiger-striped, zebra-striped, barred, troubled, constellated, gorgeous, torrential, and turbulent, incendiary. (Serres 1985: 20)[14]

The soul is there in the garment to be pointed out (rather to be seen), but it is volatile escaping easily a passive, objectified position. However, one may alternatively approach it in its determination as it unfolds itself in the human being. As Steven Connor puts it, for Serres "The soul of the pilot of a ship extends coenesthetically into the whole of his vessel, just as the driver parking a car feels his fingertips extending all the way to the front bumper." (1999). Serres's "stretching of limbs" and "bursting into flames" thus means that the writing soul is now seeking to make full use of its bodily medium. In an earlier work, *Genèse* ("Genesis," 1982), Serres observes that

> The hand is no longer a hand when it has taken hold of the hammer, it is the hammer itself, it is no longer a hammer, it flies transparent, between the hammer and the nail, it disappears and dissolves, my own hand has long since taken flight in writing. The hand and thought, like one's tongue, disappear in their determinations. (Serres 1995: 30)

The volatility of the soul is that of the transparency of the hand with a hammer or a pen as it disappears in the determination of a body. Serres calls it a "naked faculty," that is, something that is impossible to determine by its function, but is given as an open set of possibilities and by the actual bodily determination. Comparing again the hand and the soul, he asks:

> So what is a hand? It is not an organ; it is a faculty, a capacity for doing, for becoming claw or paw, weapon or compendium. It is a naked faculty. A faculty is not special, it is never specific, it is the possibility of doing something in general. To talk about the faculties of the soul is a great misnomer, when we are differentiating between them: the soul is also a naked faculty. It is nakedness. We live by bare hands. (Serres 1995: 34–5)

The soul and hand – which thus becomes emblematic of the former – are volatile because of the impossibility of differentiation; they are naked as possibility, but when they are actualized, when reaching out into the world by their the bodily determination, they are not to be unveiled as folds in the world of tissues.

Following this, the soul – and the hand – is fundamentally asymmetrical, chimera-like entities in Serres. A hand may either touch another or may be touched, like the right hand touching the left. Unfolding by the determinations of the body, the soul may thus take on an active side in the bodily determination; a side which may touch upon itself in a local fashion, literally speaking as a person's tongue in the cheek, or the concentrated fingers on a chin. Or it may reach out in the world, potentially in a global determination, for instance by making use of telecommunications.

To Serres, consciousness awakes in these folds and in the bodily determinations of the soul:

> I touch one lip with my middle finger. Consciousness dwells in this contact. I start to explore it. Often consciousness conceals itself in folds, lip resting on lip, palate closed on tongue, teeth against teeth, eyelids lowered, tightened sphincter, the hand closed into a fist, fingers pressed against each other, the rear surface of one thigh crossed on the front of face of the other, or one foot resting on the other. I bet that the homunculus, tiny and monstrous, of which each part is proportional to the magnitude of sensation, swells in

those automorphic places, when the skin tissue folds upon itself. By itself, the skin takes on consciousness [...]. (Serres 1985:19, translation mine)[15]

In Serres, consciousness is volatile, automorphic, and autopoietic; volatile since it depends entirely on the materiality that may unfold it; the human body, which "hosts" the soul in the interplay between its surrounding environment. As in Epicurean philosophy and indeed in Lucretius, the soul is supposed to vanish by the death of its body, for only the body may unfold a human soul; it is genealogically conditioned by its medium. Consciousness is thus auto-morphic and auto-poietic in Serres; it is in this sense entirely a matter of form. What remains then for the subject is to acknowledge, explore, and experiment with this genealogical material to realize the basic formal properties of its knowledge and thought. For Serres, this is fundamentally a matter of touching and skin being touched; not as a primordial subject standing before the world "touching out," as it were, but, as Connor puts it, 'being amidst it', touching and being touched, continuously and eternally in the huge bunch of linnet. This leads us to a third important principle in Serres's aesthetics, namely *the principle of contingency*:

> The skin is a variety of contingence: in the skin, with the skin, through the skin, the world and my body touch, defining their common border. Contingency means mutual touching: world and body meet and caress in the skin. I do not like to speak of the place where my body exists as a milieu, preferring rather to say that things mingle among themselves and that I am no exception to this, that I mingle with the world, which mingles itself in me. The skin intervenes in the things of the world and brings about their minglings. (Serres 1985: 82)[16]

What is important in Serres is that this complex superficiality of tactility leads to a *variety of contingency* on any possible level of touching, and

153

that the subject is given in a *mutuality* of touching; hence the importance of the term mingling. What is left for the philosophical subject to do is to mingle on in a reflective manner; not eventually to unveil or stripping bare the world, but gradually threading it together, like a text, taking as its starting point what is at hand, what is intermittent. To Serres, "Tissue, textile and fabric provide excellent models of knowledge, excellent quasi-abstract objects, primal varieties: the world is a bunch of clothes." (1985: 85) It is up to each of us, alone or together, mingling, to design, create, and recognize patterns.

Tactility and Vision in Bonnard

What remains for the philosophical subject is thus to touch and be touched by those screens, veils, and skins which are floating by and which one may mingle with and learn from. This leads us to approach the dimension of aesthetics not primarily addressed in Serres, namely that of art. In a brief, suggestive section in the first chapter on tactility, "Screen, Veils, Skin" (*Toile, Voile, Peau*, 1985: 27 ff.) Serres shows us how this aesthetics of the senses may find its "models of knowledge" in pictorial art.

As mentioned, Serres takes here Impressionism for a "laboratory of the senses" since this project in painting is supposed to emphasize the physical impression of the world upon the canvas and the sensory apparatus. It should be noted that Serres does not seek to capture Impressionism as an art historical category as such; his aim is to develop further his aesthetics of the senses by reflecting on mingling surfaces – *in casu* French painter Pierre Bonnard's play with the surface of bodies, canvases, and painting. Hence "Le Kimono" (app. 1890, oil on canvas screen, 152 x 54 cm), the painting on a screen depicting a dark-haired woman dressed in a spotted kimono: "The slightly fluttering dress fills the space, the screen is erect leaning towards the body, vertical as a Chinese roll. The leaves cover the background, covers parts of the fabric, but only slightly so that the painting almost only consists of the textile." (1985: 27)[17] Observing this dominance of the fabric, Serres asks rhetorically:

> Why didn't Bonnard paint directly on the kimono, why didn't he exhibit the fabric of the kimono, its very own textile, rather than the screen? Why doesn't he paint directly on the textile of the fabric rather than on another one, that of the screen?
>
> If you remove the leaves and the cloak, will you then touch the dark haired woman or the canvas of the painting? Pierre Bonnard rather lets us touch than see these membranes and fine layers of things, the leaves, the fabric, the screen and its firm plates, the fall of leaves, the undressing, the sophisticated coverings, the thin caressing veils: his tactful, tactile art does not make the skin a vulgar object for the gaze, but a sensing subject, the active, always underlying subject. Screens cover screens; veils are covering each other, thus veiling only veils […] (Serres 1985: 27)[18]

That which at *first glance* may appear as a confusion between the surfaces of body, canvas, and painting, is to Serres a tactful and indeed graceful way of depicting the body and thus an exemplary model for the knowledge of the material of sensation. One may say that this confusion of the "first glance," that is, the eye, is used deliberately by Bonnard to demonstrate that one cannot present anything in a true, beautiful fashion without veiling it at the same time. Emphasizing veiling by the title ("The Kimono"), in the pictorial theme by foregrounding the fabric, as well as actually painting on dressing screens, the painter lets his model appear by means of a disappearance. However, by confusing the surfaces and foregrounding literally the texture of fabric, of the kimono as well as the canvas of the screen, Bonnard establishes a peculiar flatness in the pictorial expression, which seems to abolish concepts of presence and absence usually connected with the veiling and unveiling of bodies. This leads Serres to realize a paradoxical character of Bonnard's impressionistic practice, namely that:

> The eye looses its preeminence in the very domain of its dominance, pain-
> ting. At its extremity, Impressionism returns to its really original sense, that
> of contact. (Serres 1985: 35)[19]

One recognizes here the key principle of contact in Serres's aesthetics referred to above. Contact in the field of vision should thus actually not be understood as a confusion of sight but as reaching another, more fundamental level in sensation, namely that of tactility. Following Serres, the principle of contact in Impressionism leads the artist to show the spectator a more "profound" albeit literally superficial way of looking at the world, a looking by means of mingling, of touching and being touched at.

However, the question remains who is touching who in Bonnard's paintings. Whereas it is true that the term mingling in Serres implies that there is no part in touching that is given by being essentially the active one, we also saw that the starting point of *Les Cinq sens* was a question of action in the relationship between consciousness and the soul: that knowledge of the world is realized by means of reaching out into the world or of touching oneself. In the passage on Bonnard's "The Kimono" above, Serres seems first to suggest that the spectator is the one reaching out seeking with his look to touch and explore the environment depicted, the woman with the kimono, yet reaching out in a bunch of textiles. This perception of looking is stressed in the fourth chapter of *Les Cinq sens,* "Visite", (1985: 255 ff.) which lays out vision as the look's wandering around, visiting, and thus touching things in the world; visiting in the same manner as one's hand may reach out to explore things: another body's textures, shapes, firmness, etc. Accordingly, this active aspect of sensation is evident in *Les Cinq sens.* Returning to Serres's starting point, that is the question of the soul and the coming into being of consciousness, one may say that the notion of "visiting" the world by means of looking seems to substantiate the old saying that the soul is resting in the eyes. It is by the eternally restless and searching look, its desire as well as its involuntary, saccadic movements, that one may locate the soul unfolding and consciousness emerge.

Although the active dimension of looking is evident, this is actually not the point in Serres's analysis of Bonnard's paintings. In the passage above, he observes that the painter's 'tactful, tactile art does not make the skin a vulgar object for the gaze, but a sensing subject'. One might even say that the painter is just a tool for the woman thus depicted, that he forms part of the "complex of tissues" that makes out her appearance. Whereas it is true that the reaching out, mingling, and visiting the world with one's volatile look will not make objects out of things, the look is indeed not only to be seen as an active agency here. Returning to Lucretius, Serres seems rather to attribute activity to the painter:

> The old Epicureans designated them simulacra, those fragile membranes, that fly in the air, emitted everywhere and received by everybody, and whose function is to produce signs and to make meaning. Bonnard's, and maybe also other's canvas make out the function of such simulacra. Surely these membranes simulate. But more than anything else: leaving the painter's skin and the fine envelope of things, one's veil meets the others's, the canvas catches the thrown-off sloughs in their momentary union. A simultaneous simulacrum. (Serres 1985: 36)[20]

What is especially important to Serres's interest in Impressionism is the way it thematizes – and in a certain sense even realizes – an emission of membranes, a throwing off of sloughs, and especially, contact, impression. Contact here is first of all that of the painter and the world: The painter who opens himself to the impressions of the "fine envelope of things," but also the one who throws off sloughs before the spectator, as if the canvas and the gestures of the brush formed part of the artist's body. Serres points at this affiliation between artist and model by stressing the moral aspect of work; a moral that includes himself as a philosopher:

> The painters sell their own skin, the models lend us theirs, and the world gives its skin for free. I have not saved my own, here it is. Carved, printed, soaked with meaning, often a sudarium, sometimes happy. (Serres 1985: 36)[21]

The Cartesian pun made early in *Les Cinq sens*: "I think, therefore I am beautiful; the world is beautiful, therefore I think", is here taken for an obligation that constitutes the morals of models as well as painters. In the name of Beauty, it is the duty of both parties to give "their skin for free" that is to engage themselves fully in the mingling of bodies and the exchange of skins. In Serres's perception, the open economy of art is thus primarily based on a morality of beauty, of aesthetics. And whereas "beauty contains truth", it is the duty of the philosopher to engage himself in this exchange in order to lay it out in a beautiful fashion. The dictum that 'knowledge cannot exist without beauty' may thus also lead to an understanding of an aesthetic necessity of philosophy, i.e. that beauty makes knowledge necessary.

Shroud and Sudarium: A Veronican Approach to Images

In order to explain further the particular kind of contact in Bonnard's paintings, Serres had recourse to metaphors, which are also found in other realist notions of pictorial arts, namely the sudarium and the shroud. The analogy between dress, canvas, paper, and sudarium was already made in the passage on morality above. Turning towards another painting by Bonnard, "Nu à la baignoire" ("Naked woman in the bath," 1937, oil on canvas, 93 x 147), he notes that:

A sudarium is a cloth, a tissue meant for wiping off sweat from the skin; a shroud when it is has received the sweat of a dying person. The skin is covered by transpiration, secretes its fluids, and becomes marbled, spotted, and mottled, as does the nude model. The sudarium materializes the liquid veil, the mask soaked in blood or sweat: the cloth reminisces the liquids, slightly plastic like it, but firm because of the remaining secretes, and almost gaseous because of the evaporation. The film between the skin and the bath is receiving the transitions of the phase, the exchanges. The robe in the bathroom, in the vaporized environment could be called a sudarium. (Serres 1985: 34)[22]

For Serres, the sudarium and the shroud capture as metaphors perfectly the particular instance of contact addressed in his special interest in Impressionism. The sudarium epitomizes here the bodily association of the canvas; that the latter in a certain sense originates from the painter's body when reaching out into the world trying to catch those fine emissions of light. Like the sudarium, this contact implies the capturing of volatile, viz. fluid matters (blood, sweat, tears) and making these transient secretes firmer, "slightly plastic" as it were; yet secretes which might again evaporate right before the spectator – vaporize and fill his eyes as well as the rest of his sensuous apparatus as an ethereal gaseous substance. In this manner, Serres seems to attribute those basic bodily fluids a certain nobleness: Mingling with the surfaces of the textile and the senses they once more become "alive," not as part of an organism but as part of a sensuous body.

In order to stress the "active" part played by the painter, Serres has recourse to the biblical scene where Saint Veronica approaches Christ on Golgotha before crucifixion:

Tradition calls her Veronica, the saintly woman who wiped the crucified's saintly face, covered by a liquid mask, soaked in sweat and blood, and this name means, in the antique languages, the true icon, the authentic [*fidéle*] image. True, authentic, because it is imprinted, impressionistic. (Serres 1985: 34, my insert)[23]

The nobleness of the fluids is certainly emphasized by the parable of St. Veronica. The referent is not just any "object"; it is a unique and in this case unearthly instance, an object of love, sympathy, and religious sentiment, which is embraced by a weeping woman:

Veronica becomes the patron saint of the painters: eyes blinded with tears, of sorrow and pity, she took in her hands the imprint of the skin, the mask of pain, this saintly woman with open, touching and caressing hands and without a gaze. (Serres 1985: 35)[24]

The "activity" thus addressed in Serres's analysis of Bonnard is that of a gentle caress, of hands touching out into the world without the determination of a gaze nor even with the curiosity of a look "visiting" the world. As Serres has it in his analysis of Lucretius above, this is a "phenomenology of caress." For the painter touching out into the world is thus associated with blindness, although this scene also implies a radical *openness* with the woman embracing Christ with her open hands, her tears streaming towards the blood and sweat of the one loved and soon lost. As a medium, the sudarium itself seems less important here compared to the mingling of bodies – and especially – the mingling of bodily fluids, which precisely assumes a material yet ethereal quality in Serres's account. One may thus say that the parable of St. Veronica emphasizes the principle of flux identified in Serres's analyses of Lucretius. This seems to indicate that flux is not only an inherent quality of the world of ideas, as we saw above, but also of emotions. So, regardless of the vulgar connotations that one may attribute to the term "bodily fluids," these "matters" epitomizes, at least in the parable, the basic principles of sensation and knowledge, i.e. flux, contact, and contingence.

The metaphorical definition of picture and contact is developed further by reference to the shroud of Turin:

> In Turin, one can visit the shroud that covered the body of Christ in his grave, the veil of his face. Exposed when still alive to the hardest of tortures, covered by sweat, blood, saliva, scarred by flagellation, nailed by the spikes, pierced by the point of a lance, his dead body was covered by this linen tissue, which itself slipped in between the atrocious world and the imprinted skin, and finally buried the body as a veil. Loosened carefully, stretched and spread out, straightened and pinned up, the tissue becomes a canvas, it exposes the traces of the body and the face: here is Man. (Serres 1985: 34)[25]

We recognize in this passage the thematization of bodily fluids, which also characterizes the parable of St. Veronica. Although atrocity, i.e., Sin substitutes Love as the central motif, the shroud metaphor is no less "soaked with meaning" in comparison with the sudarium of Veronica. Serres seems to require a religious dimension to make the metaphors epitomize the basic principles of sensation and knowledge. And what is more, although to Serres, Veronica is the patron saint of the painters, the sudarium and especially the shroud motifs still imply a sense of presence and absence which we do not find in the analysis of Bonnard, nor in the basic principles of the "philosophy of mingling bodies."

In the following part of I would like to elaborate a little on this need of story and the significance of presence and absence in Serres's perception of images. Having an eye to the traditions of the study of pictorial art, the Veronican motif evoked in Serres's *Les Cinq sens* may be found also in the realist theories of photography and cinema; theories which precisely emphasize the physical and chemical connection between light, the referent and the photographic material of expression. Roland Barthes, in his mediations on photography, *La chambre clair* (1980, "Camera

Lucida"), is perhaps the most explicit in this regard, stating that:

> Always the Photograph astonishes me, with an astonishment which endu-
> res and renews itself, inexhaustibly. Perhaps this astonishment, this
> persistence reaches down into the religious substance out of which I am
> molded; nothing for it: Photography has something to do with resurrection:
> might we not say of it what the Byzantines said of the image of Christ
> which impregnated St. Veronica's napkin [*dont le Suaire de Turin*]: that it
> was not made by the hand of man, *acheiropoietos*? (Barthes 1984: 82, my
> insert)[26]

Although it is true that the English translator of *La Chambre clair*,
Richard Howard, seems to confuse the holy shroud of Turin for St.
Veronica's napkin, the Veronican motif is clear enough in Barthes
himself, for whom love and loss are also pivotal. We also recognize in
Barthes the "religious substance" which seems to determine Serres's
choice of metaphors, and which seems to characterize not only the
philosophical subject (Serres, Barthes), but also the ethereal matter that
is soaked into the tissues and the photographic paper. The term
"*acheiropoietos*," that it was not made by the hands of a human being,
stresses the noble, if not religious character of the image, which paradoxically stems from the most basic substances. In a paragraph nearby,
Barthes elaborates further on the character of this substance:

> It seems that in Latin "photograph" would be said "imago lucis opera
> expressa"; which is to say: image revealed, "extracted," "mounted,"
> "expressed" (like the juice of a lemon) by the action of light. And if
> Photography belonged to a world with some residual sensitivity to myth,
> we should exult over the richness of the symbol: the loved body is
> immortalized by the mediation of a precious metal, silver (monument and
> luxury); to which we might add the notion that this metal, like all the
> metals of Alchemy, is alive. (Barthes 1984: 81)[27]

In Barthes's account, photography seems attributed with the same sense of unearthliness as the ethereal substance of the sudarium. Moreover do we recognize here a special connection between referent and picture similar to that of the painter and the model in Serres. Somehow "automatically," the referent and the image express themselves together; to borrow a technical term, they "develop" themselves together before the subject in a fashion similar to that of Serres's tactile images. Although Barthes makes an early, rigid, distinction between *Operator* and *Spectator* (1984: 9); it ends up being impossible for him to maintain a separation of these concepts. Like Serres, Barthes becomes involved as a philosophical writer because of an aesthetic necessity inherent in the material.[28]

The Tactile Image: Bodies Mingling in the Light

Dichotomies of distance and proximity, absence and presence play a major role in Barthes's argumentation. The so-called *noeme,* or "essence" of Photography identified in the course of the book is formulated as "That-has-been" (1984: 77 ff.); a sentence, which captures both presence and loss, and distance in terms of space as well as time. However, despite this seemingly fundamental character of photography, Barthes occasionally outlines a different perspective, which seems closer to that of Serres's principle of contact:

> The photograph is literally an emanation of the referent. From a real body, which was there, proceed radiations which ultimately touch me, who am here; the duration of the transmission is insignificant; the photograph of the missing being, as Sontag says, will touch me like the delayed rays of a star. A sort of umbilical cord links the body of the photographed thing to my gaze: light, though impalpable, is here a carnal medium [*milieu*], a skin I share with anyone who has been photographed. (Barthes 1984: 80-81, my insert)[29]

The "umbilical cord" between referent and subject thus referred to here does not contradict the *noeme* of Photography. On the contrary, the *noeme* "That-has-been" implies inevitably a sense of contact. Barthes' notion of light leads us back to the concept of general tactility underlying the perception of image in Serres's analysis of Bonnard's painting. In this environment (*milieu*) of light, Barthes identifies a "skin" that he "shares with anyone"; an environment of mingling, perpetual contact, where object and spectator may find themselves as forming part of and being subjected to one and the same "thing." Barthes ventures to designate this environment a "skin" and a "carnal medium," and obviously "light" cannot be reduced entirely to a physical substance (photons/waves). Light is an environment in which all parties involved may mingle, leave imprints, and thus express themselves in terms of sudaria, simulacra, thrown off sloughs, etc. Light in Barthes is thus an environment that not only facilitates contact, but also "develops" contact as a separate instance, that is, as an image. This *genealogical dimension* of the image is difficult, if at all possible to identify in Serres, but possible, seemingly, in Barthes's account. In *La Chambre clair*, "light" seems in a sense to be a prerequisite for the set of relations distended by the photograph; yet this "skin of light" is something that is "shared with anyone who has been photographed"; a sentence which seems to indicate that "Photography," in a genealogical sense, somehow precedes the tactile environment, the "room of light" (*chambre clair*). In this perception, Barthes's quasi-ontological concept of Photography would imply not only an environment of "carnal light" but also a "gaze" before which this environment unfolds. This idea seems related to Jacques Lacan's concept of gaze in his theory of the visual drive (1977) and Maurice Merleau-Ponty's concept of the "flesh of the world" (1969); a pre-phenomenological dimension, from which spectators emerge as conscious subjects, perhaps not unlike in the fashion by which consciousness awakes in the endless "bunch of clothes" of Serres's cosmology.

Returning finally to Serres's concept of general tactility, we seem to recognize in Barthes's perception of photography the basic principles of flux, contact, and contingency outlined in Serres's (and Lucretius's) aesthetics of the senses. Whereas Barthes may offer us a genealogical account of the constitution of images, Serres in turn gives Barthes and the realists an entire philosophical system in which one may understand the fundamental connection between aesthetics, sensation, and consciousness. In this sense, the concepts of general tactility and tactile images may perhaps finally free Barthes and the radical realists in image theory who still dare to insist on the truth of the image and the truth of beauty.

1 "La tradition appelle Véronique la sainte femme qui essuya la sainte face du crucifié, couverte d'un masque liquide, ruisselant de sueur et de sang, et ce nom signifie, dans les langues antiques, la vraie icône, l'image fidèle. Vraie, fidèle parce que imprimée, impressionniste." (Serres, 1985: 34)

2 There exists no published English translation of this work so far. The original French version is published as a first of two (or more?) volumes. However, despite the fact that today, 17 years after the publication of the original *Grasset* version, Serres is still publishing new works, nothing indicates that a successive volume should still be expected. Moreover, this book makes out a finished and fully integral piece of work that has been and should be approached as such.

3 As Lyngsø notes (304-5), Serres has also advanced a theory of aesthetics in a more modern sense, that is, as an aesthetics of Fine Art (Michel Serres: *Esthétiques. Sur Carpaccio*, Paris, 1975). However, this perspective will not be dealt with in this paper.

4 The citation system used here refers to the division of Lucrete's manuscript into books ("vol.") and verses ("v.").

5 "Observez maintenant le fouillis fluctuant qui séparé et unit le bord et l'adhérence, la surface limite et la croissance infinie des plis. À la lettre et sans métaphore, cet espace est fluent. Il est l'écart mobile d'une fine fidélité. Voilà, tout simplement, *la généalogie des simulacres*, de ces idoles motiles émanées des surfaces, des bords limites, de l'ειδος, eidos."

6 As the editor of *De rerum...* notes, "There is a lacuna of uncertain length after line 216" (cf. Lucretius 2001: 106, n. 17).

7 "Au but, à la réception, l'appareil sensoriel entre en contact avec cette robe fine. Dès lors, la vue, l'odorat, l'ouïe, et ainsi de suite, ne sont que des touchers. La sensation est un tact généralisé. Le monde n'est plus à distance, il est à proximité, comme tangible."

8 "Comme tous les philosophes passionnées du réel objectif, Lucrèce a le génie du tact et non de la vision [...]. Savoir n'est pas voir, c'est prendre contact, directement, avec les choses [...]. Les objets, à distance, échangent leur peau, ils s'envoient des baisers [...]. Phénoménologie de la caresse."

9 "Le monde se remplit de voiles complexes. [/] Une tradition veut que la vérité soit un dévoilement. Une chose, un ensemble de choses couvertes, d'un voile, à découvrir.[...] Cela paraît puéril. [/] Non, la chose ne gît pas sous voile, ni la femme ne danse sous ses sept voiles, la danseuse est elle-même un complexe de tissus.'

10 "Le monde est un amas de linges."

11 "la connaissance n'est pas différente de l'être."

12 "Je pense donc je suis beau. Le monde est beau donc je pense. Le savoir ne peut pas se passer de la beauté."

13 Connor's article is published on the WWW and has no pagination.

14 "Il résiste maintenant à dessiner, ou à peindre. Isolez, si possible, les petites zones secrètes ou l'âme, à l'évidence, réside toujours, coins ou replis de contingence, isolez

encore, si possible aussi, les zones instables qui savent jouer à l'âme avec une autre comme à la balle, entourez les boules ou pavés qui ne deviennent sujets qu'en face des objets, les régions denses ou compactes qui demeurent objets, toujours, seules ou face à celles qui les objectivent, déserts qui manquent d'âme, noirs; le dessin n'entoure que rarement des zones compactes, celles-ci explosent, fusent et fuient en couloirs étroits, forment des cols, des cheminées, des parcours, passages, flammes, zigzags et labyrinthes, voici, sur la peau, en surface, l'âme changeante, ondoyante et fugace, l'âme striée nuée, tigrée, zébrée, bariolée, chinée, troublée, constellée, chamarrée, diaprée, torrentueuse et tourbillonnaire, incendiée."

15 "Du majeur, je me touche une lèvre. En ce contact gît la conscience. J'en commence l'examen. Elle se tapit souvent dans un repli, lèvre posée sur lève, palais collé à la langue, dents sur dents, paupière baissées, sphincters serrés, main fermée en poing, doigts pressés les uns contre les autres, face postérieure de cuisse croisée sur la face antérieure de l'autre, ou pied posé sur l'autre pied. Je parie que l'homuncule, petit et monstrueux, dont chaque part est proportionnelle à la grandeur des sensations, grandit, se gonfle aux automorphismes, quand le tissu de peau se plie sur soi. La peau sur elle-même prend conscience, ainsi sur la muqueuse et la muqueuse sur soi-même."

16 "La peau est une variété de contingence: en elle, par elle, avec elle se touchent le monde et mon corps, le sentant et le senti, elle définit leur bord commun. Contingence veut dire tangence commune: monde et corps se coupent en elle, en elle se caressent. Je n'aime pas dire milieu pour le lieu où mon corps habite, je préfère dire que les choses se mêlent entre elles et que je ne fais pas exception à cela, je me mélange au monde qui se mélange à moi. La peau intervient entre plusieurs choses du monde et les fait se mêler."

17 "L'habit, un peu flottant, occupe l'espace, la toile monte le long du corps, verticale comme un rouleau chinois. Du feuillage règne au fond, envahit un peu, l'étoffe, si peu qu'à la limite le tableau se réduit au tissu."

18 "Pourquoi Bonnard n'a-t-il pas peint directement sur le peignoir, pourquoi n'a-t-il pas exposé la toile du peignoir, son étoffe en place de la toile? Pourquoi ne peint-il plus sur tissu mais sur une autre contexture?

Otez les feuilles, ôtez le peignoir: toucherez-vous la peau de la femme brune ou la toile du tableau? Pierre Bonnard donne moins à voir qu'à sentir sous de doigts pellicules et couches fines, feuillage, étoffe, toile, à-plat, effeuillage, déshabillage, dévoilements raffinés, rideaux minces, caressants: son art plein de tact ne fait pas de la peau un objet vulgaire à voir, mais le sujet sentant, sujet actif toujours dessous. La toile se recouvre de toiles, les voiles s'entassent et ne voilent que de voiles..."

19 "L'œil perd sa prééminence dans le domaine même de sa domination, la peinture. A l'extrême de son effort, l'impressionnisme en vient `a son vrai sens d'origine, au contact."

20 "Les anciens épicuriens appelaient simulacres des membranes fragiles qui volent par l'air, émises partout, reçues par tous, chargées de faire signe et sens. Les toiles de

Bonnard, et d'autres peut-être, remplissent la fonction de simulacres. Certes, elles font semblant. Mais surtout: partant de la peau du peintre et de la fine enveloppe des choses, le voile d'un rencontre les voiles des autres, la toile saisit la jonction instantanée des mues. Simulacre simultané."

21 "Les peintres vendent leur peau, les modèles louent la leur, le monde donne les siennes, je n'ai pas sauvé la mienne, la voici. Ecorchée, imprimée, ruisselante de sens, suaire souvent, heureuse quelquefois."

22 "On appelle suaire un linge conçu pour essuyer la sueur, linceul quand il a reçu la sueur d'agonie. La peau se revêt de transpiration, exsude et se marbre, perlée, nuée comme celle du nu féminin. Le suaire matérialise le voile liquide, le masque ruisselant de sueur ou de sang: le tissu ressemble au fluide, un peu souple comme lui, solide pourtant par les dépôts laissés, quasi aérien par l'évaporation. Le film entre peau et bain reçoit les transitions de phase, les échanges. Le peignoir, à la salle de bains, au milieu des vapeurs, pourrait s'appeler suaire."

23 "La tradition appelle Véronique la sainte femme qui essuya la sainte face du crucifié, couverte d'un masque liquide, ruisselant de sueur et de sang, et ce nom signifie, dans les langues antiques, la vraie icône, l'image fidèle. Vraie, fidèle parce que imprimée, impressionniste."

24 "Véronique devient la patronne des peintres: les yeux pleins de larmes, aveuglée de chagrin et de pitié, elle prit de ses mains l'empreinte de la peau, le masque de douleur, sainte femme de contact et de caresse, mains ouvertes sans regard."

25 "On peut visiter, à Turin, le suaire qui, dans son tombeau, enveloppa (sic!) le corps du Christ, le voile de son visage. Plongé vif dans les tortures les plus dures, couvert de sueur, de sang, de crachats, de poussière, sacrifié par la flagellation, troué de clous, percé du fer de lance, son cadavre fut roulé dans ce tissu de lin, glissé lui-même entre le monde atroce et la peau imprimée, il fut enterré sous ce voile. Retiré doucement, étiré, déplié, aplani, exposé, le voile devient toile, donne à voir les traces du corps, du visage, voici l'homme."

26 "Toujours, la Photographie *m'étonne*, d'un étonnement qui dure et se renouvelle, inépuisablement. Peut-être cet étonnement, cet entêtement, plonge-t-il dans la substance religieuse dont je suis pétri; rien à faire. La Photographie a quelque chose à voir avec la résurrection. New peut-on dire d'elle cd que disaient les Byzantins de l'image du Christ dont le Suaire de Turin est imprégné, à savoir qu'elle n'était pas faite de main d'homme, *acheïropoïétos*?" (Barthes, Roland: *La Chambre clair*. Gallimard/Seuil, Paris.1980 : 129)

27 "Il paraît qu'en latin 'photographie' se dirait: 'imago lucis opera expressa'; c'est-à-dire: image révélée, 'sortie,' 'montée,' 'exprimée' (comme je jus d'un citron) par l'action de la lumière. Et si la Photographie appartenait à un monde qui ait encore quelque sensibilité au mythe, on ne manquerait pas d'exulter devant la richesse du symbole : le corps aimé est immortalisé par la médiation d'un métal précieux, l'argent (monument et luxe) ; à quoi on ajouterait l'idée que ce métal, comme tous le métaux de l'Alchimie, est vivant." (Ibid 127)

28 Indeed, this moral aspect is often stressed in the last part of Barthes's work. In *Roland Barthes/ par Roland Barthes* (1975) referring to Nietzsche, he thus addresses this final part as a stage of morality, driven by aesthetics.

29 "La photo est littéralement une émanation du référent. D'un corps réel qui était là, sont parties des radiations qui viennent me toucher, moi qui suis ici; peu importe la durée de la transmission ; la photo de l'être disparu vient me toucher comme les rayons différés d'une étoile. Une sorte de lien ombilical relie le corps de la chose photographiée à mon regard : la lumière, quoique impalpable, est bien ici un milieu charnel, une peau que je partage avec celui ou celle qui a été photographié." (Ibid.126–7)

Literature

Barthes, Roland. 1975. *Roland Barthes/par Roland Barthes*. Paris: Seuil.

Barthes, Roland. 1984 (1980). *Camera Lucida*. London: Penguin.

Connor, Steven. 1999. "Michel Serres's Five Senses". Paper for the Michel Serres Conference held at Birkbeck College, Centre for Interdisciplinary Research in Culture and the Humanities, May 29th, 1999. Located at http://www.bbk.av.uk/eh/eng/skc/5senses.htm by June 1st, 2001.

Egholm, Jesper, Lyngsø, Niels, and Søndergaard, Morten. 1991. *Omkring Michel Serres: Form og objektivitet Vol. II*. Aalborg: Nordic Summer University/RES.

Johansson, Troels Degn. 1991. "Mise en Obscène." In Klaus Bruhn Jensen, Troels Degn Johansson, and Lars Bo Kimergård (Eds.): *Sekvens 91 – Lars Von Trier*. Copenhagen: Department of Film & Media Studies, University of Copenhagen.

Lacan, Jacques. 1977 (1973). *The Four Fundamental Concepts in Psychoanalysis*. London & New York: Penguin.

Lucretius. 2001 (1969). *On the Nature of Things*. Transl. by Martin Ferguson Smith. Indianapolis: Hackett.

Lyngsø, Niels. 1994. *En eksakt rhapsodi: Om Michel Serres' filosofi*. Copenhagen: Borgen.

Merleau-Ponty, Maurice. 1969 (1957). *The Visible and the Invisible*. Evanston, Illinois: Northwestern University Press.

Serres, Michel. 1977. *La naissance de la physique dans le texte de Lucrèce: Fleuves et turbulences*. Paris: Éditions de minuit.

Serres, Michel. 1985. *Les Cinq Sens: Philosophie des corps mêlés - I*. Paris: Bernard Grasset.

Serres, Michel. 1995 (1982). *Genesis*. Ann Arbor: University of Michigan Press.

Prosthesis Unbound

Esben Krohn

SEMICHORUS I
    We, beyond heaven, are driven along;
SEMICHORUS II
    Us the enchantments of earth retain;
SEMICHORUS I
    Ceaseless, and rapid, and fierce, and free,
    With the Spirits which build a new earth and sea,
    And a heaven where yet heaven could never be;
SEMICHORUS II
    Solemn, and slow, and serene, and bright,
    Leading the Day, and outspeeding the Night,
    With the powers of a world of perfect light;
        Percy Shelley, Prometheus Unbound, *1820*

What may not be expected in a country of eternal light? I may there discover the wondrous power which attracts the needle; and may regulate a thousand celestial observations, that require only this voyage to render their seeming eccentricities consistent for ever.
    Mary Shelley, Frankenstein: Or The Modern Prometheus, *1831*

Introduction

IN THE SHELLEYS, the myth of Prometheus was cultivated and reformulated. The dream or nightmare of revolt against the realm of God and Man's dominion over fire found a new expression marked by the political and technological currents of the time. They brought to life in words a utopia of the unbound or modern Prometheus and the perfect or eternal light.

But the difference between the two authors' utopias is striking. In Percy Shelley, human potential is set free and therefore remains at one with itself. Man becomes complete and the utopia becomes the whole world, while in Mary Shelley the potential is materialised in an other who constitutes a monstrous autonomy, and the utopia simply becomes a point at which no-one in the novel actually gets to, but it is hinted that the monster will get there. In Percy Shelley, the resolution is achieved within Man's natural self, in Mary Shelley Frankenstein seeks resolution via an external artificial extension. In Percy Shelley Man achieves freedom, in Mary Shelley Man's creation and mirror image struggles for and achieves autonomy. In Percy Shelley enlightenment is complete, in Mary Shelley the place with the eternal light is the place where Frankenstein's prosthesis is laid to rest. Both Percy and Mary strive towards the light at a time when technological discoveries are being made that are capable of framing it.

With photography and moving pictures later generations could see for themselves this light, which in its own way had become a reality. The light could be taken or recorded from nature and stored and repeated for ever in this world.

For example, in 1913 a small expedition arrived on Samsø with the aim of, among other things, setting up a telegraphic spy post, blowing up a boat and setting fire to a mill. They were stopped on the quay in Selvig Havn by the island's lone policemen with a braid hat and an alsation. He protested in vain against the car they had brought over, which he thought might frighten or otherwise injure people and animals. He was also unable to prevent their other activities, as they were part of the making of a film, *Arvingen til Skjoldborg* (Alfred Cohn, 1913), and the aforementioned mill had also been bought and paid for by the film company for Kr 5000. The filming aroused great interest, all the more so because the mill was going to be blown up after having served faithfully for 16 generations. Three-quarters of the island's population turned out for this special Midsummer bonfire.

The film-makers were not deterred by the authorities. They had things under control and their own direction. Control over the power of the fire in the car's combustion engine and the spark in the telegraph, which in the fictional story could both create words and would set off the aforementioned explosion. But things almost went awry at the mill. The fire became more intense than expected and an actor's life was put in danger. This element of reality then on the other hand had a greater dramatic effect in the film.

All thus ended well, as it did otherwise in the film itself. But the legacy of Prometheus: the fire and moreover the light and electricity and all Man's dominion over forces that are thus not without an echo in the realm of fiction. As modern technology has influence on the world, in the fiction it plays a role too in the play of shadows.

It is this play that we will examine in the following. How the photographic process itself in its own way implies a specific expression of a form that can also be seen in the written word, and how this is expressed in the actions of fictional figures in words and particularly in moving images.

Nature is images

Before images began to move they were frozen, but already on their way to thaw the new perspective that would haunt the shadows of film, and where we will see it directly influence actors who are fictional in more than one sense. The shift from photography to moving images brings to life a perspective that film technology makes it possible to play out and place on show. What was created, or rather formulated, was the Modern, the new age.

But in reality, time is the wrong expression, for it is space that is pregnant. For if we say that a picture says more than a thousand words, we have to ask ourselves whether all these words are written or spoken, sound or image, or, time or space. What was new in photography and later in moving pictures was that they created the fullness of space in an aesthetic but nevertheless concrete sense, like a reflection of the secular rejection of the belief in the fullness of time, as expressed by the transcendent and life-giving word. With photography the movement that had been implicitly expressed in the art of printing itself, was brought into direct contact the aesthetic: the relationship between speech and writing, vision and hearing, authenticity and reproduction, authority and revolution, spirit and body were turned around. Gutenberg offered people a chance to see for themselves, provided self-vision instead of omniscience.

Photography caused a sensation in its day. Contemporary descriptions can put us on the track of the aesthetic potential of this new perspective. In this light, photography is not only an invention but also the fulfilment of a utopian idea of space that is at one and the same time emptied and all-embracing in the modern age. What struck people at the time was, among other things, the automatic quality of the process: It is nature itself that develops the pictures.

The article "The pencil of nature. A New Discovery" (*The Corsair*, 1839), says, for example:

All nature shall paint herself – fields, rivers, trees, houses, plains, mountains, cities, shall paint themselves at a bidding, and a few moment's notice. Towns will no longer have any representatives but selves.

And if nature has this power to create images in its own image, then perhaps it follows that: "the whole universal nature [is] nothing more than phonetic and photogenic structures". Nature itself can, in this light, be viewed as a large film projector that projects images of a world that human beings then have to act within; a world of reflections which not only comprises everything but which also possesses the possibility of registering everything.

> What will become of the poor thieves, when they shall see handed in as evidence against them their own portraits, taken by the room in which they stole, and in the very act of stealing!

The new medium is not only an invention but also a door into a whole new world of new possibilities and challenges. This new world is far more clever than the old world, but also imaginary to a greater degree. The craft of recreating creation, such as the work of the painter, has been surpassed by nature itself, which creates itself in its own image, in which the image might be just the image of an image. The new world demands new artists. The article ends with a prediction: "It may be presumed that the number of artists will be greatly reduced, and that a few will attain greater excellence."

Words are images

One of those who accepted the challenge was Edgar Allen Poe. We cannot know for certain whether Poe read the article cited above, but we do know that he was aware of the new invention. In 1840 he wrote a short article on the daguerreotype. The article is not particularly interesting: it limits itself to the facts about the process. What is interesting is how we can see Poe's eye for photography in his fiction.

Poe "invented" the detective genre, "the private eye," and this "invention" seems to hide another invention: the photographic process. Seeing writing as surface, that is, as space, in "The Purloined Letter" (1844), is, for instance, an implicitly photographic point of view. Poe's use of this perspective does, however, not limit itself to the stories about Dupin. In Poe's cryptic stories the point of view is also buried up. And of course: in Poe's fiction, subjects themselves are often walled up – dead or alive or in some intermediary state.

Poe's great interest in cryptography is interesting in itself. It represents a search behind writing for the hidden meaning. But in Poe's stories this penetration seems not so much to reveal a rational subject, but rather an imaginary borderland between cleverness and madness, between I and eye (that sound identical in speech, but look different in writing). In Poe's stories, partly in opposition to his poetry, vision rather than hearing is the primary sense. Writing is to be seen rather than heard, which is also the case with the cryptographic message, the patterns and substitutions of which demand space in order to be deciphered.

The most obvious example is perhaps *The Tell-Tale Heart* (1843), where the narrator kills an old man – presumably because of the latter's "evil eye". "I think it was his eye! Yes, it was this! One of his eyes resembled that of a vulture – a pale blue eye, with a film over it". Faced with this terrible eye the narrator shines a light from a lantern: "a single dim ray, like the thread of the spider, shot from out the crevice and fell upon the vulture eye." The old man dies. "Yes, he was stone, stone, dead." The narrator hides the body under the floor and puts the boards back in place. "I replaced the boards so cleverly, so cunningly, that no human eye – not even his – could have detected anything wrong." The police show up, but the narrator lets them in "with a light heart". They examine the room carefully without finding any clues. But the narrator hears a sound and goes pale. "No doubt I now grew very pale." It is the sound of the dead man's heart beating: "*much such a sound as a watch makes when enveloped in cotton.*" And the narrator reveals himself: "'Villains!' I shrieked, 'dissemble no more! I admit the deed! – tear up the planks! – here, here! – it is the beating of his hideous heart!'"

The story progresses through mirrors, in which the old man and the narrator are mirrored in each other, much like I and eye mirror each other's sound. The old man is really just an eye; an eye that sucks the life out of the narrator, like a vulture sticking its long neck through the hide of an animal, eating everything inside and leaving nothing but the shell. The narrator's solution to this predicament is to turn the situation on its head by projecting a thin ray of light from a dark lantern into the evil eye and thus petrifying the old man.

The whole process is like that of a photographic apparatus, in which writing, the narration itself, fixes everything and develops the narrator. It is a play between black and white, between light and shadow, negative and positive; an image of writing, and writing about the image; a photograph with a point of view that writes itself all the way to the bitter end. The story progresses toward its own impulse which is not the end, not silence, but the white sheet on which the text itself is written. The narrator blanches at the sound of the heart enveloped in cotton, the white textile out of which the textual motivation has been spun. Writing is not words, in the sense of speech, but letters printed on a surface.

As with the play on the similarity between "eye" and "I", the relationship between ear and eyesight is emphasised. In the last sentence the narrator draws attention not only the dead body, but also to the sound. "Here" and "hear" come together in the only direct speech of the whole story. This space is a despairing voice in a room in which everything has been flattened. The sound is space, speech is writing, hearing is eyesight. "The clock" is in reality "a watch" – time is a matter of space. The narrator's voice entails to its own cessation in spatial terms.

The narrator is a point of view that finds expression in the story, a point of view that fills space, but also empties itself. Describing his acute senses, the narrator at the same time reveals his madness. The narrator is like a camera, which describes everything clearly down to the very smallest detail, and at the same time makes everything fictitious by recording the room through a technique that poses the question of whether everything might perhaps be just a picture of a picture, "a dream within a dream".

In this self-reflexive space authenticity is impossible. The authority of the narrator is based on an oxymoron: he is aware of his own eclipse; a form of being by force of not being. The oxymoron is also the very basis of the typology of reproduction: to transform yourself into letters is a precondition for occupying space, but it is also what forces the subject into a frame. You are expressed when you express yourself, when you are seen, but you disappear in the surface and the order of words. You exist and do not exist at the same time. You exist in force of the empty shell you leave behind in the frame. This is the perspective of the modern age that Poe saw and which millions of people would see concretely in film.

Moving pictures are without spoken words

With film Poe's written testimonial became a medium that carries within itself the perspective in which the new written image comes to life. Perhaps not as radically and intensely as in Poe – but quite concretely.

In what follows we will consider the relationship between medium and human being, with a special view to tracing the new relationship brought to light by film. Our examples are Danish silent films from around the First World War. At that time Denmark was a leading actor in the international film market. Nordisk Films Kompagni, with Ole Olsen as the main person behind the scenes and Valdemar Psilander in the foreground as the company's big star, was the second largest production company in the world. Personalities like the actress Asta Nielsen and director Benjamin Christensen also created a sensation.

These films often have an interesting ambiguity. The play is doubled, actors act out performances and the stage shows a stage. A duality thus emerges which both exposes and disguises the basis of the illusion. This duality is revelatory because it draws our attention to the staging, and yet conceals the illusion by making it part of the fiction.

Asta Nielsen was born in Copenhagen 11 September 1881, but the film star Asta Nielsen, "die Asta" was born in the film *Afgrunden* (*The Abyss*, Urban Gad, 1910). In the film she plays the music teacher Magda Vang, who leaves her fiancé Knud (Robert Dinesen), the son of a minister, for the brutish circus rider Rudolph (Poul Reumert). The film ends in social come-down and a fight in which Magda kills Rudolph.

The most famous scene in the film is the "Gaucho dance," when Magda and Rudolph perform a captivating dance in a variety show. The scene is interesting enough in itself, and also as an example of stage doubling in Danish silent film, but the point of view is also worth noticing. The scene is shot from the wings with the audience to the right in the picture, and Magda does not perform for this audience but for the viewers of the film. This would not look so strange if the scene had been presented from an implicit perspective – it would, for instance, seem more logical if Knud was following the performance from the wings, but this is not the case.

Now, we can, of course, only guess as to why the scene was done this way. Some will think it is the result of the director's lack of talent for a medium that is new and has yet to find its right methods. Others might claim that the point of view gives the images a depth which would disappear if the scene was shot from the perspective of the audience, since the backdrop would then flatten the picture. But whichever explanation one chooses, the scene remains peculiar and important. One the one hand, we have a scene within a scene, which in itself emphasises the fiction, on the other hand, the audience of the film is being addressed, which breaks with the inner logic of the film.

*Asta Nielsen and Poul Reumert.
Still from Afgrunden.*

But the fact that something seems illogical in the fiction, does not mean that it is without meaning. We do not have to leave the universe of the film for the real world – the imperfect medium and the inexperienced or perhaps aesthetically conscious director with a fine eye for composition. We can remain on the borderline between fiction and reality. An imaginary realm that the film itself makes room for mirrors the fictitious characters and lets them see mirror images of themselves.

Film is born in a secularised age, which means that the relationship between reality and fiction, uttering and utterance, enters a shadow world, and it is this world we are presented with in the shadow play of the film. *Afgrunden* thus mirrors the abyss that opens up after the death of God; we gaze into it, and it, in its turn, gazes back at us. That God is dead does not mean that the idea of a controlling principle disappears, but that this principle has to be part of the performance. The ideal notion of a pact between human beings and an objective narrator has been destroyed, and what remains is a pact between the subject and the lens, within the same frame. Human beings have abandoned the divine framework for the aesthetic – just as Magda leaves the minister's son for the artist Rudolph.

The framework is in Danish silent film clearly delineated. The camera movements are minimal and the scenes are usually played out in front of a set camera setting. Within this given frame we then witness a series of spatial doubling, which correspond with the silent actors. The films reveal new rooms and spaces within rooms, such as secret passages and hidden rooms, which are used in the games of dissimulation of the villains. We are given a visual parallel between the role-play of the subject and the art form's concrete ability for spatial doubling; a matching of the silence that envelops the secular medium. A wilderness of mirrors, reflecting the world brought about by secularisation, which in its turn concretely inscribes a mechanical perspective into the frame.

Complicated forms can be played out on the doubled stage. In *Døds-angstens Maskepil* (Eduard Schnedler Sørensen, 1912) the well-known actor Frank Harvey (Valdemar Psilander), onboard a ship, must act until total exhaustion in order to avoid panic among the ship's audience, who is unaware that the ship is on fire. He is helped by Oda (Ellen Aggerholm) who was taken with the star in the theatre.

Valdemar Psilander was the great star of his day, and the star can be seen to incarnate an ambiguity implicit in the new perspective, and which is also expressed explicitly here. In the film, Frank Harvey collapses from exhaustion in a concrete gap between the reality of the fiction, the burning ship, and the fiction within the fiction, the stage where he performs his act. Significantly, the star Frank Harvey, alias Valdemar Psilander, is thus in a space between fiction and reality, and in which he fits perfectly with our view of the star.

The star is more than the fiction and more than reality. The star is not only interesting by virtue of the role that he or she plays, but this extra value can presumably not be cashed in by a real subject in real life. The same is true of the world of the film. It is not fascinating solely by virtue of its concrete fictions, but is also a world in itself. This can, of course, also be said to be the case for the worlds of the theatre and the circus, from which we are familiar with the double and revealing scene in *Hamlet* (William Shakespeare, approx. 1601). What is new is this massive and concrete focus on the imaginary world as the subject's motivation, contained within a secular framework in which the objective perspective depends on a mechanical inscription.

The actors in the fiction appear to be guided by an ambiguous or inscrutable motivation, in which they perish. In *Vampyr-Danserinden* (August Blom, 1912) Oscar Borch (Robert Dinesen) falls hopelessly in love with the vampire dancer Silvia Lafont (Clara Wieth). In spite of all his efforts, his love is not returned. He therefore drinks poison before

Still from Vampyrdanserinden.

hc and Silivia enter the stage together for the fatal dance, and thus dies a double death; in the dance, where Sylvia squeezes life out of him, and in the world of the film, from the poison.

Vampire dancing was a relatively familiar term at the time. *Hver 8. Dag* of 12. February 1911, for instance, describes a performance by Alice Eis and Herbert French in Cirkus Variété: "Based on a poem by Rudyard Kipling and a painting by Burne-Jones... The whole act is presented with a realism that is striking and quite extreme for a Danish audience." The painting in question must be Phillip Burne-Jones' "The Vampire" from 1897, and the poem the one of the same title that Kipling wrote the same year, inspired by Burne-Jones' painting. Phillip Burne-Jones and Rudyard Kipling were, incidentally, related, and the year was also a big one for vampires with the publication of Bram Stoker's *Dracula*. The painting and the poem, though, are hardly as bloody as the book: they do not deal with proper vampires, but with women who suck power and money out of a man.

The two real-life dancers Eis and French also dance in the film *The Vampire* (Robert G. Vignola, 1913), and Kipling's poem also inspired a film with a title based on its first line, *A Fool There Was* (Frank Powell, 1915), in which Theda Bara plays "the vampire." So is born the first "vamp" in film.

The fictions keep doubling; from painting to poem, and from dance to film, with increasing realism and perversity. The film bears the subtitle "The Drama at 'Central Variétée'" and promises "The Sensation of the Now". It thus surpasses the fiction that was already a part of reality, vampire dancing on stage, in order to find the spirit of the age.

In the film, we follow three plays within the same frame, perspective or level of knowledge: That of the audience, Sylvia's, and Oscar's. One party knows more than the other, who again knows more than the third, constituted by the fictive audience, which again mirrors the real audience, which knows everything. What we are dealing with is an intricate structure of doubling, in which Silivia and Oscar play for the fictive audience, while the real audience peeps in behind the scenes. So is created a perpetual back-and-forth motion, which can be compared with the effect achieved when two mirrors face each other. You get a corridor of frames that at one and the same time seems to be disappearing into nothingness and to be coming back from the same place. It can be compared to secular death, which is both the end of the subject and the motivation for creative thought. A death which is both the endpoint of this concrete fiction, and that which it is the task of the new perspective to frame and thus to conquer by filling in the perpetually doubled frame – the cinematics of cinematographic subjects fill out the frames of the cinematographic machine.

Silent film copies and steals stories with arms, legs and gestures, but they do not content themselves with copying. The secular perspective gives a new dimension to the two-dimensional surface. This can happen concretely through the perspective or by introducing an extra dimension into the action.

In *Døds-Spring til Hest fra Cirkus-Kuplen* (Eduard Schnedler Sørensen, 1912) Count Willy von Rosenörn (Valdemar Psilander) is suddenly ruined and is forced to sell his property. He takes a room in an "Artists' Hotel" where he meets artists from "Circus Carino". The count consents to taking part in a risky circus act: mounted on a horse, he is going to let himself be hoisted up under the circus cupola on a platform where a large fireworks will be set off. Before the film reaches this climax, the count has time to become infatuated by the sly equestrienne Doré (Mrs. Ræder) and to save the shyer dancer Evelyn (Jenny Roelsgaard), who is deeply in love with the him, from a hotel fire. Confused and tipsy he falls down to the circus floor, but is nursed back to his senses by Evelyn.

The upward and downward motions create a concrete third dimension in the film, which is seen both during the hotel fire, in which the lift plays a major role, and in the fatal platform in the circus. In themselves, the hotel and the circus also constitute borderlands between high and low. In the artist world, the count is given the chance of substituting his lost position at the top of society with fame by taking place in an aesthetic performance. The films thus shows us the world of film itself, in which it is possible to become much more famous than any count. From being a prominent person, he is now given the chance of performing as an artist. As a count, he existed by virtue of tradition, in the new world, he exists by virtue of his own appearance in public which offers him the possibility of both a retired position and of being himself, which is mirrored in Psilander's status as star. He can step in and out of the *demi-monde* presented by the artists' hotel and in which mistakes and death threaten. The film is a three-dimensional carnival, in its setting, plot, and imaginary motivation, which goes beyond the fiction.

The new perspective makes room for another world within the world; a world which fascinates, thrills and takes the audience away from everyday life. Already on 23 September 1906, that is, before Danish silent film had started producing fiction in earnest, *Hver 8. Dag* wrote: "Motion pictures are obviously the solution and hunger of the day." The same article also revealed how film created its illusion through the use of film tricks and mechanical means. The last mechanical explanation is also worth taking note of: "The presentation of motion pictures is based on the curious fact that the human eye is only able to register 15-16 impressions per second." This is hardly a sensational revelation. The phenomenon was well known at the time. But the choice of words reminds the viewer that man is imperfect. We can only do so much. What the article emphasises, and what film in itself expresses, without taking the action into consideration, is that human beings are imperfect. Paradoxically, by its potential to show all places and everything, repeatedly and anywhere, film has the potential of surmounting our limitations. Film gives and takes, letting human beings step in and out of a new, secular and imaginary frame. These are the rules of the game.

The mechanical as guiding principle is also a theme in Danish silent film, implicitly as well as explicitly. It is obvious that characters within a fiction are controlled, but by repeatedly focusing on doubling and the concrete preconditions of the medium (which is mechanical reproduction) film gives a mass audience the change to finally see for themselves the situation brought about by secularisation: the grand narrative is gone, but many small performances, with their own hidden but worldly directors, must still be played to their end. These performances reveal plays with masks, that are thrown off only to expose new masks.

In *Othello* (Martinius Nielsen, 1916) a famous actor, Ludvig Romey (Vlademar Psilander) falls in love with Melitta (Ebba Thomsen), and turns down his former girlfriend the walk-in Lene Becker (Inger Nybo). The conflict between the two comes to a head, and Lene swears to take revenge. Six years pass. Ludvig and Melitta are married, but their marriage is crumbling. Ludvig has no talent for bourgeois idyll. After a death Melitta travels south to rest, while Ludvig remains behind. He falls fatally for the foreign star actress Amata Mayro (Inger Nybo) who in reality turns out to be the very same Lene Becker he rejected in his youth. She has come to take her revenge. Ludvig becomes obsessed by Amata, promises her anything she wants in return for her love, and watches any man who approaches her like a jealous Othello. Just before the curtain rises for a theatre performance of exactly *Othello* (William Shakespeare, 1604), Amata takes off her mask and reveals that the great actor is playing a walk-on part in the play she herself, the former walk-on, has staged. On stage, play and reality come together, and Ludvig kills Amata in Desdemona's death scene before the eyes of Melitta, who has returned and is sitting in the audience.

What we have here is an actress (Inger Nybo), playing an actress (Lene Becker), playing an actress (Amata Mayro). And we have a theatre audience watching a play which is really a very different play from what they think they are watching. Compared to, for instance, *Vampyrdanserinden*, in which Oscar's private play was his own concern and his own death, and in which the vampire dance was an aesthetic phenomenon in the real world, the play of doubling receives yet another turn of the screw here, in the literal copying of an already written textual surface. The fiction comes alive within the fiction when Ludvig takes the role of Othello and kills Desdemona alias Amata Mayro alias Lene Becker. When the curtain falls the audience has watched a paranoid performance; the actors became actors in a play that was the fatal re-enactment of a play. It is a play in which everything is given, in which the actors are marionettes, and which is brought on by inner demons – obsession and revenge. And what is more: The intense emotions are not even authentic, since the actors have to repeat a form that is given, a play that is already written.

But the outcome of a film hardly needs to be this bad. In *Pjerrot* (Hjalmar Davidsen, 1916) there is also marital trouble. Jean Riot (Gunnar Tolnæs) loves his wife Gabrielle (Janny Petersen), but has to scrimp and scrape because he has taken over his father in law's (Frederik Jacobsen's) gambling debt and has fallen into the hands of a money lender. Layette has left the country to get away from the gambling. Tired of her admired but stingy husband, Gabrielle is tempted by director Garoche (Erik Holberg). Jean surprises the two together and leaves both his wife and their small daughter. For four years he roams around the world. He does, however, return to his own country, where he accepts to play the role of Pierrot on the condition that his name is not mentioned. He meets Layette again, who is now director at the theatre. As fate will have it, Gabrielle and his daughter are in the audience. His daughter is thrilled by the performance, and on her own, seeks him out in his dressing room. Layette has recognised his grand-child, and in apparent desperation he hits the bottle, thereby accidentally starting a fire. Jean, still wearing his costume, saves his daughter, but is not recognised by Gabrielle. The daughter is very ill, but begs to see Pierrot one more time. Jean shows up in his costume and plays his part. The daughter is delighted and her life saved. Old Layette, on the other hand, dies, but only after having written a letter that explains the whole wretched business, including the reason for Jean's miserliness in his marriage. Husband, wife and daughter are then unified.

Again the play doubles. Unlucky Lafayette's gambling, forces Jean to play a role, which again forces him from house and home, and later into acting anonymously, first in the theatre, then at home. After her husband left her, Gabrielle has made her living as a music teacher. Everyone plays in this story, with more or less luck. They are all victims of deception, of interrelated playing and acting. Unlike the films mentio-ned above, Jean's performance as Pierrot in the theatre is straight-for-ward and without any underlying play. But this film does contain a scene leaden with meaning: Harlekin in the play about Pierrot plays a mechanical statue which is wound up. This is an excellent image of a plot which in this, as in many other silent movies, might seem contri-ved to the point of pure mechanical construct. But it also contains an implicit recognition of man's room for action in a mechanical age. The scene is at once comical and desperate, as in Gustav Wied's words from the strange "stageplay" *Dansemus* (Dancing Mice, 1905), where direction and spoken lines intersect: "Yes, we are all dancing to the tune of a higher hurdy-gurdy, your Excellency."

Words are moving images

We do not know whether contemporary audiences saw these stories as mechanical constructs, but the films nevertheless convey a mechanical view of narrative which is interesting in relation to the written motives the films explicitly or implicitly present, either through titles or in their programmes.

The point of titles is, of course, to overcome the silent scene. But in films from this period, titles are not just a substitute for speech. The titles are often woven into the action itself, as letters, telegrams, posters, newspapers, etc. They can be seen as a foreign element in the silent film. *Hver 8. Dag* for 30 July 1912 compares two films with the same source, William Magnay, that are showing at the same time: *Kansleren Kaldet den Sorte Panter* (Holger Rasmussen and Einar Zangenberg, 1912) and *Den Sorte Kansler* (August Blom, 1912). It is said about the latter that "the presentation is marred by too many printed lines and a deluge of letters that always seem irritating to the cultured viewer." Viewers can see for themselves whether there is anything in this, but the intrusive titles can also be regarded in a different light: As a way of emphasising that the world of the film is not presented without effort, and that it is not without mechanical elements.

In the world of film, we are completely in the power or the word, which may suddenly turn a person's entire existence on its head. We are not referring to *Logos*, in which the word is transcendently incarnated, but to the secular word. This is a ruthless word, but also a liberated word; an autonomous and automatised word. The words actually determine the course of the action. They break into the life of the fictive characters. Unexpected letters with fatal contents change everything in a moment, posters in the street lure audiences to performances that cause complications, newspapers describe the performances of the famous and feed the fascination of the reader, and telegrams either bring important news, like newspapers, or are forged with exciting consequences. And all this is achieved through flat words, written images.

In the fictive world, existence is not longer given by an absolute provider of signs on the outside, but is a world filled with signs, put into play by an implicit perspective. Writing in the silent film is not natural.

It is writing which exists by virtue of the perspective implied by silent film. It is reproductive writing; what is supposedly private can be read by others than the indented recipient and telegrams can be forged with fatal consequences. On the silent stage, writing is not only speech, understood as an extension of the person's own expression, but often something that takes characters out of themselves in a concrete way. Writing initiates thrills, devotion and abduction, deprivation, forgiveness, disruption, resurrection, etc. Writing moves people – it is ultimately kinetic, cinematographic, and thus mechanical, and even more when the action is taken into consideration.

A silent film may seem mechanical in the extreme, particularly when we also take its programme into consideration. In addition to a plot summary, this contains a list of the film's parts. Reading such a list of say 50 short indications of the action of the film, we may think we are holding Vladimir Propp's functions from 1928 (*Morfologija skazki*). Here, the plot of the magical fairytale is boiled down to a model. The programme of a silent film comes very close to rendering concrete a formalistic view of the structure of narrative before structuralism. But this does not mean that a later historical period exposes the programme, which in its turn exposes the expression of the film. We also have to say that the film in itself reveals, and in its time exposes, a new view of writing.

The secular perspective implies a re-evaluation of the incarnate and living word, in which the religious has been exchanged for the aesthetic. Thus, the word does not lose its power, but its control is transformed from the metaphysical to the physical – that is, the mechanical. It is not silenced, but must perform in a medium where it is the carrier of automation. The word becomes writing, which points toward an unsafe and fascinating aesthetic ground, opposite to the religious turn to the safe ground of fate. We are dealing with words that give life, in an aesthetic sense, as the word in religion gives life. We are dealing with words incarnated in an aesthetic perspective, as the word is incarnated in an absolute narrator in faith.

The titles in these films have to be seen literally as written images. It follows that we cannot claim that the writing precedes the film, for instance that the film is just an expression of its writing. On the contrary, the film expresses a view of writing, both quite openly in the titles placed within the frame itself, and in the agreement between the secular perspective and the causal effect that words have in cinamatographical terms. The films are really very concrete. They express an inscribed perspective by doubling the stage and letting the words in the titles initiate the action. The titles are surfaces, reflected in the film images, the written images and the pictorial language, with fatal consequences for the double-acting people.

The rest is talk

In our view, the films discussed here, and many others from the same period in Danish film history, give equal status to form and content, medium and human being, to a degree that is quite rare. In later silent films (even if these too might be re-evaluated bearing the written word in mind) narration seems to take over, and the medium recedes into the background. The acting subjects become indifferent to the demands of the medium. The narrative is simply transported by means of film, and can be presented through any medium, even if the aesthetic potential of film of course makes possible a greater immediate fascination for the viewer. But the fascinating written image disappears and normal speech takes over the titles.

In *Nedbrudte Nerver* (Anders Wilhelm Sandberg, 1923) a clever journalist, Erik Brandt (Gorm Schmidt), believes he is witnessing a murder, which of course brings him into a whole series of calamities. In the end it turns out that what he witnessed was in fact only the shooting of a film, under the instruction of none other but the real director Sand-

Still from Himmelskibet.

berg. It is an imaginative idea and the dialogue is smart, but the fixed idea bordering on obsession found in earlier films is gone. Speech as speech has taken over the titles, replacing the secular written image.

There are 181 titles in this film. About two thirds are dialogue and the dialogue is natural. *Døds-Spring til Hest Fra Cirkus-Kuplen*, for instance, only has 38 titles. It is only half as long as Nedbrudte Nerver, but the difference is still marked. Further, the speech that fills about a quarter of the titles in *Døds-Spring til Hest fra Cirkus-Kuplen* is not natural. It is rather a kind of summarised speech, in which the concrete text of the titles contains the content of what is said rather without being a direct transcription of the speech of the characters. Finally, the two films belong to different genres, comedy and melodrama, and the latter is more suited to fateful words. With a film like *Nedbrudte Nerver* silent film has reached the end of its capacity for expression, and can only wait for the talking picture, which naturally is better at expressing such forms. The film is not silent, it is without speech. It does not have written images, but is waiting for optical sound.

The speech of light

A further and for us more interesting development in Danish silent cinema as regards the written image is idealism. This is connected with the struggle of film to become respectable and the shadow of the Great War. These peace films and programmatic films such as, e.g., *Pax Æterna* (Holger Madsen, 1916) and *Himmelskibet* (Holger Madsen, 1918), attempt to allow the new medium to present a new utopian ideal. Both films are about the idea of creating peace and harmony in the world, in *Pax Æterna* by bring peoples together, in *Himmelskibet* by means of an expedition to Mars, where the locals' ideal society appears as an inspirational power for man.

In both films, Ole Olsen, managing director of Nordisk Films Kompagni, was himself involved in the manuscript. In connection with

Pax Æterna, he writes in his memoirs, *Filmens Eventyr og mit Eget*:

> Certainly, during the war everyone wanted peace fervently, not least Nord-isk Films, whose business had suffered a lot of damage in various countries. I aired the idea, which people have since been working with, that peace could come if the states of Europe united in a League. (p.114)

Apart from good business instincts, Olsen also saw the movies as an educational factor. He writes with the agenda of the day (1940) in mind that: "in the new world that will be created after the apocalypse that we are at present going through the film will take on an even greater mission than it has had to date, by spreading understanding and enlightenment over the entire earth" (p.169).

Ole Olsen's clever mixing of business and idealism was given a more aesthetic twist by Sophus Michaëlis, who wrote the prologue to *Pax Æterna* and co-wrote the manuscript of *Himmelskibet* with Olsen as well as the prologue to the film. Michaëlis saw a direct link between the potential of the medium and idealism. In the program for *Himmelskibet* he writes:

> Intellectually and spiritually, the Martians have advanced much further than Earthlings. They have found the language of unmediated expression, which reflects every thought in the mimicry expressions of the face, in the speaking naturalness of every outward movement [...] Writing is unknown, only the unmediated language of living images is.

And in an interview in *Berlingske Tidende* (21.12.1918), he says:

> Film can no longer be avoided. All the forces of Good should now unite to make it realise its potential as the greatest factor in international education in the modern age, sovereign in its national independence as music, but even more direct in the means it uses.

There is in these manifestos a dream of crossing the boundaries that are given by the disposition of the world and the subject as well as language. But here the medium becomes a means of achieving a utopian goal in contrast to the relationship in the doubled scene, where the scenes are reflected in the foundation and written image of the new perspective. It is a matter of two sides of the same coin to the extent that both forms pull toward an aesthetic resolution. But the forms are nevertheless different. The doubled scene expresses the demonic and the possessive aspect of the project, i.e., the aesthetic challenge that secularisation makes. The idealistic film invokes a romantic and elevated rationality that is intended to serve as a surrogate God – as it is put several places in the prologue to *Himmelskibet*: "The high almighty messenger of Love/is that radiant force you call God."

It is easy to poke fun at the naive well-wishing that flows out of *Pax Æterna* and *Himmelskibet*. In the prologue to *Pax Æterna*, we find:

> Den evige Fred! O, skælvende Haab!
> Paa Havet forstummer i Støn de Almægtiges Raab.
> Den evige *Fred* – Du *forjættede* Land!
> O, vis os, Fata Morgana, din palmevajende Strand! […]
> – Vi flyder om i Grave, i isopfyldte Have:
> der er som Vandet gurgler i vore egne Struber.

> Eternal Peace! Oh, trembling Hope!
> On the sea the roars of the Almighty ones fade to groans.
> Eternal *Peace* – you *promised* land!
> Oh, show us, Fata Morgana, your palm-waving strand! [...]
> – We float about in graves, in ice-filled seas:
> it is as if the water gurgles in our own throats.

The last verses may recall for later generations of Danes the famous Donald Duck song, "The sobbing seaman": "Oh, give me a grave/on the ice-green sea/... where only the waves hear me cry." (Sonja Rindom, 1952 – after Carl Barks).

Nor were his contemporaries blind to the naiveté. Although the age was rather cruel, words like the beginning of the prologue of *Himmelskibet* were too much to swallow, or rather, too airy:

> Hvad op vi bygged, slog vi ondt i Stykker
> – et Ragnarok hen over Jorden raser,
> Lemlæstet løfter Verden sine Krykker
> mod Himmelørkenens fjerne Freds-Oaser.

> What we built up, we evilly destroyed
> – an Apocalypse raged around the world,
> maimed, the world raises its crutches
> against the distant Peace oases of the heavenly desert.

Many contemporaries note that the idealistic beautification does not correspond to the concrete images. Thus, in *Filmen* No. 10, 1 March 1918, we read that:

> but there was no great victory, because script and direction – the body and soul of the film – somehow do not fit together. It was pulled in two directions. One part sought to raise it up into space, the other to create a kind of Martian realism in which only ideas held any interest for the writer.

Sophus Michaëlis seems to simply distance himself from the film in his subsequent 1921 novel of the same title, where he describes "Light plants".

> These living image tissues replaced books and were used in a visual instruction that required neither language nor writing, but spoke immediately via sight. In contrast to Earth, whose film images seem like a fantastic

197

toy, a living puppet theatre in which painted actors played comedy or tragedy, lyric zing for the edification of Hottentot brains, these image tissues were a natural theatre, where real life events were reflected as truly as those of the living. (p. 189)

There is a clear element of synesthesia in *Himmelskibet*. In words, song, music – there was a specified "Musical guide to the film" – the written word and living images, the aim was to evoke utopia as possible for the audience. To become part of a greater whole. The sensing body, split by the demands of the age, was to be unified again. The attempt did not get off the ground, but what remains is nevertheless the dream of a resolution on another plane. This is formulated by Charles Baudelaire, who worshipped Edgar Allan Poe, in *Les Fleurs du Mal* (1857) in his poem "Elevation" as a place where one effortlessly understands the language of flowers and silent objects: "comprend sans effort / Le langage des fleurs et des choses muettes!" But *Himmelskibet* did not make of the silent movie a "Light plant". The ideas anchored the film to the earth, and the film never really took off. At the same time a vain attempt was made to roar out and wake up the silent God and express His words through the imaginary power of living images.

Conclusion

Both the idealistic film and the films with the doubled scenes objectify for a mass audience in a medium, born out of secularisation a worldly striving to substitute the aesthetic for the religious. It is the challenge of the modern time, one that requires new forms and a new medium. But while the idealistic film attempts this by means of a rather airy reference to utopia, in our opinion the double scene is an ideal presentation of the modern. Things are connected by cog wheels and mirrors.

Both types of film play on the utopian, but the idealistic film refers to something that it is incapable of expressing, while the doubled scene expresses the expression itself expressly in the expression. The camera, the instrument of doubling records and stresses the double scene with its doubled actors in the frame of doubling. The mechanical reproduction calls forth the modern and modern man. It is a matter of a concrete objectivisation of something that cannot be mediated in the same way in words. A new medium is required.

Poe's words on reflections between object and subject, walled-up perspectives, the dream of being able to transcend out the perspective or escape from the frame and the text as a surface and textual game, all of it in a fateful frame, points to the technology and inventory of the silent movie. Poe has, perhaps better than the silent cinema, survived the ravages of time. The silent movie appears out-dated to many people today, in spite of the above mentioned modern perspective that we see in it.

Why the modern perspective within the modern perspective, in the medium of doubling, went out of fashion is a question to which we cannot offer a definitive answer. Perhaps part of the explanation lies in the fact that the new perspective became an integrated part of reality. Film in itself ceased to be a novelty at the same time as the secular perspective became an incarnate part of reality. Fiction and reality became in harmony with one another.

The silent cinema was quite literally talked to death, but in its own way before the talkie saw the light of day. A shift occurred from picture texts and written images to titles which clearly related the speech of the fictional characters. Hence the characters ceased being expressed merely in the surface and began to express themselves. With the sound cinema the senses were again united into something resembling reality, and the characters also took on a life that transcended the frame of the representation. The sense-less, which was the sphere of the silent movie, was brought brought to its senses, and it all ended in a petit bourgeois idyll.

But what remains is basically a series of forms that are still alive and filled with light. Not because they are seen or attributed artistic value. It is in fact no longer necessary for them to be seen by eyes out there in the real world. They themselves have eyes, and once created, they recreate themselves in an eternal repetition of automatic self-reflection and self-recording. Monstrous as Frankenstein's monster, but nevertheless shadows that ultimately achieves eternal light, which, even if God is dead, keeps moving. Created in the schism between the divine tale and the modern secular age, where the requirement is that man must be his own creator, and where man must regard himself as fictions, because the transcendental authority has gone. Fictions that create fictions, that are reflections of self-reflection, that with their form are freed so that they are autonomous as an unbound prosthesis with inscribed phantom pains of transcendental amputation.

Filmography

Afgrunden (*The Abyss*). Urban Gad, 1910.

Arvingen til Skjoldborg. Alfred Cohn, 1913.

Dødsangstens Maskespil (*Ablaze on the Ocean*). Eduard Schnedler-Sørensen, 1912.

Døds-Spring til Hest fra Cirkus-Kuplen (*A Fatal Decision*). Eduard Schnedler-Sørensen 1912.

Himmelskibet (*A trip to Mars*). Holger Madsen, 1918.

Nedbrudte Nerver (*Shattered Nerves*). Anders Wilhelm Sandberg, 1923.

Othello (*The Actor's Love-Story*). Martinius Nielsen, 1916.

Pax Æterna (*Pax Æterna or Peace on Earth*). Holger Madsen, 1916.

Pjerrot (*The Pierrot*). Hjalmar Davidsen, 1916.

Vampyr-Danserinden (*The Vampire Dancer*). August Blom, 1912.

Literature

Baudelaire, Charles (1857). *Les Fleurs de Mal*, Paris.

Michaëlis, Sophus (1921). *Himmelskibet*, Copenhagen: Gyldendal.

Olsen, Ole (1940). *Filmes Eventyr og Mit Eget*, Copenhagen: Jespersen og Pios Forlag.

"The pencil of nature. A New Discovery", in *The Corsair. A Gazette of Literature, Art, Dramatic Criticism, fashion and Novelty* Vol.1, no 5, 13 April 1839, http://www.daguerre.org/resource/texts/corsair.html (augusti 2002)

Poe, Edgar Allan (2000). *The Purloined Letter*, in *Tales & Sketches*. Volume 2: 1843–1849, Urbana & Chicago: University of Illinois Press.

Poe, Edgar Allan (2000). *The Tell-Tale Heart*, in *Tales & Sketches*. Volume 2: 1843–1849, Urbana & Chicago: University of Illinois Press.

Shelley, Mary (1993). *Frankenstein: Or The Modern Prometheus*, London: Wordsworth Editions Limited.

Shelley, Percy (1967). *Prometheus Unbound*, in *Poetical Works*, London: Oxford University Press.

Holy Shit!

Quentin Tarantino's Excremental Aesthetics

Claus Krogholm Sand

"Butch glances to his right, his eyes fall on something. What he sees
is a small compact Czech M61 submachine gun with a huge silencer
on it, lying on his kitchen counter.

BUTCH (softly): Holy shit.

He picks up the intimidating peace of weaponry and examines it.
Then... a toilet FLUSHES."[1]

THE WORD *SHIT* is used quite frequently in Quentin Tarantino's
Pulp Fiction (1994). In fact, it is used about 80 times during the film.[2]
The word is heard in the very first line of the film's prologue, even
before the first image is seen: "No, forget it, it's too risky. I'm through
doin' that shit" (p. 7). What Pumpkin (Tim Roth) is through doing is
robbing liquor stores. He is not giving up a life in crime. It is only that
robbing liquor stores has become too risky. So *shit* does not mean crime
as such. The question is, what does it mean?

Tarantino's films are often regarded aesthetically interesting but ethically problematic. The are seen as cynical, amoral, as glorifying violence, etc. Danish film critic Morten Piil often laments Tarantino's lack of morals. He sees Tarantino as cynically depicting violence without any moral or human context. Piil claims to be a skeptic who can see the talent (you only have to look), but he is repelled by the cynicism. Yet it takes more than eyes to recognize the talent or quality in a Tarantino film. It takes ears, too, even more so. What elevates Tarantino above the average Hollywood production is not so much the violence – which is much more explicit in many other films – but, rather, the dialogue. The amount of words in Tarantino's films is impressive. There is talking, chatting, disputing, quarreling and philosophizing – and there is moralizing in long, equilibristic chains of words. To recognize the quality of Tarantino's films one must listen to the words. Even the foul ones.

The accusation that the violence is depicted without any moral or human context is both right and wrong. Right, because there is often a lack of narrative motivation for the violence. In the average Hollywood film, the narrative motivation for the violence will be, that the initial use of violence, the crime, is a disturbance of the ruling order. The task of the hero is to re-establish order by fighting the initial violence with the violence of the law. Dirty Harry might be acting outside the law, but the violence is justified by the narrative of re-establishing order. The violence is not accidental or arbitrary. It is the necessary means in a narrative causality. The violence is motivated by a morality that is above the law.

This is not how violence works in Tarantino. There is no order that is violated. The law is more or less absent. The violent actions occur by accident, as when Vincent Vega (John Travolta) shoots Marvin in the head. The gun is fired and the issue discussed by Vincent and Jules (Samuel L. Jackson) is whether the car hit a bump in the road or not. And this is what the violence is all about: bumps in the road. The car functions literally as a "narrative vehicle" bringing the protagonists from action to action. But cars will crash, hit bumps in the road and so on. The narrative journey "hits bumps" time and again. This way the violence becomes arbitrary or contingent. Things happens *by accident* (Botting, 1998). The violence becomes a representation of a society marked by meaninglessness. It is society as a profane space, amorphous and contingent (Eliade 1993: 17). It is a society of accidental, sudden and violent death. But it is exactly the meaninglessness and contingency that is the subject of the frequent ethical considerations in Tarantino's films. It might be that the violence is blossoming in a moral void, because the action takes place in a society devoid of ethical content and values. But it does not take place without ethical reflection.

Shit is a word frequently used in *Pulp Fiction*. In the citation above, it appears in an interesting context, as *holy shit.* The contrast between the exalted – the *holy* – and the low, the abject – *shit* – is obvious. In the scene in the film it is followed by the sound of a toilet flushing, that points out how shit is normally perceived: as a waste product that is done away with. But here it is put in context with the sacred. The sacred and the profane point to the action that follows. Butch (Bruce Willis) shoots and kills Vincent. The two characters represent two different perspectives on *shit*.

The juxtaposition of the sacred and the excremental is not altogether paradoxical. In a certain sense, the two phenomena are even closely related. The opposition between the sacred and the profane is often considered as an opposition between the ecclesiastical and the secular, which is not necessarily correct. Rudolf Otto, in *Das Heilige* (*The Sacred*, 1917), proposed a notion of the sacred that was emptied of any connotations of good, of morals and the exalted. Rudolf Otto was concerned with the manifestation of the sacred. He claimed that the manifestation of the sacred – *hierophany* – was met with fear and a sense of terror – *mysterium tremendum*. Simultaneously, the sacred appears as a tremendous attraction to man – *mysterium fascinans*. This contradictory experience was labeled *the numinous* by Rudolf Otto (Eliade 1993: 7). Face to face with the numinous, man will feel his own being as a complete nothingness. The numinous is the radical Other – *Das ganz Anderes*. In the revelation of the sacred – *the hierophany* – there is not yet any difference between good and evil, exalted and abject, ecclesiastical and secular etc. Hierophany is a foundation of the world. It is the ontological constitution of the world, where a fixed ground is established, a center in the amorphous and indifferent space (as in Genesis). The establishing of a center becomes the basis for any succeeding orientation and thereby for the differentiation between good and evil, etc.

George Bataille tried to create a science of the radical Other, *heterology*. He considered other names such as *hagiology*, from *hagios* that can both mean defiled and sacred (analogous to the word *sacer* (french *sacré*) that means sacred, but also condemned, doomed, rejected). Or he would simply call it *scatology* – the science of the excremental (Bataille 1972: 200, note 47). This science should be concerned with the two types of social facts: 1) religious facts (prohibitions, commands and rules) and 2) profane facts (civil, political, legal). These two types correspond to two contradictory human drives: a) discharge, the excremental drives, the heterogenous, and b) accumulation, the political, legal and economical institutions, the homogenous (Bataille 1972: 295). The homogenous society is the productive and utilitarian society accumulating profit in a general economy. Any form of accumulation of, for instance, knowledge is productive for the homogenous society, in that the heterogenous elements threatening social stability are integrated and homogenized. You can talk of a profane heterogenity.

The homogenization of the heterogenous elements is not absolute, but the sign of an exclusion of the heterogenous from the social institutions (including the church). The proper heterogenous elements are thus deported to the religious sphere as *le part maudite* (the condemned part). This means that different heterogenous elements like excrements, corpses, perversion and religious ecstasy have a common ground: "The concept *foreign body* (heterogenous body) allow us to highlight the elementary *subjective* identity between the excrements (sperm, menstrual blood, urine, feces) and all that has been considered as sacred, divine or wonderful" (Bataille 1972: 296, my transl.). Freud notices the same phenomenon in his investigation of the concept of taboo. He, too, claims that there is no primordial difference between *sacred* and *unclean* (Freud 1981: 24). Freud observes that taboo has two contradictory meanings: on the one hand *sacred, consecrated* and on the other *uncanny* ("*unheimlich*"), *dangerous, prohibited, impure*. In his speculation on the origin of the social in the primal horde, Freud states that there are three fundamental taboos: on incest, murder and cannibalism. In the myth of the primal horde, the Father has a monopoly on women. The sons are therefore reduced to a (latent) homosexual relationship. The sons conspire to kill the Father, but after the deed they feel guilty. The Father is then exalted through a ritual, cannibalistic feast, where the Father is both incorporated and exalted as a moral institution – the Law. A social culture is thereby established, based on commands, prohibitions and rules: the taboo on incest – you should not marry women of the same tribe; the taboo on murder – to prevent a repetition of the killing of the Father; and the taboo on cannibalism – the incorporation of the Father. This becomes the foundation of the Name of the Father and the symbolic order (the homogenous). Jacques Lacan has pointed out that the Name of the Father – *Nom-de-Pere* – simultaneously is the "No" of the Father *Non-de-Pere*. The No that constitutes prohibitions and commands. Finally, as Slavoj Zizek has pointed out, the Father is a ambiguous figure. There is the exalted, dead Father. But he was, because of the monopoly on women, simultaneously the perverted father – *Pere-version*. This is the ambiguity between the sacred and consecrated on the one hand and the uncanny, dangerous and impure on the other.

You can claim that the main part of the heterogenous world is constituted by the sacred world and that the *heterogenous* things, that cannot be considered sacred in proper sense, bring about reactions similar to those the sacred things provoke. These reactions consist in that the *heterogenous* thing is supposed to be incorporating a unknown and dangerous force (like the Polynesian *mana*), and that a certain social prohibition on contact (*taboo*) is what separates it from the *homogenous* or common world (corresponding to the profane world's opposition to the strictly religious world). (Bataille 1994: 14, my transl.)

In *Pulp Fiction, shit* is such a heterogenous body floating between the sacred and the profane, thereby constituting a kind of *excremental ethics*. In the beginning of the film, Vincent shares his experience of Europe with Jules. The topics of conversation are Dutch hash bars and the French names for McDonald's burgers. As Vincent observes:

VINCENT: But you know what the funniest thing about Europe is?
JULES: What?
VINCENT: It's the little differences. A lotta the same shit we got here, they got there, but there they're a little different. (p. 14)

The difference between Europe and America is that it is *a little different*, but basically it is the *same shit*. It is about globalization and perhaps post-modernity. You will find McDonald's everywhere. Maybe a *quarterpounder* will be called something else, but the substance will be the same. It is all about the little differences, like *the metric system*. The difference is the unit of measurement, but substantially it is *the same shit*. It is the disenchanted modern world, characterized by contingency, nihilism and the loss of meaning. It is the homogenous society. What is left are the little differences in everyday life, such as the erotic-moral significance of foot massage.

VINCENT: You don't be givin' Marsellus Wallace's new bride a foot massage.

JULES: You don't think he overreacted?

VINCENT: Antwan probably didn't expect Marsellus to react like he did, but he had to expect a reaction.

JULES: It was a foot massage, a foot massage is nothing, I give my mother a foot massage.

VINCENT: It's laying hands on Marsellus Wallace's new wife in a familiar way. Is it as bad as eatin' her pussy out? No, but you're in the same fuckin' ballpark.

Jules stops Vincent.

JULES: Whoa… whoa… whoa… stop right there. Eatin' a bitch out, and givin' a bitch a foot massage ain't even the same fuckin' thing.

VINCENT: Not the same thing, the same ballpark.

JULES: It ain't no ballpark either. Look, maybe your method of massage differs from mine, but touchin' his lady's feet, and stickin' your tongue in her holiest of holies, ain't the same ballpark, ain't the same league, ain't even the same fuckin' sport. Foot massages don't mean shit.

VINCENT: Have you ever given a foot massage?

JULES: Don't be tellin' me about foot massages – I'm the fuckin' foot master.

VINCENT: Given a lot of 'em?

JULES: Shit yeah. I got my technique down man, I don't tickle or nothin'.

VINCENT: Have you ever given a guy a foot massage?

Jules looks at him a long moment – he's been set up.

JULES: Fuck you. (p. 20–21)

Jules has been set up. Foot massage is not insignificant (*don't mean shit*). There is a difference, and it is an ethical difference. *It's laying hands on Marsellus Wallace's new wife in a familiar way* – which is a transgression of certain ethical norms. The Big Man's wife is taboo. Antwan *should* expect Marsellus to react (although not necessarily expect to be thrown out from a third floor window). *Shit* does make a difference. It is a difference belonging to the practice of profane everyday life.

It is a completely different story in what is perhaps the most crucial scene in the film. Again *shit* makes a difference, but in quite a different way. Jules and Vincent have executed the men who had tried to cheat Marsellus Wallace. But a fourth man has been hiding in the toilet (again the toilet is a significant place). He fires his gun at them, but, miraculously, no one is hit.

> JULES: We should be fuckin' dead!
> VINCENT: Yeah, we were lucky.
> *Jules rises, moving toward Vincent.*
> JULES: That shit wasn't luck. That shit was somethin' else.
> *Vincent prepares to leave.*
> VINCENT: Yeah, maybe.
> JULES: That was… divine intervention. You know what divine intervention is?
> VINCENT: Yeah, I think so. That means God came down from Heaven and stopped the bullets.
> JULES: Yeah, man, that's what is means. That's exactly what it means! God came down from Heaven and stopped the bullets.
> VINCENT: I think we should be going now.
> JULES: Don't do that! Don't you fuckin' do that! Don't blow this shit off! What just happened was a fuckin' miracle!
> VINCENT: Chill the fuck out, Jules, this shit happens.
> JULES: Wrong, wrong, this shit doesn't just happen. (p. 137–139)

This is not a question of little differences. It is not *the same ballpark*. Shit represents – in Jules' eyes – the radical Other – *that shit was somethin' else*. The question is whether shit is contingent or arbitrary – *this shit happens* – or an act of divine intervention – *holy shit*, the radical Other or heterogenous. For Jules, the event will be an epiphany – "I had what alcoholics refer to as a 'moment of clarity'." (p. 175) – a revelation that will have radical consequences for his future existence.

> JULES: What's an act of God?
> VINCENT: I guess it's when God makes the impossible possible. And I'm sorry Jules, but I don't think what happened this morning qualifies.
> JULES: Don't you see, Vince, that shit don't matter. You're judging this thing the wrong way. It's not about what. It could be God stopped the bullets, he changed Coke into Pepsi, he found my fuckin' car keys. You don't judge shit like this based on merit. Whether or not what we experienced was an according-to-Hoyle miracle is insignificant. What is significant is I felt God's touch, God got involved. (p. 172–173)

His whole existential ground will shift from profane to sacred. It is a kind of "death" and "rebirth". In a certain sense, the bullets have killed Jules. That is why he is talking about "quitting the life" (p. 173). After that, he will "walk the earth … until God puts me where he wants me to be" (p. 173–74). It is a retirement from the profane, contingent life. Jules puts his life in the hands of God in a sacred, determined existence. He is in a void, but it is not the disenchanted, meaningless world. He is on his way into a new space. He does not know where but is convinced there is an intention behind what happens. Mircea Eliade talks about an "ontological homesickness" (Eliade 1993: 76), a kind of contrast to what George Lukács has found characteristically of the modern, profane world: the transcendental homelessness (Lukács, 1994).

Jules is in a transitional phase, which will show in two ways. Again *shit* will make a difference. After all the trouble, Jules and Vincent are having breakfast at a diner. Vincent is offering Jules a sausage, but Jules says no thanks, referring to the fact that he does not eat pork: "Pigs sleep and root in shit. That's a filthy animal. I don't wanna eat nothin' that ain't got enough sense to disregard its own feces" (p. 171). It is not a question of religious conviction ("I ain't Jewish"), but can be related to a differentiation between what is pure (the inner) and filthy. The body is a threshold between inner and exterior. This threshold is a symbolic representation of the boundary between the sacred and the profane space (Eliade 1993: 18). A little later, Jules is referring explicitly to the transitional phase when he is confronting Pumpkin and Honey Bunny:

> JULES: Now this is the situation. Normally both of your asses would be dead as fuckin' fried chicken. But you happened to pull this shit while I'm in *a transitional period*. I don't wanna kill ya, I want to help ya. But I'm afraid I can't give you the case. It don't belong to me. Besides, I went through too much shit this morning on account of this case to just hand it over to your ass. (p. 183, emphasis added).

Because *this shit* happens while Jules is in *a transitional period*, Pumpkin and Honey Bunny are saved. The accidental and contingent – *happened* – is suspended and will not have the consequences it would were it to occur in the profane space: a sudden and violent death.

In Butch' (Bruce Willis) story, it is again the contingency that is thematized. After having cheated Marsellus Wallace in a fixed fight, Butch is escaping in a cab. He is conversing with the female cab-driver:

> BUTCH: …Esmarelda Villalobos – is that Mexican?
> ESMARELDA: The name is Spanish, but I'm Columbian.
> BUTCH: It's a very pretty name.
> ESMARELDA: It mean "Esmarelda of the wolves."
> BUTCH: That's one hell of a name you got there, sister.
> ESMARELDA: Thank you. And what is your name?
> BUTCH: Butch.
> ESMARELDA: Butch. What does it mean?

BUTCH: I'm an American, our names don't mean *shit*. (p.93–94, emphasis added)

Where Europe and the United States were characterized by the *same shit*, there is a difference between American and Hispanic names. The American name does not mean anything, it is contingent. As it turns out, this is, after all, not true in this case. Butch' name does in fact mean something. Rather, it is the name of the father, that means something. This is revealed in the story of Butch's ancestors. A watch has been passed on from father to son through generations. It is a special watch – a *war watch* – that is supposed to bring luck. In reality, the forefathers all died in war. Butch's father wore the watch in Vietnam, where he was a prisoner of war, and he had to hide the watch in his rectum. As a consequence of this, he died from dysentery. The watch was then passed on to Butch by Captain Koons, who took on the task of fulfilling the father's last will: "I hid this uncomfortable hunk of metal up my ass for two years" (p. 86). Here the paradoxical juxtaposition of waste and value becomes explicit. Gold (watch) and feces are one and the same, as Freud pointed out in the anal economy of drives (Freud, 1955). To Butch, the watch is a sacred object, while at the same time it is in a certain sense *a piece of shit* (both literally because it has been hidden in the rectum and symbolically because it did not bring his ancestors luck in war). For the honor of his ancestors, however, he is willing to risk his own life to secure the watch. His code of honor even compels him to save his deadly enemy Marsellus Wallace from his destiny: anal rape. The weapon Butch chooses is significant for his code of honor. It is a samurai sword. Like the samurai, he neglects his own interests in the service of the warlord.

Vincent is the only one who remains in the profane space. This is what will determine his faith. He is the only protagonist who dies. This destiny has in a way been indicated when he tells his dealer Lance about his car. Someone keyed it: "I had the goddamn thing in storage for three years. It's out five fuckin' days – five days, and some worthless piece of shit fucks with it" (p. 42). Vincent is talking about a *worthless piece of shit*, in contrast to the *piece of shit* we saw in Butch' story: the watch that was not worthless, but a sacred *piece of shit*. In Vincent's universe there are no such values. It is a profane and contingent universe. But it is characteristic of the disenchanted world that there are private, sacred spaces (Eliade 1953: 17). As we have seen, Vincent has his own ethics of every day life, concerning foot massage and the boss' wife, for instance. But this is not an ethic that will form a foundation for a human, social sense of community. Vincent's ethical concerns are first and foremost centered upon his own survival. His own private sacred space, where he withdraws when ethical questions are bothering him, is the toilet. Three times he withdraws to the toilet. The first time is when he has taken Marsellus' wife Mia (Uma Thurman) out. When they return to Marsellus' house, Vincent retreats to the toilet to have a moral conversation with himself: "it's a moral test of yourself, whether or not you can maintain loyalty. Because when people are loyal to each other, that's very meaningful" (p. 69). Vincent's loyalty is in a sense concerned mainly with the name of the Father – Marsellus Wallace. It is significant that this chapter is called "Vincent Vega and Marsellus Wallace's wife" and not "Vincent and Mia". She is "the big man's wife" (p. 22), and as such, she is taboo. This is why you cannot even touch her feet "in a familiar way".

The second time Vincent withdraws to the toilet is after Jules' revelation and conversion, where they are discussing the existence of miracles. In a certain sense, it is once again the name of the father that is troubling Vincent. This time it is not the profane father (Marsellus), but the Holy Father:

VINCENT: Stop fuckin' talkin' like that!
JULES: If you find my answers frightening, Vincent, you should cease askin' scary questions.
VINCENT: I gotta take a shit. To be continued.
Vincent exits for the restroom. (p. 174–175)

Confronted with the sacred and numinous, Vincent retreats. The sacred is precisely terrifying – *mysterium tremendum*. Vincent's reaction is a withdrawal to the homogenous, where the heterogenous body can be expelled ("I gotta take a shit"). It is the same reaction when he was tempted by Mia to violate the taboo and the name of the father. "I'm gonna take a piss" (p. 67), Vincent explains before he goes to the toilet to morally pull himself together and go home without touching Mia.

Finally there is the last and fatal withdrawal to the toilet, when Vincent will stand face to face with Butch. Vincent's faith corresponds to his moral conviction: *shit happens*. It is a sudden and violent death, if not released by a bump in the road, then by Pop Tarts popping from the toaster. There is some ambiguity to what happens. Vincent dies a violent, arbitrary death – a profane death. At the same time, however, it is the violent break-in of the heterogenous in the homogenous space that kills Vincent. The violence is not homogenized. The violence is not a re-establishing of order motivated by the narrative. The violence is contingent and meaningless when seen in the optics of a profane ethic. However, seen from another angle, as Jules will do, the violence is the heterogenous ("that shit was somethin' else"). It is the sacred manifesting itself as an abyss in the profane, disenchanted space. There is an emphatic manifestation of the heterogenous when Vincent accidentally shoots Marvin in the head. Jules is already agitated by the miracle that they were not killed in the apartment. With Marvin's body in the backseat, they are really in a foreign space: The Valley where Marsellus does not have any "friendly places". Simultaneously, however, the Valley is the way to the kingdom of death – *The Valley of Death*. Jules' conversion will have him re-evaluating the biblical passage – Ezekiel 25:17 – he used to recite before liquidating his opponents. Part of the passage goes like this: "Blessed is he who, in the name of charity and good will, shepherds the weak through *the valley* of darkness. For he is truly his brother's keeper and the finder of lost children" (p. 186). After the events he has been through – the *hierophany* – he has realised: "I saw some shit this mornin' made me think twice. […] I'm the tyranny of evil men. But I'm tryin'. I'm tryin' real hard to be a shepherd" (p. 187). He did not succeed in bringing Marvin safely through the valley. But Marvin's violent death – the break-in of the heterogenous in the profane space – has convinced him he should try to be the shepherd – *his brother's keeper and the finder of lost children*. It is an ethical choice that will constitute a social community. So there is a moral sense that is both olfactory and tactile. *Shit* does make a difference.

---

1 Quentin Tarantino: *Pulp Fiction* (1994), p. 117. References to the publiced manuscript.
2 That is not as often as fuck that is used about 160 times (in constellations like *fuck*, *fuckin'*, *motherfucker* and so on).

Literature

Bataille, Georges (1972). "D.A.F. de Sades brugsværdi", In *Den indre erfaring.* Copenhagen: Rhodos, pp. 289–308.

Bataille, Georges (1994). "Fascismens psykologiske struktur", In René Rasmussen & Asger Sørensen (eds.), *Excesser: Af og om Georges Bataille.* Århus: Forlaget Modtryk, pp. 9–34.

Botting, Fred & Scott Wilson (1998). "By Accident: The Tarantinian Ethics". *Theory, Culture & Society,* vol. 15, nr. 2, pp. 89–113.

Davis, Todd F. & Kenneth Womack (1998). "Shepherding the Weak: The Ethics of Redemption in Quentin Tarantino's *Pulp Fiction*". *Literature/Film Quarterly,* vol. 26, nr. 1, pp. 60–66.

Eliade, Mircea (1993). *Helligt og profant: Om religionens væsen,* Peter Thielst trans, Copenhagen: Det lille Forlag, 2nd ed.

Freud, Sigmund (1981 [1912–13]): "Totem and Taboo: Some Points of Agreement between the Mental Lives of Savages and Neurotics". In *The Standard Edition of the Complete Psychological Works of Sigmund Freud,* vol. XIII, London: The Hogarth Press.

Freud, Sigmund (1955 [1917]): "On Transformations of Instinct as Exemplified in Anal Erotism". In *The Standard Edition of the Complete Psychological Works of Sigmund Freud,* vol. XVII, London: The Hogarth Press.

Kristiansen, Claus Krogholm (1996). "'A Wax Museum with a Pulse': Om repræsentationsproblematikken hos Godard og Tarantino", In *Alebu: Tidsskrift for danskfaget,* vol. 2, nr. 3, pp. 52–74.

Lukács, George (1994). *Romanens teori: Et historiefilosofisk essay om den store epiks former,* Rolf Reitan trans., Århus: Klim.

Tarantino, Quentin (1994). *Pulp Fiction: Three Stories about one Story,* London: Faber and Faber.

Willis, Sharon (1993). "The Father's Watch the Boys Room". *Camera Obscura,* nr. 32.

Taste as a matter of pedagogical concern

Helle Brønnum Carlsen

TASTE IS ONE of the body's five senses. However, taste also refers to a larger system, where intersubjective values and understandings structure the validity of a judgement. This common intersubjective understanding is not private, as is physiological taste, nor is it unchangeable. Rather it changes due to a sociological framework. The position of the subject in historical, cultural and social structures is decisive for the general preferences of taste which are established during our lifetime, but especially in childhood. None of these kinds of taste can be distinguished in our relation to food. Whereas physiological taste gives the condition of registering a taste, sociological taste frames the communication through food and meals, and the aesthetic taste constructs the very content in the communication by being interrelational. In this way, the aesthetic work of food is a specific kind of communication explained by sociology and understood by philosophy. This affects the way we think of food in education, how we construct our aesthetic experiences and how the choices we make are influenced by these experiences.

To identify some of the factors involved in planning educational and general work on food and meals, this model can help us in sorting out the different aspects of the construction of aesthetic experience.

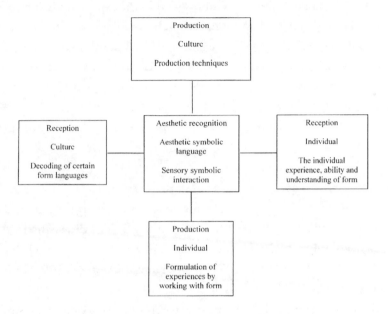

Figure 1. Aesthetic interaction as a basis for aesthetic learning. Adapted from Hohr (1994: 181).

The vertical axis is connected to the immediate experience (*Erlebnis*) where the individual experiences from his or her own position based on prior experience (*Erfahrung*), which will always will be embedded in the existing culture that limits and evaluates what is to be accepted as food in socio-cultural terms. The horizontal axis is connected to the expression, from which point of view one could discuss the didactical question of creativity. In a certain culture, people learn to produce and develop certain ways of food. In everyday language, this competence is often called "how to cook", and if the individual is able to express itself in an aesthetic communication, it presumes certain knowledge of those techniques practised in food preparation. Through the experience, the fantasy is developed, the techniques give the possibility to express the result of the fantasy, and the symbols used in the expression is summed up in the aesthetic language of taste. The aesthetic consciousness is not established by scientific language and analyses, but through work based on senses. But the process goes much further than that. The aesthetic consciousness works in the tension between the individual as sensing and symbol-creating person, and the cultural and historical horizon, which also draws our patterns of life influenced by the ways of production.

Sense, pleasure, and aesthetic experience

In this article, I highlight the problems involved in placing the experience of taste – if this is at all possible – within the field of the aesthetic. As background, I use Carolyn Korsmeyer's *Making Sense of Taste* (1999), but I shall also include my earlier research into the aesthetic recognition as a sensory interaction (Carlsen 2000: 204).

Before confronting the main issue, we must step back and consider how the different senses have been perceived over the last few centuries. These perceptions still influence the philosophical way of interpreting the five different senses, and the experiences resulting from this. These historical leftovers still influence our mode of understanding and are deeply embedded in our frameworks of organising our experiences of the senses.

The next step will be a mapping of the phenomenology of taste (understanding taste as the sense and not the abstract metaphor deriving from philosophers of the 18th century). This will encompass some scientific reflections on the sense of taste; where anthropological and sociological studies will help us in understanding the difference between the aesthetic features of food and/or drink on the one hand, and the sensual pleasure often experienced in the gustatory taste, on the other.

Finally, I shall elaborate on which aesthetic value should be attached to the experience of taste. I shall develop the thesis set out by Korsmeyer (1999), that foods qualify as symbolic and meaningful because they are representational and expressive. These categories have been taken from Nelson Goodman's *Languages of Art* (1967), and even though Goodman did not reflect on food at all, several of his symptoms of the aesthetic apply to food and help us in finding the symbolic significance in it. What I will do is to consider the aesthetic from a cognitive perspective, as this puts us in a position from which the aesthetic appreciation "requires a certain understanding and insight that constitute aspects of the pleasure they deliver" (Korsmeyer 1999: 6).

The sense of taste and its hierarchy

First of all, we must be prepared to accept that the sense of taste is two-directional, pointing both in the direction of the subjects who do the tasting and in the direction of the objects being tasted. In everyday discussion – and unconsciously accepted as historically factual – any references to the sense of taste and to the senses in general are focused on the subject who senses.

Furthermore, we in the Western tradition have based our hierarchy of the senses upon the rankings established by Plato and Aristotle. Since this is deeply rooted in our frames of concept, and responsible for our experiences of the senses, we cannot just ignore or dismiss this hierarchy. We must investigate it, and then try to develop from it whatever can be fitted into a late modern theory, in order to understand the world of the senses through philosophy.

Briefly stated, the ancient and still-functional hierarchy divided the five senses into two categories. The lower senses: touch, taste and smell, were opposed to the higher senses: sight and hearing. The former require direct contact with the object to be sensed, whereas the latter function at a distance. Since Plato thought the intellectual soul to be immortal and rational, it was the divine part of the human, and accordingly the distance senses were the ones that could provide objective information and reflection – in other words, the cognitive senses. The lower, bodily senses were – like the flesh and the demanding soul – unreliable and mortal, and linked to desire and pleasure. They had to be tamed. Nevertheless, Plato developed a huge list of basic tastes, which referred to the very physiological result of the sense of taste. But the lower bodily senses never had any essential influence on the intellectual soul. Aristotle was somewhat more human (neither so realistic nor so strict) and pragmatic. He admitted the need of both a soul and a body. But he still regarded the distance senses as the highest, as the cognitive senses, and therefore more important. For Aristotle, the sensuous pleasures could be a fulfilling part of a good life, but they still had to be controlled. He was the first to see differences between the two pleasures resulting from either the bodily senses or the intellectual senses. Without using the exact words, he studied disinterested pleasure and sensuous pleasure, the latter, of course, being the lowest. In modern philosophy, this concept subsequently became one of the cornerstones in differentiating between the beautiful and the pleasant.

Even though all five senses are established in time and place, the information delivered from sight and hearing has been bound up in a mutual language which qualifies it as logic. But the distance senses are expressed in a symbolic language, as are the bodily senses. As senses, they are – all five – not detached from time and place, and it is therefore tempting to seek out a theoretical understanding of the distance senses in philosophy, to afford some help in expanding the understanding of – in this case – the sense of taste. As Korsmeyer puts it: "The sense of taste has long provided a provocative comparison for theories of aesthetic perception and discrimination of artistic qualities" (Korsmeyer 1999: 4). Korsmeyer argues that certain parallels between food preparation and artistic creativity make aesthetic theory relevant for the understanding of taste, eating, and food.

We need a mutual language and a common frame of reference from which we can understand the sense of taste theoretically. The further development of the aesthetic in the 18th century did not open the doors for the bodily senses. On the contrary, these doors were closed even more by the distinction between aesthetic and non-aesthetic senses. Taste was now both a literal gustatory taste – being non-aesthetic – and an analogical metaphorical and aesthetic taste which referred to the ability to discriminate. Nevertheless, the gustatory taste is the metaphoric basis for the aesthetic taste, and in some respects they work the same way: (1) they both require individual experiences, they need to be experienced; (2) their objects have to be "tasted" before being judged, and (3) they are both bound up with pleasure or disgust. But from Kant's pinpointing the disinterested pleasure as a criterion for aesthetic theories, the literal taste has a problem of existence within the theory. Eating is obviously a practical activity connected to intimate interests. The interest of hunger will never release the pleasure of desire. Literal taste was left; in theory, it appeared an uninteresting act.

Hegel introduces a further division between the senses, writing about the theoretical and practical methods of perception. Since art to him had to be persistent, food was almost the lowest object perceptible, as it had to be destroyed to be tasted. Hegel makes the connection between the aesthetic senses and the artistic senses, maintaining the demand of the other Enlightenment philosophers for aesthetic perception to be universal. What must not be forgotten in this understanding is the ideology behind the Enlightenment philosophy. Today this Enlightenment project can be seen to manifest a set of social presumptions and exigencies peculiar to its time, and many contemporary critics, e.g. Terry Eagleton, have interpreted philosophies of Taste sceptically as components of the historical developments of class interest. I shall not elaborate on Pierre Bourdieu, who wrote his criticism in *Distinction: A Social Critique of the Judgement of Taste* (Bourdieu, 1979), where he most unusually rejects the qualitative distinction between literal and aesthetic taste. But even though his attack has been useful, and his criticism of a certain class-interest expressed in classical philosophy has been necessary, he makes several important mistakes. As Korsmeyer observes (Korsmeyer 1999: 64), Bourdieu assumes a correlation between universality and philosophical interests, and he implies that philosophy in general is a groundless enterprise based on the fiction of pure contemplative inquiry. He furthermore invents a concept of the aesthetics of the necessary, which is expressed by working-class people. He expects this concept to be backed up by a search for healthy and nourishing food, instead of the refined search for upper-class status symbols (Bourdieu 1979). Unfortunately, the so-called lower-classes have not shown themselves to have chosen from this point of necessity, and general investigations into eating habits show us that those eating the poorest food – with regard to health and nourishment – are the lower-classes. They are the only ones buying the instant powder-puddings, and they are not the ones preparing celery and other basic foods. This might just be one result of Bourdieu throwing the literal and the aesthetic taste into the same pot without arguing for the aesthetic value of food. Bourdieu makes taste a sociological way of eating, and leaves the prejudices untouched.

Although Bourdieu has had great influence, his failure to make a sociological statement points to the necessity of elaborating a map of phenomenology of taste, if not a Philosophy of taste.

While taste throughout history has been pushed further and further away from the fields of philosophy, it has gained more and more interest in other scientific studies. Both within the genre of cookbooks and anthropological or sociological studies on food, eating habits, etc., food is taken very seriously – whereas the sense of taste is left without any noteworthy interest within philosophy, literature and art.

Brillat-Savarin (1825), being one of the first gastronomic journalists in European writing, is always mentioned in this connection, because he argued for the sense of taste as a serious matter in our way of confronting the world. He observed that in gastronomy, the sense of taste, preparing and eating food, are components of a civilising power that brings people together and keeps them together.

The factors involved in the taste experience

First of all, we find the bodily factors universally determined in the individual. We utilize all three senses connected to the body – smell, touch and taste – to do the tasting, and this has been used as an argument for the low-level status of these senses. Strictly speaking, however, the actual sensing of taste takes place in the mouth, on the tongue.

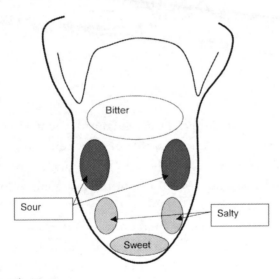

Figure 2. The Tongue.

In the papillae on the tongue we find the taste buds, looking more or less like an onion, with each bud containing between 50 and 150 taste receptors.

225

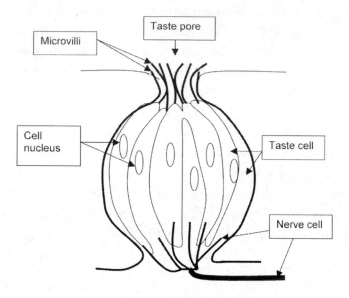

Figure 3. The taste bud.

It is possible to draw a rather precise map of the tongue and its papillae, where each taste receptor cell is capable of responding to more than one class of stimulus. Moreover, the stimuli for any one of the four classic taste modalities (sweet, sour, salty, bitter) may come from several different types of chemicals.

At the molecular level, taste is quite similar to our other senses. A gustatory stimulus activates a taste receptor cell, which in turn conveys the message to a sensory neuron. A nerve impulse then relays the message to the gustatory centres of the brain, where it registers as a taste (McLaughlin 1994: 538). The shape of a molecule that stimulates taste determines which taste modality it stimulates.

Sensorians (people working scientifically with the flavours and taste), could take over here and map out more than 300 possible taste nuances in a carrot. The interesting point here is the validity of what is derived through the sense of taste. The scientific mapping of what happens when we taste is not a basis for the philosophy of the aesthetics. We have no need to know what is going on in our cells and biochemistry to develop the theory which I will discuss on the pages that follow. However, the capacity to taste is required in order for us to be aware of the existence of taste.

For centuries, scholars have debated whether or not there were only four taste modalities. At the end of the 16th century, one finds a description of nine basic tastes, and this number increased in the following century. For the descriptive taste categories used today, we operate with the well-known four. These four taste modalities should not be confused with the hundreds of "flavours", which reflect the blending of modalities. A flavour, strawberry for instance, is a particular type of blending, either natural or chemical. The mixing of flavours can be compared to the mixing of colours, whereas this cannot be done with the four modalities of taste (Levinson 1995: 14). At present, scientific knowledge on taste modalities still leaves many questions unanswered, but research has shown that salt and sour work in the membrane of the cell, as the act of receiving and translating the sensory information to a useful signal for the nervous system involves the direct interaction of the sodium ion or hydrogen ion in the cell membrane. I will not try to teach biochemistry here. It is only to show how simple the transduction (the receiving and translating process) looks for salt $(Na+)$ and sour $(H+)$, compared to the complex process involving cell surface receptors and messenger molecules when bitter and sweet are registered at the tongue. Bitter-taste stimuli are the most chemically diverse of all the taste-modalities (McLaughlin 1994: 541). But understanding this diversity is, of course, a job for a physiologist. Very rarely are the isolated tastes found in real life, but the four taste modalities are those that can be registered as categories, although containing many differences within the same category. Just think of lime, lemon and orange. They are all sour, but not the same kind of sour. It is not customary to utilize a wide vocabulary for the tastes of the food we eat, but oenologists and sensorians have developed a very specific vocabulary to enlarge our awareness of tastes.

In this way, we use the chemistry embedded in accumulated experience (*Erfahrung*), sensorian science, food science, craft, etc. to acquire special taste expressions influenced by the social, anthropological, the cultural and the individual. It is precisely this relationship that I shall approach from a philosophical point of view, in order to discover the aesthetic possibilities in tasting and using food.

The science of taste is thus more than the experience of taste registered by the receptors of the tongue. However, this aspect – neglected by Philosophy – is definitely an important part of the experience as a whole. One might say that the experience of taste is both the *experience* of taste and the experience of *taste*. So far, we have investigated the former. When we emphasise the experience, all the senses are working together, resulting in a broad gastronomic pleasure, as Brillat-Savarin, for example, tried to explain with his three disparate descriptions of the "full taste": the direct, the complete, and the reflective senses (Brillat-Savarin 1986: 64). Later on, Roland Barthes mapped the interpretation of the perception, but the key problem seems to be that reflection about the experience of senses involves confronting some philosophical issues (Barthes 1997).

One of the most well-known of these issues is that we do not taste in the same way. We are physiologically different – only 20% of us are super-tasters (Levenson 1995: 13). Some of us register the bitter taste of phenylthiocarbamid (ptc) in the cabbage types – especially broccoli – very clearly, whereas others hardly notice. On the other hand, it would appear to be proven that genetically we all prefer the sweet, and to a lesser degree the salt. We can identify universal similarities in our experience of taste, but our biological needs and preferences are rudimentary as compared to other influences. As the anthropologists and sociologists have shown, the cultural factors seem to be of considerably greater influence in our choice of food, music, art, etc. This is incompatible with scientifically seeking after the determinants of taste. Our experience of taste is indeed influenced by our knowledge of what we are eating. The pure form is not enough to describe the complexity of an experience of taste, and this is why the sensorians are very useful and indeed necessary, but inadequate in their mapping of flavours and the function of the tongue. By eliminating the experience of taste, the information on what is tasted can be scientifically relevant. As soon as this aim has been achieved, however, the purity disturbs the totality of the aesthetic experience. How knowledge and cultural preferences are powerful influences can be illustrated by an experience I myself had recently.

I had been invited to visit Bordeaux. Included with the visit was an overnight stay at a château producing wine. I was fortunate to be staying in one of the best châteaux in the Pomerol district. I had dinner with the family, who were very friendly and very committed to the production of a small – but excellent – quantity of Pomerol wine. To show me the best of the region, they had also prepared a typical Bordeaux meal, and I was served a starter which looked more or less like eel in red wine – a famous French dish. The family – and especially the dynamic slim-line lady who was the wine-producer in person – looked happy to serve me this, and to eat it themselves. I confronted the dish with an open mind and used my pure taste to find out if I liked it. The texture of the eel was a little too much like rubber, and the fish had a peculiar vapid or flat taste, but the sour taste of the red wine sauce helped. I encountered some small, dark lumps in the sauce, but somehow I felt it best to ignore them. The next day I was told what I had eaten. It was a speciality of Bordeaux. At the mouth of the Garonne River as it flows into the Atlantic Ocean lives an enormous leech. A leech is not a vertebrate but much lower in the zoological scale, belonging to the analides (the worms). This leech is killed, scraped to remove the slime, and the blood it has sucked from other water-animals is stored in a bowl. Then the leech is cut in pieces and boiled in red wine, and this wine sauce is thickened with its own blood. I have never felt the need to vomit because of something I have eaten, but I did now. It was definitely not the sensorious taste that gave me the disgust, but the later information about what I had really eaten. It is also an example of the culturally different taboos, which Norbert Elias and Stephen Mennell have written about in their investigations of our history of mentality in European civilization (Elias 1980; Mennell 1985). I must add that in the airport at Bordeaux I saw a small jar of this self-same leech in blood-sauce, at a price of 125 Franc for about the same amount that I had eaten.

The phenomenology of taste

The pleasure in eating is more complex than the pleasures in tasting, and often it is knowledge that makes the difference. The knowledge might be wrong; our perception of what we eat can mislead us, just as I thought it to be eel instead of leech. But I still gave it a name. I didn't just taste this dish and think of the taste alone. I accepted the so-called eel and judged the taste of what I had incorrectly perceived it to be. It is rather difficult to change one's taste and preferences established in the early years. The changing of one's taste is not just a change of one's feeling pleasure or disgust, but also of one's being embedded in a culture. Tastes are acquired both within a society and between cultures (Korsmeyer 1999: 93).

The standpoint for a pedagogical approach could be suitably located here. We are able to expand our taste and preferences, and the more we challenge the taste and tastes, the more we learn to make refined distinctions between foods which used to appear the same to us. What makes taste much more than a biological sense or a chemical sense is the unique human ability to – with experience and attention – let the taste emerge on our own tongues. The human education of the palate. This is also seen in the consequences. All animals eat, but only humans develop cuisines.

That is why writing on food exists: reflecting what we eat, when we eat it, and why we eat it. Here there could be a connection to a philosophical system, but to take this a further step we need to give structure to the taste, and to examine the different elements participating in the experience of taste.

I shall now draw a mental map of the function of taste, and also of the object for consumption – because one of the usual errors in talking about taste lies in the one-sided focus on the subject, without consideration of the object.

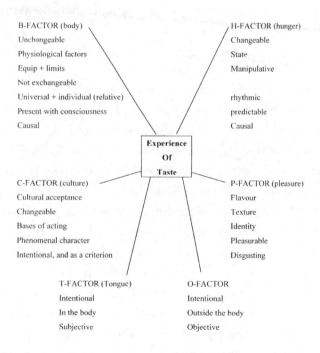

Figure 4. Factors affecting the experience of taste. Adapted from Korsmeyer (1999: 94).

The O- and the T-factors are two related aspects. Taste is therefore an intentional activity – a conscious act directed towards some kind of object.

With the argument that taste is only subjective, one could consider the above model as maintaining that taste is both subjective and objective, i.e. the attention is directed towards an object. The subjectivity of taste is correctly understood, as it has to do with the condition of the subject (the T-factor, B-factor and H-factor), just as one could regard the P-factor as an adjunct to the T- or C-factors: I like it because of the pleasure at my tongue (e.g. sweet), or it i is disgusting to my cultural taste (e.g. leech).

Taste is not only subjective, telling us about the subject doing the tasting. It also concerns the relation between subject and object. When we taste, we learn about the world. My example from Bordeaux refers to a T-factor becoming revolting, because O's identity was recognized as unacceptable within C.

The model could be set in relation to the aforementioned model. The establishing of the aesthetic symbolic language for which I have argued takes place in the interaction where the sense is directed intentionally towards an object. Here it will also be possible for taste to convey meaning, thus having a cognitive dimension. Foods function in symbolic systems, as shown by my elaboration of Hansjörg Hohr's model – symbolic systems that extend from the ritual ceremonies of religion to the everyday choice of breakfast. But it is not in the study of cultures that the philosophical point of view is placed (by anthropologists, sociologists etc.), nor in the individual understanding of form (by gastronomers, sensorians), but in the relationship where the intentionality establishes symbols – aesthetic symbols to be used in an aesthetic language, totally different from the discursive, analytical language. If theorists had been more considerate in allowing the cognitive and complex elements of taste to expand, the gustatory and the aesthetic tastes might have become closer.

Since I have claimed that taste possesses an objective component as well, I shall, finally, review some of the aesthetic possibilities it affords. The scientific studies of taste fail to understand the perceptions reflected in the cultural prejudices and the object of the taste. Preferences of taste indeed share a common base; anthropologists have found associations between the expressive and symbolic elements involved in tasting. However, too many gastronomes and some sociologists have claimed taste to be discriminating and refined only. What might be investigated next is the revelation of the ethical and social dimensions in food embedded in symbol systems which are basically aesthetic. This, too, could be an important argument for the aesthetic dimension or position being taken seriously. My hypothesis is that knowledge about the ethical, social and scientific dimensions in food will not in itself influence our choice of food. However, through the intentionality of the aesthetic experience (in the interrelationship just shown), we encounter these dimensions as having meaning in the object to which we address our intention.

The object relation in taste makes it possible to draw similarities between art and food, to a certain degree in the way they are experienced, and within the frames of the aesthetic. So, can an experience of taste (and not just the taste of refined foods/high gastronomy) be legitimately understood as being an aesthetic experience? Taste can be artistic, by reacting to the visual pleasure, but it can also be object intentional, establishing symbol-systems. And in this respect, it reveals general aesthetic features. Therefore, I will leave behind that part of the taste experience which leads to pleasure, since this will not bring us further in the search for taste as an aesthetic activity in a philosophical mening (but I shall not reject it as being important for the totality of taste experience). Even the perceptual discrimination used for pleasure is familiar to aesthetic understanding and discrimination; the gustatory enjoyment stops before reflection of the objective intentionality.

Taste is a cognitive sense

Following Korsmeyer, I shall regard taste as a cognitive sense that directs attention to objects and events in the world. Korsmeyer uses Nelson Goodman's analysis of symbol systems, specifically directed at art (Goodman 1976: 252). Goodman does not mention food, but his understanding of symbols and their aesthetic characteristics can be very useful in this investigation. Goodman introduces what he calls Symptoms of the Aesthetics:

> Repeated failure to find a neat formula for sorting experiences into aesthetic and non-aesthetic, in rough conformity with rough usage, suggests the need for a less simple-minded approach. Perhaps we should begin by examining the aesthetic relevance of the major characteristics of the several symbol processes involved in experience, and look for aspects or systems rather than for a crisp criterion, of the aesthetics. A symptom is neither a necessary nor a sufficient condition for, but merely tends in conjunction with other symptoms, to be present in, aesthetic experience. (Goodman 1976: 252)

Goodman mentions four types of symptoms of the aesthetic: (1) syntactic density, (2) semantic density, (3) syntactic repleteness, and (4) the feature that distinguishes exemplificational from denotational systems and combines with density to distinguish showing from saying. Two of the categories under semantic density, according to Goodman, are representation and expression; and it is those two symbolic functions of food, as well as the exemplificational functions, that Korsmeyer applies to food and its consumption. The symbolic functions penetrate all forms of eating. From the humble oatmeal to the most elaborate gourmet dinner. Let us follow Korsmeyer's analysis of the application of the three symbolic functions (Korsmeyer 1999: 115).

The representational food

Representation demands either that something real is denoted, or that the representation denotes an abstract concept.

Examples are legio: Jelly-babies, juicy fruit candies and what-have-you from the sweet industry; the Asian art decorations of radish-roses, melon-boats, etc. etc.; 19th. century carvings created by Carême; sugar skulls from the Day of the Dead in Mexico; Easter eggs; pretzels; croissants, and finally, the most outstanding representation: the bread and wine of the Eucharist.

Some of these are produced just for fun, but many have a considerable representational background. Let me give two examples. The pretzel originated in Italy and is called "bracciatelli", which means "folded arms". It was invented by a monk as a reward for the pupils who knew how to say their daily prayers, symbolising the correct way to fold the arms during prayer. The croissant was invented by the bakers of Vienna to celebrate the defeat of the besieging Ottoman Turks in 1683. It illustrates the crescent moon of Islam, now being swallowed by its enemies.

Many of these are representational to the sight and not the taste, few using taste representationally. But when the Jews eat bitter herbs at Passover to commemorate the bitter life in Egypt, the direct connection between taste and representation is present. Much representational food is commercial, sweets for example, or the culinary stunts as exemplified in the works of Câreme. This is only to illustrate that eating is a complex experience involving more than one, two, or three senses.

The exemplificational food

This is the most common type of symbol, where an object both posses-ses a property and refers to it. For instance, the food refers to some of the properties regarding what is to be eaten, focusing on these during the direct experience.

It is not just the directly noticeable properties in foods which expand the yum-yum reaction, but other aspects concerning the food that clamour to be appreciated. It might be that it is local, prepared by my favourite chef; that it is organic; that the sour taste reminds me of all the C-vitamins I am getting, and so forth.

> Attention to exemplified properties is attention directed to the object of perception, via the taste sensations that it is capable of delivering. Goodman's catalogue of symbolic relations neatly demonstrates the cognitive elements of tasting and eating, [...] and exemplification thus provides a handy classification of perceptual/cognitive experience. [...] The symbolic relation of exemplification refers to qualities possessed by the object of experience. (Korsmeyer 1999: 128)

The aesthetic characteristic experience in the mouth (since the sense receptors are located here) is the version of taste of aesthetic pleasure and might be found in appreciation of a meal, but not very often, since many return to "What I can taste?" (the B- and T-factor), and not what is reflected by the product and its qualities (the O-factor).

The exemplification expands the pleasure of the taste experience into a universe of meaning, which, as a result of our cultural practice, is so deeply embedded in our behaviour that it might as well be unconscious.

The cultural practice	The aesthetic experience	The perception
(C-factor)	(O-factor; interrelational)	(T-factor)

The structuralist anthropologist Claude Levi-Strauss and the theoretician Roland Barthes has elaborated on the influence of the C-factor in their works, but further reference to their discussion goes beyond the scope of this article.

The expressive food

The exemplification can be directly expressed in a certain property to be enjoyed in the food (a P-factor applied to an O-factor), or it could be an implicit property found at a certain place in the rhythm of the meal.

This symptom concerns tradition and routine. Here we find rituals, religious acts, caring, and everyday life. Sweet expresses caring, whereas salt expresses survival and friendship; to share the salt, the subjective experience is needed to express the power of love. Often we see expressive symptoms in food as incorporating the uniquely particular insight of life and experience, which is received through the aesthetic understanding of this experience of taste. The metaphorical exemplification of the taste experience might induce a high complexity of meaning. Taste sensations alone are not conveyers of meaning, just as a small sample of a certain shade of blue will not be. Meanings of many kinds will become part of the eating experience – sometimes because of a greater social context, sometimes provoked by the taste-experience of what we are eating.

The cognitive significance of food is:
– An effect of reference
– Representation
– Expression
– Exemplification
– The social conditions involved in its preparation and serving.

Not all forms of eating have high levels of significance, but ceremonial meals abound with significance.

Registration of these qualities requires a recipient who pays attention to the cognitive, the emotive, and the aesthetic. More than mere identification is required. We need to dwell on the experience, embracing all perceptive and emotive experiences in this aesthetic attention. Pleasurable as it may be, Goodman's analysis maintains that aesthetic appreciation is basically cognitive because it requires attention, recognition and affective response in the apprehension of the varieties of symbolic activity. Goodman maintains that the emotions function cognitively.

We can conclude by reiterating that food is more than just a discursive means of communication. Food also embodies cognitive elements which encourage the taste experience beyond the empirical experience to become a fabricated experience, which can be corroborated or invalidated by means of the culturally in-built sense perceptions. As Korsmeyer puts it: "The cognitive elements embedded in the various symbolic relationships extend the concept of aesthetic appreciation considerably beyond pleasure, to the insight and emotional depth for which art is valued" (1999: 117).

Literature

Barthes, Roland (1997 [1961]). "Toward a Psychosociology of Contemporary Food Consumption", in C. Counihan et al. (eds): *Food and Culture*, Routledge: New York.

Beauchamp, Gary and Bartoshuk, Linda (1997). *Tasting and Smelling*, New York: Academic Press.

Bourdieau, Pierre (1979). *Distinction. A Social Critique of the Judgement of Taste*, London: Routledge & Kegan Paul.

Brillat-Svarin, Anthelme (1986 [1825]). *Smagens Fysiologi* , Copenhagen: Gyldendal.

Carlsen, Helle Brønnum (2000). "Aesthetic learning processes with particular emphasis on the subject of home economics", in Jette Benn (ed.): *Home Economics in 100 years. Home economics in the 21 st century – History, Perspectives & Challenges,* Copenhagen: Danmarks Lærerhøjskole.

Drotner, Kirsten (1995). *At skabe sig selv*, Copenhagen: Gyldendal.

Elias, Norbert (1980). *Über den Prozess der Zivilisation*, Frankfurt am Main: Suhrkamp Verlag.

Fink-Jensen, Kirsten (1998). *Stemthed – en basis for æstetisk læring. Det musiske i et livsfilosofisk lys*, Copenhagen: Danmarks Lærerhøjskole.

Goodman, Nelson (1976). *Languages of Art*, Indianapolis: Hackett Publishing Company Inc.

Hohr, Hansjörg (1993). "Estetisk dannelse i didaktisk perspektiv", in Susanne V. Knudsen (ed.): *Æstetik og Didaktik. Didaktiske studier*, Bidrag til didaktikkens teori og historie, bind 5, Copenhagen: Danmarks Lærerhøjskole.

Hohr, Hansjörg (1996). "Det æstetiske som kundskabsform", In *Perspektiver på Æstetiske Læreprocesser*. Viborg: Dansklærerforeningen.

Hohr, Hansjörg (1999). "Den estetiske erkendelsen", *Kvan* 53, pp. 16–26.

Kant, Imanuel (1974). *Kritik der Urteilskraft*, Hamburg: Felix Meiner Verlag.

Korsmeyer, Carolyn (1999). *Making Sense of Taste*, Ithaca: Cornell University Press.

Levenson, Thomas (1995). "Studies from Life. Accounting for Taste". *The Sciences* Jan.–Feb., pp. 13–15.

Mclaughlin, Susan and Margolskee, Robert (1994). "The Sense of Taste". *American Scientist* vol. 82, pp. 538–545.

Mennell, Stephen (1985). *All Manners of Food*, Oxford: Basil Blackwell Ltd.

Vejledning i hjemkundskab (1995), Faghæfte 11, Copenhagen: Undervisningsministeriet.

Contributors

Per Bäckström. Associate professor at the Department of Documentation Studies, University of Tromsø. Ph.d. candidate with the project "Aska, tomhet & eld. Outsidertematiken hos Bruno K. Öijer", an analysis of the poetics of the Swedish poet Bruno K. Öijer (b. 1951), at the Department of Comparative Literature, University of Lund. Fil.Mag. (MA) in comparative literature, philosophy and history of art, University of Lund. Recent publications: "Michael Riffaterre och poesins semiotik: En kritisk läsning", *Norsk Litteraturvitenskapelig Tidsskrift* 2000:2; "'Vi lever i ett sönderfall': Ruin och melankoli hos Bruno K. Öijer", in Troels Degn Johansen, Claus Krogholm Kristiansen & Erik Steinskog (eds.), *Ruinøs modernitet*, Aarhus: NSU Press, 2000; "Avant-garde, Vanguard or 'Avant-Garde': What we are talking about when we are talking about avant-garde", in Karin Granqvist och Ulrike Spring (eds.), *Representing: Gender, Nation and Ethnicity in Word and Image*, Tromsø: Kvinnforsk Occasional Papers, 2001.

Helle Brønnum Carlsen. Assistant professor at N. Zahles Seminarium, Copenhagen. Ph.d. candidate with the project "Aesthetic learning-processes in connection to food and meals", at the Department of Educational Philosophy, The Danish University of Education, Copenhagen. Mag.art. (MA) in comparative literature; a trained teacher, BA in nourishment and bio-chemistry. Recent publications: "Aesthetic learning processes with particular emphasis on the subject home economics", in Jette Benn (ed.): *Home Economics in 100 Years: Home Economics in the 21st Century – History, Perspectives & Challenges*, Copenhagen: Danmarks Lærerhøjskole, 2000; "Smag og behag: en didaktisk udfordring", in *Dansk Pædagogisk Tidsskrift* 2002:2.

Mischa Sloth Carlsen. Cand.mag. (MA) in Comparative Literature and History of Ideas, and exam.art. (BA major) in Dramaturgy from the University of Aarhus, Denmark. Co-editor of *Flugtlinier: Om Deleuzes filosofi*, Copenhagen: Museum Tusculanum Press, 2001 (with Kim Su Rasmussen and Karsten Gam Nielsen). Recent publication: "Billeddannelse som et udløb af erfaringen! De kantianske spor i Gilles Deleuzes teori om 'billed-bevægelse'", in Mischa Sloth Carlsen, Karsten Gam Nielsen & Kim Su Rasmussen (eds.): *Flugtlinier: Om Deleuzes filosofi*, Copenhagen: Museum Tusculanum Press, 2001.

Troels Degn Johansson. Assistant Professor at The IT University of Copenhagen, Department of Digital Aesthetics and Communication. Research field: pictorial media and virtual spaces in computer-mediated communications, with special reference to computer games, virtual worlds, digital art, and visual culture. President of the Nordic Summer University (NSU), 1999–2000. Ph.D. project: *Landscapes of Communications: Pictorial Representation in the Visualization of Lands-*

cape Change in Web-Served Computer-Mediated Communications (Danish Forest and Landscape Research Institute, 2002). Cand.mag. (MA) in Film Studies from the University of Copenhagen. MA in Psychoanalytic Studies in the Humanities, University of Kent at Canterbury. Co-editor of, e.g., *Iconicity: A Fundamental Problem in Semiotics*, 1999, *Ruinøs modernitet*, 2000 (with Erik Steinskog and Claus Krogholm Sand); and *Sekvens 91 – Lars von Trier*, Department of Film & Media Studies, University of Copenhagen.

Esben Krohn. Ph.d. candidate, working on a project on Danish silent film from the Danish Film Institute, Copenhagen. Cand. phil. 1993, and mag. art. (MA) 1998 from the Department of Film & Media Studies, University of Copenhagen. Recent publication: *Det Første Filmarkiv/The First Film Archive*, Det Danske Filminstitut/The Danish Film Institute, 2002 (texts and research for a bilingual DVD production with and about 70 Danish non-fiction movies from the period 1899-1913, co-edited with Thomas C. Christensen).

Karen Hvidtfeldt Madsen. Assistant Professor at the Department of Contemporary Cultural Studies, University of Southern Denmark. Ph.D. from the Department of Languages and Culture, University of Roskilde; Cand.mag. (MA), from the Department of Comparative Literature and Modern Culture, University of Copenhagen. Recent publications: *Modstand som Æstetik & Æstetik som Modstand: Peter Weiss og Die Ästhetik des Widerstands* (doctoral thesis), Roskilde Universitetsforlag, 2000. "Fortællinger og fortrængninger. Heimat som erindring", in *Kultur & Klasse* 91, 2001.

Michael Penzold. Repetent (tutor and teacher) at the Evangelisches Stift in Tübingen. Ph.D.-candidate, working on the romantic female authors Thomasine Gyllembourg and Bettina von Arnim, at the University of Tübingen. Research on Jakob Böhme, Friedrich Nietzsche and Peter Handke. Has studied drama, German, theology, pedagogy and philosophy in Erlangen, Tübingen and Aarhus, and has worked as a teacher.

Claus Krogholm Sand (b. 1960). Associate Professor in Danish Literature and Director of Danish Studies, Department of Communication, Aalborg University. Current research project: "Utopia and Auto-geography. The Novels of Per Olov Enquist". Ph.D. in Danish Literature, Department of Communication, Aalborg University. Recent publications: "Ustedets poetik. Pablo Henrik Llambías' Rådhus", in *Kultur & Klasse* 90, 2000; "Erindringsbilleder", in Troels Degn Johansen, Claus Krogholm Kristiansen & Erik Steinskog (eds.): *Ruinøs modernitet*, NSU Press: Aarhus, 2000; "Faderen og loven. David Lynch og det obskønes politik", in *Politologiske Studier*, 2001:3.

Erik Steinskog (b. 1969). Presently working on two projects related to post-Wagnerian opera, focusing on questions of the voice, technology, subjectivity and performativity. Dr. art. (Ph.D.) from the Department of Musicology, Norwegian University of Science and Technology (NTNU), Trondheim, Norway. Degrees in musicology (with a thesis on Olivier Messiaen) and in philosophy (with a thesis on Walter Benjamin), both from NTNU. Recent publications: *Arnold Schoenberg's* Moses und Aron: *Music, Language, and Representation* (doctoral thesis), Trondheim: NTNU, 2002. "Meaning, Message and Medium: Arnold Schoenberg's *Moses und Aron* and the Question of Mediality", in Joyce Goggin & Michael Burke (eds.): *Travelling Concepts II: Meaning, Frame and Metaphor*, Amsterdam: ASCA Press, 2002; "Figur og topografi, om 'Sejrssøjlen'", in Marianne Barlyng & Henrik Reeh (eds.): *Walter Benjamins Berlin. 33 læsninger i Barndom i Berlin omkring år 1900*, Hellerup: Forlaget Spring, 2001. Co-editor of *Ruinøs modernitet* (with Troels Degn Johansson and Claus Krogholm Kristiansen), Århus: NSU Press, 2001.